P9-CEZ-702

QUICK ESCAPES®
PITTSBURGH

25 WEEKEND GETAWAYS
FROM THE STEEL CITY

BY

MICHELLE PILECKI

The Globe Pequot Press

GUILFORD, CONNECTICUT

Photo Credits: All photos by Thomas Clinton, except for the photo on page 89, courtesy of the Greater Columbus Convention and Visitors Bureau, © Rod Berry, and the photo on page 239, courtesy of the Pennsylvania Center for Travel, Tourism and Film.

Cover photo by Index Stock Imagery
Cover design by Laura Augustine
Text design by Nancy Freeborn/Freeborn Design
Maps by M.A. Dubé

Library of Congress Cataloging-in-Publication Data

Pilecki, Michelle.
      Quick escapes Pittsburgh : 25 weekend getaways from the Steel City / by Michelle Pilecki.
         p.   cm. — (Quick escapes series)
      Includes index.
      ISBN 0-7627-0912-X
      1. Pittsburgh Region (Pa.) — Guidebooks. I. Title. II. Series.
      F159.P63 P55 2001
      917.48'860444—DC21   2001033087

Manufactured in the United States of America
First Edition/First Printing

To Bob D.

I always said I'd dedicate my first book to you—I just didn't realize it would take this long.

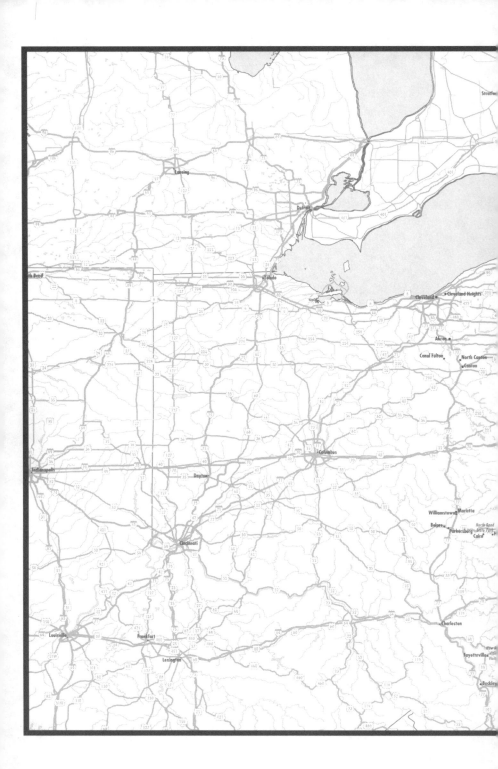

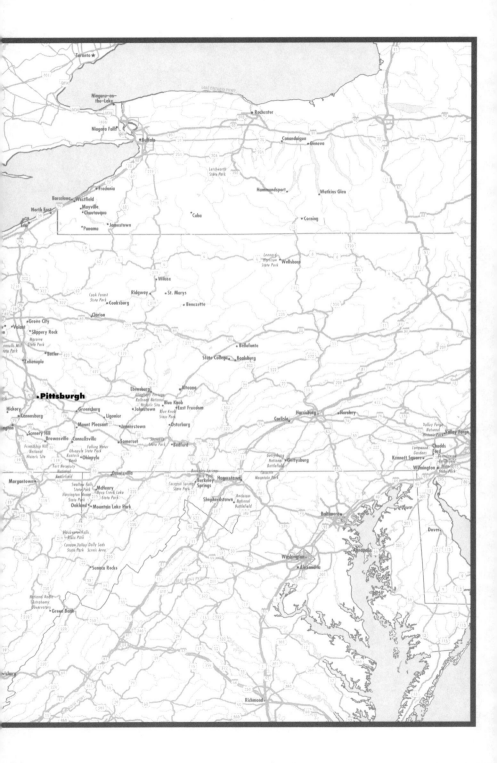

CONTENTS

The information and rates listed in this guidebook were confirmed at press time. We recommend, however, that you call establishments before traveling to obtain current information.

ACKNOWLEDGMENTS

This book could not have been written without the input and assistance of a lot of people: traveling Pittsburghers and relocated Pittsburghers Mark Aksoy, Bill Arble, Sujoy Basu, Alex and Susie Bellotti, Alice Carter, Jim Cunningham, Sam Edelmann, Winnie Flynn, Ian Gallacher, Dean Geibel, Janne Hunter, Jim Kempert, Jeff Leonard, John McIlvaine, Doug Root, and Rick Sebak. I drew on the resources of dozens of tourism bureaus, as you can see at the end of each chapter, and a lot of the folks really went the extra distance to help: Matt Turner of West Virginia's tourism division and the many people in the local bureaus, including Sharon Cruikshank in Fayetteville, Kim Cooper in Lewisburg, Bill Smith in Davis, and, especially, Jeanne Mozier in Berkeley Springs; Scott Dring and his crew in Ohio Travel and Tourism, and Brent LaLonde and Beth Ervin in Columbus; Marijo Martinec in South Bend; Odette Yazbeck and Tori Reep with the Shaw Festival in Niagara-on-the-Lake; Cathy Rehberg in Stratford; Leigh Anne Sperry in the Laurel Highlands; Connie Yingling in Maryland; Joni Sadley in Elk County; Karen Lenehan in Cleveland; Jennifer Boes with Delaware Tourism; and Laura Overstreet in Alexandria.

I also need to thank my colleagues at *Pittsburgh* magazine for taking up my slack and putting up with my whining: Chris Fletcher, Mike May, Dana Black, Michael Maskarinec, and Joyce DeFrancesco. And my editor at Globe Pequot Press, Laura Strom, for her patience. But most of all, I need to thank (and blame) Tom Clinton for insisting that I could do this book and then helping me accomplish it with his navigation, photography, and suggestions.

INTRODUCTION

Welcome to my party. In one sense, this book is a celebration of the history, scenery, and culture of that part of North America reasonably close to Pittsburgh. But in a more practical sense, these twenty-five itineraries are set up like parties, with a mix of people, activities, and foods. I've set up each trip as I would a party buffet: I don't really think that everybody is going to take a big helping of everything I've laid out, but I want to make sure to have a lot of different things so that everybody gets plenty to enjoy. This museum doesn't interest you so much? Well, maybe you'll like that park, or that shop, or that monument. I've got other things, too, in "There's More" at the end of each chapter, with other ideas of things to see and do, plus more suggestions on restaurants, lodgings, and special events. We'll get your plate filled.

These two-dozen-plus weekend trips travel to nine states and one province in two countries, with battlefields and historic sites from six wars, plus dozens of house museums, art museums, history museums, natural history museums, science museums, sports museums, music museums, military museums, railroad museums, and a streetcar museum. We've got wineries, breweries, chocolatiers, farm markets, markethouses, and, ah yes, blessed are the cheese makers (they're in here, too). And I've got some covered bridges to sell you while leading you down many a garden path.

I found lots of surprises while exploring for this book: A subarctic ecosystem a few hours south of Pittsburgh. A prairie north of town. A valley higher than any of our hills. And more than a few stereotypes shattered. Just as outsiders have outdated expectations of Pittsburgh, so some of us may be surprised to find such cultivated beauty in Youngstown, a nineteenth-century utopian society in Butler, and the ultimate in arts shopping in West Virginia.

Putting together a book like this, however, is like taking a snapshot of a moving train. A number of museums and visitors centers opened anew or reopened after extensive remodeling while I was researching this book in 2000, and more of them are soon to be opened, reopened, built, or planned in 2001. I've tried to make note of them. Same with route number changes. For example, New York's Southern Tier Expressway, long known as NY 17, was renamed I–86. And when the book was half written, Pennsylvania's Turnpike Commission announced that it would phase in new numbers of all the exits according to their distance from the state line, as so many surrounding states have done.

This is one way of saying that while phone numbers, Web sites, hours, admission prices, and descriptions were verified as accurate when this book was written, things change. It's a good idea to call first to confirm, especially with Sunday hours and especially in smaller cities and towns. Ditto if you want to know about discounts for groups, senior citizens, or other age groups. And if you have your heart set on a particular restaurant or B&B, make a reservation. There are many desirable restaurants and B&Bs that are booked weeks, even months in advance. The good news is that many of them now take reservations online as well as by e-mail and phone.

The trips are arranged geographically: north of town, primarily along I–79; west into (and through) Ohio; east, with the Pennsylvania Turnpike as your starting route; south below the Mason-Dixon Line; and what I've called "Into the Heartland," primarily using state and national roads into the mountains of Pennsylvania. A few are barely an hour from The Point. A few more require some serious drive time: five or six hours. Most are about three hours away, give or take half an hour. The destinations have three-season and even four-season possibilities, from gardens blooming in spring and summer to stunning foliage in fall to great shopping and snow sports in winter. Most places are pretty casual, and I've taken note of the more dress-up possibilities. Assume that you can always see a lot more on foot than from your car. In most cases this means packing comfortable walking shoes; others may need more serious athletic shoes, and a few, real hiking boots.

I know I'm going to be hearing from people (I've already heard from a few) as to how I could possibly leave out their favorite town or restaurant or museum or activity. Hey, I tried to get in as much as I could, but I knew I had to leave out a lot. For the record, I will note that there are great fishing possibilities in pretty much every state park mentioned. I couldn't detail them all. There are more golf courses than I could cram in. There are gardens I had to pass by, wineries I couldn't stop to taste, and shops where—this time, at least—my credit cards had to go uncharged.

I had fun exploring. I hope you do, too.

NORTHERN

ESCAPES

Butler County

IN HARMONY

---

1 NIGHT

Antiques Road Show • Farms • Utopian Society
Lake Adventures • Romance

Pittsburgh's northern neighbor covers a lot of territory, capable of appealing to a remarkably wide audience, from toddlers building sand castles on the "beaches" of Lake Arthur to weekend jocks challenged by extreme sports to bargain hunters on the antiquing circuit. There's the well-preserved first home of the Harmony Society for history lovers, a prairie habitat for nature lovers, and a romantic mill and covered bridge for the rest of us lovers.

Surprisingly enough, local officials have barely awakened to the notion of tourism, with nary a visitors guide nor visitors center in sight at the end of the twentieth century. Historic villages and pristine lakes that would be overrun in more heavily marketed parts of the nation lie awaiting discovery. This is especially ironic given the suburban sprawl eating away at the southern portions of Butler County's rural beauty. But you really don't have to travel far to escape the strip malls and housing tracts and congestion. Agriculture remains the county's chief "industry," and the area is still home to more golf courses (seventeen) than any other county in the state—practically in our backyard.

DAY 1

Morning

Head straight north on PA 8 to the county line. Just opposite the Butler Valley exit of the Pennsylvania Turnpike is the Venus Diner.

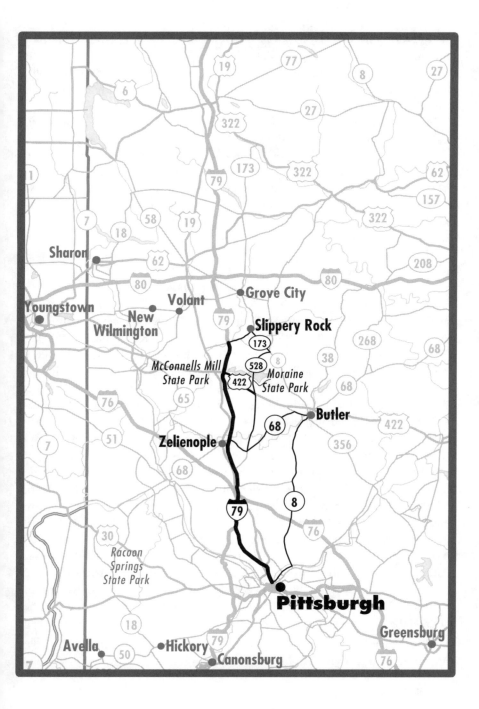

BREAKFAST: The Venus (5315 William Flynn Highway; 724–443–2323) is not a modish, hip re-creation of an old-fashioned diner, but a real old diner, right down to the jukeboxes in the booths, corned beef hash, constant coffee refills, and complete lack of concern about cholesterol. (Cash only.) Open seven days a week 5:30 A.M. to 7:15 P.M.

Mosey along on PA 8 and, as the strip malls fade (or at least get smaller), watch for antiques shops and signs for the farm markets tucked off the main roads. One of the best selections of antiques, primarily nineteenth century (with the occasional eighteenth), is at **Wagon Wheel Antiques** (724–898–9974), on your right about a mile beyond the Venus Diner. The various dealers carry a lot of great old furniture, some toys, and fairly decent jewelry as well as knickknacks. (Open Monday through Saturday 10:00 A.M.–5:00 P.M.; Sunday noon–5:00 P.M.)

The county's many farm markets generally sell bedding plants or preserves as well as local produce, and are fun to explore. In a few more miles is the intersection with PA 228 west; take a left to **Hawkins** (724–625–1211), a farm market and nursery with (in season, July through September) the best sweet corn around. Or continue along PA 8 until PA 228 (yes, it follows PA 8 for a while) heads east, and go to the **Joseph King Farm Market** (724–898–3487), well off the road and next to the farmhouse. Say hello to the dogs and the kids running around, and look for fresh old-fashioned flowers like snapdragons and sweet williams, or dried statice and strawflowers in Lisa's Touch of Country, in an outbuilding next to the market. (Both generally open 9:00 A.M.–5:00 P.M. daily.)

Continue north on PA 8 as development makes itself known again and downtown Butler looms ahead. The county seat, like many small cities, has lost a lot of its oomph and bustle, but not all its charm, like its old-fashioned town square in front of the **County Court House,** a National Historic Landmark at 290 South Main Street (the parking lot is tucked behind the park). Once flush with oil money, Butler is a still-proud dowager selling off the occasional treasure—and a lot of collectibles and tchotchkes—in an array of antiques shops, most notably **Alley Antiques** (120 East Birch Street), **Butler Antiques and Collectibles** (119 East Wayne Street), and **Antiques** (102 North Main Street). And although the decor of the **Associated Artists of Butler** (724–283–6922) at 344 South Main Street leaves something to be desired, the changing exhibits by regional professional artists are strong. (Open Wednesday and Thursday 10:00 A.M.–4:00 P.M., Friday 10:00 A.M.–9:00 P.M., Saturday 10:00 A.M.–2:00 P.M.)

Downtown Butler is an easy, walkable grid with many notable buildings for the architecture or history buff. Tucked behind the courthouse at 123 West Diamond Street is the **Shaw House,** a National Historic Landmark currently undergoing renovation to reopen eventually as a house museum. Flanking the courthouse is another landmark, the Lafayette Apartments, along with the spiffed-up facade of the *Butler Eagle* **building.** Head north, and you'll see a local landmark designed by Benno Janssen, the **T. W. Phillips Gas Co.** at 201 North Main Street.

LUNCH: Right across the street is **Natili North Restaurant & Carry Out** (724–283–2149), for sandwiches and Italian specialties. (Open Monday through Saturday 10:00 A.M.–10:00 P.M.) But for dessert, stroll down to **Cummings Candy/Coffee Shop** at 146 North Main (724–287–3287) for a sundae in a real old-fashioned ice cream palace, complete with rich wood paneling and marble. (Open Monday through Saturday: coffee shop 7:00 A.M.–9:00 P.M., candy shop 8:15 A.M.–5:15 P.M.)

Afternoon

Back on the road, take PA 68 west past the county farm show grounds and on toward Zelienople, named for Zelie Basse Passavant, daughter of the town's founder, Baron Dettmar Basse, a former German diplomat. Both their home, **Passavant House** (243 South Main Street, built 1808–10 and the family home for 150 years), and the nearby **Buhl House** (221 South Main Street, built 1805) are open for a joint tour that includes the original pioneer kitchen, family wedding dresses (the families were joined in marriage in 1870), and a glimpse into the way life used to be. It's a good idea to call ahead. (Admission is $3.50; tours are offered Wednesday and Saturday, May through October. Contact 724–452–9457 or zeliehistory@fyi.net/~zhs.)

Move a tad farther into the past at **Harmony** (go north on Main/U.S. 19, turn right onto Grandview/PA 68, then follow signs to the National Historic Landmark District's Main Street), the founding home of the Harmony Society. This German separatist sect, founded by vine-tender-turned-prophet Johann Georg Rapp, left Europe in 1803 seeking religious liberty, and established the Town of Harmonie (as it was spelled in 1804). After the Harmonists left in 1814 to establish New Harmony in Wabash, Indiana, Mennonites bought the town, which continued to thrive. Harmony was built with individual houses, in contrast to the communal living spaces of Economy, the utopian society's third and final home (see Old Economy in Western Escape 1). Many of the original buildings are in private hands (several are shops selling antiques, gifts, and, in the case of the former opera house, ice cream), but you can tour the former Great Haus, now the **Harmony Museum** (218 Mercer Street; 724–452–7341 or 888–821–4822; www.butlercounty.net/harmonymuseum). You'll explore not only the Harmonists' and Mennonites' role in the town, but also George Washington's adventure here. (Open Tuesday through Saturday 1:00–4:00 P.M., but it's a good idea to call first; $3.50.)

Make sure you cross Grandview Avenue to take a look at the **Harmonist Cemetery,** especially its beautifully wrought gate. It weighs two tons, but its construction is such that it can be moved easily with one hand.

DINNER: Historic Harmony Inn (230 Mercer Street; 724–452–5124; harminn@bellatlantic.net), built in 1856, serves up a more modern cuisine with serious Cajun and Mexican overtones, though not too hot. If you need more spice, ask about the resident ghost, reported to be benign. More than a few folks are serious about the haunting. (Open Monday through Thursday 11:30 A.M.–9:00 P.M., Friday and Saturday 11:30 A.M.–10:00 P.M., Sunday 11:30 A.M.–8:00 P.M.)

Evening

LODGING: The Inn on Grandview (724–452–0469 or 888–544–3481), within easy walking distance of both Harmony and the Zelienople house museums, actually did start life as a nineteenth-century inn, not far from where the Colonial building has since been moved. The B&B rooms are surprisingly modern and include private baths, one of which has a whirlpool. All offer cable TV, phone, and computer hookups, but the idea is to get away from all that.

DAY 2

Morning

BREAKFAST: After your B&B breakfast of local bacon, home-baked goodies, and more, hit the road (PA 68) through Evans City, then turn left onto PA 528. As you follow the winding road through thick woods and rolling farmland, you're more likely to see deer than any sign that you're less than an hour from the city. In about twenty to twenty-five minutes, you'll come to the edge of Moraine State Park. But first turn left onto PA 422 (and a sneak preview of Lake Arthur) to **McConnells Mill State Park** (724–368–8092 or 724–368–

8811), just over the border in Lawrence County. The mill, built in 1868, and the nearby covered bridge over Slippery Rock Creek comprise one of the area's most popular postcard scenes, and a lovely spot for a romantic picnic in the off season. Between Memorial Day and Labor Day, the old gristmill is open for tours (10:15 A.M.–5:45 P.M.; off season by appointment). Slippery Rock Gorge also offers 11 miles of rugged hiking, climbing, rappelling, and white-water rafting for the more rugged—and experienced (www.dcnr.state.pa.us).

Head back to **Moraine State Park** on PA 422, so named because at least four continental glaciers and their moraines (the rocks and debris that accu-mulate around a glacier) carved the topography of the area, including three glacial lakes. Lake Arthur, however, is artificial, built in 1968. The park was actually created during a mammoth reclamation, one of the first of its kind and the first project of the Western Pennsylvania Conservancy; it opened in 1970. From the park entrance, follow the signs to McDaniel's Launch.

LUNCH: The best introduction to the 3,225-acre Lake Arthur is *Nautical Nature,* an enclosed pontoon boat that offers a variety of guided tours, includ-ing, in summer, biweekly Sunday lunch cruises (reservations recommended; 724–368–9185). Accompany a sandwich with a discussion of lakeside flora and fauna, earlier ice ages, or continuing efforts at preservation.

Afternoon

Explore some of the 40 miles of lake coastline, which includes two sand beaches for swimming (both feature basic hot dog and hamburger snack bars), four boat launches, a windsurfing launch, a 7-mile bike trail, and six hiking trails. The most rugged, Glacier Ridge, is part of the **North Country National Scenic Trail** (616–454–5506) from New York to North Dakota. In winter Moraine is great for sledding, cross-country skiing, ice boating, snow-mobiling, and the like.

Or you can just enjoy the scenery, especially one of nature's oddities: a western prairie plopped on top of a Pennsylvania hill. Head east on PA 528. Just as you leave Moraine, you'll reach the **Jennings Environmental Edu-cation Center** (724–794–6011). The relict prairie ecosystem, left over from the true prairie that stretched from the Rockies to the Appalachians around 2000 B.C., is a flat, almost treeless home to 386 species of plants, including many wildflowers not seen elsewhere. It's most famous for the 4-foot-tall pur-ple-pink blazing stars, best seen in August.

Stroll through the prairie in Moraine State Park's Jennings Environmental Education Center.

Return to PA 528 east, turn left onto PA 8, past the Old Stone House, then turn left again onto PA 173 to Slippery Rock.

DINNER: The Wolf Creek School Cafe (664 Centreville Pike [EPA 173]; 724–794–1899) was indeed home to the last remaining one-room schoolhouse in Slippery Rock, and today is filled with memorabilia from those days (though the chairs are more comfy). Check the chalkboard for the day's specials—nicely priced chicken entrees, steaks, chops, and pasta. Maybe they'll let you ring the school bell; it still works. (Open Tuesday through Thursday and Sunday 11:00 A.M.–9:00 P.M., Friday and Saturday 11:00 A.M.–11:00 P.M.; BYOB.)

Continue north on PA 173 through downtown Slippery Rock, turn left at PA 108, and then turn onto I–79 south. You'll be back home in an hour or so.

THERE'S MORE

Heritage Center. This Butler County history museum is open Saturday and Sunday (119 West New Castle Street in downtown Butler; 724–285–5482 or 724–283–8116).

Little Red School House. Butler's first public school, built in 1838, is open every other Saturday, May through October (724–283–8116).

Moraine State Park boat rentals. See the lake aboard a sailboat, paddleboat, canoe, kayak, rowboat, or motorboat. The Rita James Co. offers two launch sites (724–368–9000).

The Old Stone House. A reconstructed nineteenth-century wayside inn and tavern just outside the Jennings Environmental Education Center. Open weekends, May through October (724–794–4296 or 724–738–2053).

Hoyt Institute of Fine Arts. Changing exhibits in an old mansion in nearby New Castle (724–652–2882).

Cooper Cabin. This 1810 cabin revisits frontier life with a springhouse, spinning house, and more. Open Sunday, May through September. Near Cabot, off PA 356 (724–283–8116).

Saxon Golf Course. A 3-star-rated nine- and eighteen-hole golf course in Clinton Township (724–353–2130).

Harlansburg Station. Its Museum of Transportation in a replica train station connects to an old passenger car filled with train memorabilia. Weekends only (U.S. 19 and PA 108; 724–652–9002).

SPECIAL EVENTS

June. The annual Butler Rodeo brings the Wild West to western Pennsylvania (724–865–9337).

July. The Big Butler Fair—146 years old in 2001—hosts top country acts at the region's biggest county fair (724–865–2400; www.bigbutlerfair.com).

August. At Dankfest, Harmony hosts a festival of eighteenth- and nineteenth-century crafts (888–821–4822 or 724–452–7341).

October. The High-Tec Adventure Race series comes to Moraine State Park. Teams compete in a 10- to 15-mile mountain bike course, 5- to 8-mile

trail run, a 1- to 3-mile kayak segment, and up to ten special tests (818–707–8867; www.mesp.com).

OTHER RECOMMENDED RESTAURANTS AND LODGINGS

Kaufman House. This longtime favorite in downtown Zelienople serves traditional American fare (105 Main Street [U.S. 19]; 412–261–2079 or 724–452–6900).

Village Inn. In a historic building, find Black Angus beef at reasonable prices. Nonsmoking (PA 108 west of I–79; 724–654–6851).

Applebutter Inn B&B. This updated 1844 inn has eleven rooms, three with a fireplace. Hot tub available. Next to Wolf Creek School Cafe (666 Centerville Pike; 888–275–3466 or 724–794–1844; www.pathway.net/applebutterinn).

As Thyme Goes By. Country Victorian meets Humphrey Bogart fans (rooms are named for Bogey films), with complimentary snacks and fresh herbs to take home, as well as breakfast. Close to Moraine State Park and Slippery Rock University (214 North Main Street, Harrisville; 877–278–4963 or 724–735–4003; www.asthymegoesby.com).

Step Back in Thyme. This combination B&B, antiques shop, and tea room (yes, with scones and dainty cups) also serves lunch in frilly Victoriana (224 North Washington Street, practically in downtown Butler; 724–283–7509; www.westernpabandb.com).

FOR MORE INFORMATION

Butler County Chamber of Commerce and Tourism, 201 South Main Street, P.O. Box 1082, Butler, PA 16003-1082; 724–283–2222.

ESCAPE TWO

NORTHERN

Lawrence, Mercer, and Mahoning Counties

OTHER OUTLETS FOR FUN

---

1 NIGHT

Shopping • Singing • Art • Flowers • GWTW

Folks come by the busload from as far away as Indiana and Ontario to shop at the Prime Outlets at Grove City, drawn not just by the hundred-plus stores, but also by our state's peculiarity in not charging sales tax on clothing. Pittsburghers head up here on a regular basis, too, but there's a lot more in the area than just the chain-store mall. Not far away, to visit instead of (or in addition to) the mall, are independently owned destination shops, a sizable Amish community, a paean to vocal groups, a top-ranked art museum, a dazzling garden, and our area's own shrine to *Gone with the Wind*.

DAY 1

Morning

Head north on I–79 for less than an hour to exit 31, but instead of turning left onto PA 208 for the outlet mall, turn right and head into town. (Yes, Virginia, there is a real **Grove City.**) Turn right onto Main Street and then right into the lot of the Grove City Diner.

BREAKFAST: The Grove City Diner (108 East Main Street; 724–458–8030) tends to be fairly quiet even when it's crowded. The kids are kept busy with a variety of small toys, and the grown-ups are busy digging into huge plates of

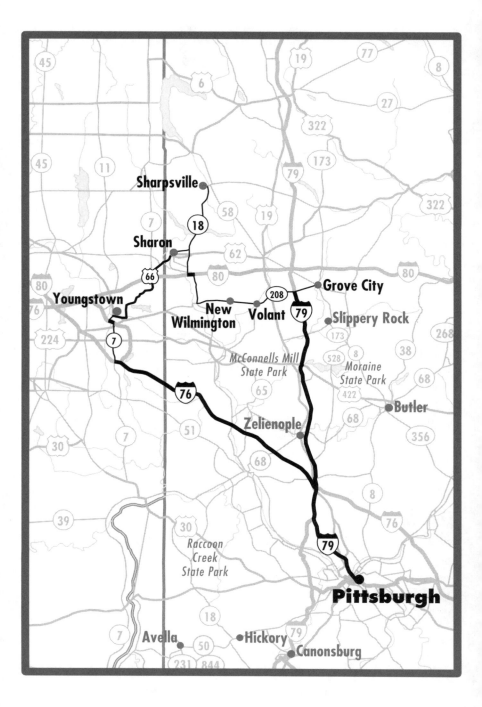

eggs, homefries, sausage, and light–as–a–feather biscuits. (Open Monday through Friday 6:30 A.M.–2:00 P.M., Saturday 6:30 A.M.–8:00 P.M., Sunday 6:30 A.M.–7:00 P.M.)

Continue south on Main Street, past Grove City College, and follow the blue-and-white signs to **Wendell August Forge** (620 Madison Avenue; 724–458–8360; www.wendell.com). This largest and oldest such forge in the United States specializes in decorative metal giftware: plates, trays, bookends, boxes, ornaments, and so on, in aluminum, bronze, pewter, and silver. Since it opened in 1923, the shop has evolved into a theme park with an overhead miniature train, nickelodeon, W. A. the talking parrot, local antiques, and, of course, artisans you can watch in action. (The shop is open Monday through Saturday 9:00 A.M.–6:00 P.M., till 8:00 P.M. Friday, plus Sunday 11:00 A.M.–5:00 P.M.; free tours Monday through Friday 9:00 A.M.–noon and 12:30–4:00 P.M.)

Double back along Main Street, but take a quick detour through the business district along Broad Street to explore some interesting independent stores. Most notable is **Joden World Resources** (144 South Broad Street; 800–747–7552), a jewelry store that specializes in top-quality antique jewelry from estate sales around the globe. Some come close to being museum quality, and drop-dead gorgeous. Newly crafted pieces are also available. (Open Monday through Saturday 9:00 A.M.–5 P.M., till 8:00 P.M. Friday.)

Head back toward I–79 and the outlet mall, but keep going west on PA 208, crossing U.S. 19 and PA 168 then dipping down into **Volant.** You're in Pennsylvania Dutch country, so be on the lookout for Amish buggies and bargains. There are some fifty shops crowding Main Street (PA 208) in this little town—in old train cars, a former gristmill, and renovated homes—open 361 days a year for shopping. Stroll around Neshannock Creek (folks are likely to be fishing) and look for fishing supplies, including Orvis, at the **Neshannock Creek Fly Shop** (724–533–3212). Or head for a more ladylike excursion in the train cars for chocolates at **Sweet Sara's** (724–533–5112; www.sweetsaras.com), lacy and frilly gifts at **Country Connection** (724–533–2733), and quilted accessories at **Quilted Collectibles** (724–533–3863). But for real local Amish quilts, furniture, baskets, hats, and toys, head up the hill a bit to **Good Earth Gallery** (724–533–2663; custom orders available). (Merchants' Association, 724–533–2591; www.volantshops.com; shops are generally open Monday through Saturday 9:00 A.M.–4:00 P.M.; Sunday noon–5:00 P.M.)

LUNCH: Head down to the depot to the **Neshannock Creek Inn** (Volant Depot; 724–533–2233), which roots for all the local teams, judging by the pennants hanging around. The salads and sandwiches aren't shy: Who can pass up the Pittsburgher, a third-of-a-pound burger with mozzarella, spaghetti sauce, and pepper rings on garlic toast? (Open Monday through Saturday 11:00 A.M.–6:00 P.M., Friday till 8:00 P.M.; Sunday noon–6:00 P.M.)

Afternoon

Farther along PA 208, in and around **New Wilmington,** the local Old Order Amish community is even more in evidence. If you explore along the side roads, some farms will have signs out for quilts, furniture, homemade pies, and more. Remember, though, that all the homes and farms, and pretty much all the shops in New Wilmington, will not sell on Sunday. Hours of business tend to be casual, but generally run 10:00 A.M.–5:00 P.M. Monday through Saturday. Between Volant and New Wilmington, **Hostetler's Quilts** (no phone) displays at least a hundred quilts plus other hand-sewn items for the home, from place mats to rugs. And just as you get into New Wilmington on PA 208 (now Neshannock Avenue), you'll spot the **Amish Peddler** (724–946–8034), which features foods as well as furniture. Turn right at the Borough Building on High Street and head up to the **Needle Nook** (4237 Bethel Road; 724–946–2837) for some examples of cross-stitch and other embroideries. Or just park south of the village square (it's the first of two traffic lights in town; both parking and hitching are free). Life here isn't much faster paced than when the area was first settled in the eighteenth century.

At the second traffic light in town (about a mile west of the town center), make a right to head north on PA 18 for about 11 miles to U.S. 62. Turn left and drive approximately 3 miles along U.S. 62 (now State Street) to downtown **Sharon,** home of shops that bill themselves as the world's largest in their fields. The sweetest is **Daffin's Candies and Chocolate Kingdom** (724–342–2892 or 877–323–3265; www.daffins.com) at 496 East State Street. Head to the rear of the store for an explanation of the chocolate-making process and the Kingdom: a display of elephants, rabbits, turtles, castles, and more, all made entirely of chocolate and all out of scale with each other. Besides its own line of handmade chocolates, the giant store also features hundreds of barrels of hard candies. (Open Monday through Saturday 9:00 A.M.–9:00 P.M., Sunday 11:00 A.M.–5:00 P.M.)

Maybe it's a good thing Imelda Marcos never discovered **Reyer's,** the self-titled World's Largest Shoe Store. It could be. The outlet store (724–981–1100) at 69 East State Street alone boasts 50,000 pairs in stock. The main store (724–981–2200 or 800–245–1550; www.reyers.com), around the corner at City Centre, figures about 175,000 shoes in some 300 brands, in women's sizes 2 through 15 and widths AAAAA through EE; men's 6 through 22 and AAA through EEEEE; and all children's sizes. There's everything from running shoes to orthotics to pink pumps for the prom. Speaking of which, it's just a short stroll to the extensive eveningwear collection at **The Winner** (724–346–9466 or 800–344–2672), the World's Largest Off-Price Ladies' Fashion Store, at 32 West State Street. There's also a children's department and a few things for the guys in this four-story, 100,000-square-foot establishment. (All three are open Monday through Saturday 10:00 A.M.–9:00 P.M., Sunday noon–6:00 P.M.)

Head west across the railroad tracks, turn left, and you'll see a black locomotive, a couple of train cars, and several other buildings around a parking lot that will likely include a lot of motorcycles and some interesting cars.

DINNER: This is the original **Quaker Steak and Lube** (101 Chestnut Street; 724–981–9464 or 800–468–9464; www.lubewings.com), now the center of an entertainment complex that includes (on a rotating schedule) live music from acoustic to alternative, karaoke, various theme evenings (Jimmy Buffett is big), and, of course, car club events. The expression *democratic as a car crash* was made for Quaker Steak. The restaurant, in an old gas station, is always packed with families, grandmothers, bikers, the pierced set, and, yes, those famous upside-down cars. While you can get great burgers, the real attraction is the wings: boneless and regular, with fourteen sauces from mild to you-must-sign-release-form hot. (Open Monday through Thursday 11:00 A.M.–1:00 A.M., Saturday 11:00 A.M.–1:45 A.M., Sunday noon–11:00 P.M.)

Evening

After dinner, hang around the Lube's **Hot Rod Cafe** (724–981–3123). Saturday night features alternative bands from western Pennsylvania and eastern Ohio. Then head east on U.S. 62 back to PA 18, turn north, and drive about 7 miles into the antebellum South.

LODGING: Tara (2844 Lake Road, Clark; 724–962–3535 or 800–782–2803) is a country inn, a restaurant, and a monument to *Gone with the Wind*. It's not just that the twenty-seven guest rooms, all different, carry out specific themes from characters and scenes from the movie, but also that one of the biggest attractions of the inn is its collection of *GWTW* memorabilia, including autographed photos of Clark Gable and Vivien Leigh. It's pricey, but sumptuous— and romantic (a favorite spot for honeymooners), set right on the Shenango River Reservoir.

DAY 2

Morning

BREAKFAST: Enjoy a simple continental breakfast served in your room. You also have the option of a full breakfast downstairs, but you don't want to fill up too much before brunch. Wake up with a dip in the indoor pool (note the hand-painted mural) or sample the spa services. Explore the 1859-vintage mansion, perhaps with a guide dressed in antebellum style, who can point out and discuss the various antiques, objets d'art, and movie items inside, and the growing collection of statuary (primarily neoclassical) in and around the gardens outside.

Brunch at Tara is both sumptuous and surprisingly priced ($18.95 per adult), with a carving station, omelettes, waffles, crepes, and a changing menu of hot dishes, salads, and desserts (11:00 A.M.–3:00 P.M.).

Afternoon

As you head back to Sharon, you'll be in **Hermitage** when you turn west from PA 18 to U.S. 62. Remember the hostage crisis in Iran in 1979–80? The Freedom Museum's **Avenue of 444 Flags** (724–346–3818) added a flag for each day of captivity, and you can drive or walk through the display. Yes, it's the world's largest display of U.S. flags.

Back in downtown Sharon, if you've had enough shopping, harmonize into the **Vocal Group Hall of Fame and Museum** (800–753–1648; www.vocalhalloffame.com). This storefront museum is still being developed, but you can browse through three floors of tributes to American vocal artists in pop music. Dominating the first floor is a representation of one of the first and greatest acts: the Mills Brothers. Upstairs, besides displays on the Supremes, Elvis, and other stars, you'll find a fun interactive display of a doo-wop group—press the button and they sing. (Admission costs $8.95; open

Wednesday through Friday 10:00 A.M.–5:00 P.M., Saturday 10:00 A.M.–6:00 P.M., Sunday noon–5:00 P.M.)

Don't doo-wop too long, because you want to make sure you leave plenty of time to enjoy **Youngstown.** For real. This much-maligned steel town is home to two jewels: a world-class art museum and one of America's premier city parks. Head west on U.S. 62, which becomes Wick Avenue as it approaches central Youngstown. After crossing U.S. 422, follow the signs to a dazzling Georgian building of Carrara marble on your right.

The Butler Institute of American Art (524 Wick Avenue; 330–743–1711; www.butlerart.com) does indeed cover the gamut of this country's art, from the colonial years of the eighteenth century to the electronic, digital, and video installations of the twenty-first century, in its new Beecher Center. The permanent collection includes sterling works by Winslow Homer (*Snap the Whip* is the museum's signature piece), the Stuarts, Mary Cassatt, Albert Bierstadt, Romare Bearden, and many more surprises, such as a gallery of sports paintings and a sculpture garden. And it's all free. (Open Monday through Saturday 11:00 A.M.–4:00 P.M., till 8:00 P.M. Wednesday; Sunday noon–4:00 P.M.)

Continue down Wick Avenue through downtown. Turn right onto Front Street, and cross the Mahoning River onto Marshall Street to **Mill Creek MetroParks** (123 McKinley Avenue; 330–702–3000; www.cboss.com/millcreek), 3,400 stunning acres of woodland, water, historic nineteenth-century buildings, and more. Amenities include golf, cabins, trails, scenic drives, three lakes, ice skating and cross-country skiing, but the crown jewel is the **Fellows Riverside Garden** (330–740–7116). It's actually well up above the lake view, with thousands of flowering bulbs in spring and a pallette of roses (from old-fashioned to the latest hybrid teas) in its formal gardens. A new visitors center provides more creature comforts and a gift shop. (Free admission; open 10:00 A.M.–dark. The Garden Center is open Monday through Friday 10:00 A.M.–4:30 P.M. year-round; Saturday 10:00 A.M.–3:00 P.M., Sunday 1:00–5:00 P.M., April through mid-December.)

When you're ready for dinner, head south on OH 7 to Boardman.

DINNER: After that brunch, you may just want a quick pizza at **Cafe Capri** (7807 Market Street; 330–726–9900). Or choose pasta and salad with a little vino. (Open Monday through Thursday 11:30 A.M.–10:00 P.M., Friday and Saturday 11:30 A.M.–11:00 P.M., Sunday 3:30–8:00 P.M.)

The Buhl Mansion in Sharon is both a house museum and a B&B.

Follow OH 7 or I–680 south to the Ohio Turnpike, and you'll be home in less than an hour via the Pennsylvania Turnpike.

THERE'S MORE

The Buhl Mansion in downtown Sharon is a stunning house museum with a carriage art gallery open for tours by reservation only; there's also a luxurious guest house and spa (724–962–3535 or 800–782–2808).

Roberta's Guide Service leads tours of the New Wilmington Amish area (724–533–2175 or 800–531–7639).

Prime Outlets of Grove City, home to 140-plus shops representing top brand names, is open seven days a week in a villagelike setting (888–545–7221; www.primeoutlets.com).

The Stavich Bicycle Trail, 12 miles, is the only rail-trail that runs through three townships in two counties and two states: Lawrence in Pennsylvania, and Mahoning in Ohio (216–536–6221).

SPECIAL EVENTS

March. The annual trout stocking in Neshannock Creek at Volant is accompanied by an all-day pancake festival and Brownie, a mascot trout.

Spring. The Sunday before Palm Sunday is Swizzle Stick Day at Daffin's, featuring free factory tours and free chocolate samples (724–342–2892).

April, October. Amish quilt auction on the third Saturday in New Wilmington.

September–December. Santa's Christmasland at Kraynak's in Hermitage (just east of Sharon) is the ultimate holiday yard display with 175 differently decorated trees, plus lights, moving figures, and more. Its spring counterpart is Easter Bunny Lane (724–347–4511).

OTHER RECOMMENDED RESTAURANTS AND LODGING

Cross Creek Cafe, right across from the creek in Volant, features dozens of sandwiches (724–533–2300).

Tavern on the Square, a longtime stop for comfort food in New Wilmington. Closed Tuesday (724–946–2020).

Ashley's Dining Room at Tara features a prix-fixe (about $76) seven-course dinner by candlelight with white-glove service. Jacket, tie, and reservations required (724–962–3535 or 800–782–2803).

Beechwood Inn (724–946–2342; www.vysion.com/beechwoodinn) and the Veazey House B&B (724–946–2918 or 724–946–8484; www.pathway.net/martyvzc) are practically right across Beechwood Road in New Wilmington.

FOR MORE INFORMATION

Lawrence County Tourist Promotion Agency, 229 South Jefferson Street, New Castle, PA 16101; 724–654–8408 or 888–284–7599; www. lawrencecounty.com/tourism.

Mercer County Convention and Visitors Bureau, 50 North Water Street, Sharon, PA 16146; 724–346–3771 or 800–637–2370; www.mercercountypa.org.

Youngstown/Mahoning County Convention and Visitors Bureau, 100 Federal Plaza East, Suite 101, Youngstown, OH 44503; 330–747–8200 or 800–447–8201; www.youngstowncvb.com.

Erie

NORTH BY NORTH EAST

1 NIGHT

Beaches • Lighthouses • Tall Ship • Wine

Waves crashing on rocks, sandy beaches that stretch for miles, a horizon where water blends with sky almost seamlessly. To get there from Pittsburgh, you'd go—north? Yup. The most popular state park in the commonwealth is a real people magnet for its beauty and its many recreational amenities as it sticks out into Lake Erie. The "almost island" (that's what Presque Isle means) is just one of the attractions of Erie, a city with its own charm, good food, and a bit of a wine industry, not to mention its history as the site of one of America's few victories in the War of 1812. We're still proud of that. In fact, Pennsylvania may well be the only one of the fifty states with its own seaworthy warship.

Erie has always been a bargain. Pennsylvania paid only 75 cents an acre for the area—a whopping $151,640.25—in 1792 so that the state could have access to Lake Erie. Today, the state's third largest city is still a bargain. And there's a lot happening there: historical restorations, lakefront developments, cultural expansion, and an awful lot of attention to tourism development. Gee, is it just coincidence that Pennsylvania governor Tom Ridge calls Erie home?

DAY 1

Morning

Head north on I–79 to exit 41 (Kearsarge) and turn right at the end of the exit ramp onto Interchange Road, which becomes PA 99 north. Turn right at U.S. 19. In less than half a mile you'll see on your left a large **Wegman's** store

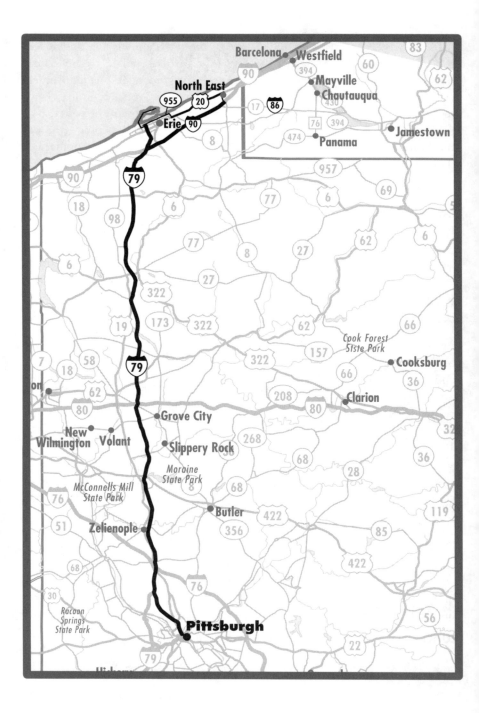

(6143 Peach Street; 814–866–6870), one of the few Pennsylvania outlets for the legendary Rochester, New York–based supermarket. The twenty-four-hour store includes the popular take-out areas for sandwiches made to order (814–866–2479), salads, bakery, pizza, wings, even sushi. Stock up on roast beef or Italian subs for a picnic lunch (maybe with an extra muffin or pastry, and plenty of chocolate-chip cookies) and add a few things to take home—maybe the house-brand fruit-only preserves. (Open seven days a week, submarine stand 10:00 A.M.–8:00 P.M.; wings, pizza, and other areas 11:00 A.M.–8:00 P.M.)

Return to I–79 and head north. The interstate soon ends and leaves you on Bayfront Parkway in **Erie.** Turn left onto Eighth Street (at Reed Manu-facturing) then just past the BelAire Hotel, turn right onto Peninsula Drive. It's about a mile to the entrance of **Presque Isle State Park** (814–833–7424). The 3,200-acre sandy peninsula is a long narrow curve that seems like lace (or Swiss cheese) with all its coves, inlets, and ponds. Along the northern coast are more than a dozen sandy beaches, all suitable for swimming and with various amenities like changing rooms, volleyball areas, playgrounds, food concessions, and, of course, picnic tables. But make your first stop the **Stull Interpretive Center** (814–833–0351), on your left near Barracks Beach (watch for the signs) soon after you enter the park and Peninsula Drive becomes a divided road that loops, with the help of bridges, at the farther end of the park. Check out displays on the glacial action that created this unusual formation (it's still moving) and the six distinct ecological zones that comprise the park. (Open June through August, 10:00 A.M.–5:00 P.M. every day; April, May, September, and October, Thursday through Sunday only, 10:00 A.M.–4:00 P.M.)

Follow the 13-mile Peninsula Drive around the park. Make sure you see all three lighthouses. **Presque Isle Lighthouse,** on the northern shore, has a companion exhibit area as you look north to Lake Erie. The **North Pier Lighthouse,** at the farthest end off the road, looks eastward to the lake; look-ing southward, you can see the **Erie Land Lighthouse** on the mainland. On your way to the North Pier, you'll pass Horseshoe Pond with its incongruous array of houseboats (they look exactly like houses, but floating). Continue your loop around Misery Bay. Commodore Perry (you'll hear lots more about him tomorrow), victor in the Battle of Lake Erie, lost many sailors to cold and disease here, and then buried them in nearby Graveyard Pond.

LUNCH: Head to the **Perry Monument** park area for a lovely picnic spot. There are scenic boat tours available (the *Lady Kate,* 814–836–0201 or

800–988–5780), and great views of downtown Erie along East Fisher Drive. (*Lady Kate* operates May 1 through mid-June, Saturday and Sunday 11:00 A.M., 1:00 P.M., and 3:00 P.M.; mid-June through Labor Day, every day, 11:00 A.M.; 1:00, 3:00, and 5:00 P.M.; and forty-five minutes before sunset.)

Also consider the various walking trails, boat rentals, and just nature-watching. With its key spot along the Atlantic Flyway, Presque Isle is Pennsylvania's best spot for bird-watching—one of the best in the United States—with more than 300 species spotted during migration. Peak times are April to mid-May, and September to early December.

Afternoon

When you're ready, take PA 832 south from the park to U.S. 20 east, I–79 south, I–90 east, and PA 89 north to **North East** (www.ne.lakeside.net), a nineteenth-century town that's on the National Register of Historic Places. Stroll around the village's Main Street (U.S. 20) and Lake Street (PA 89), and stop at the shops and galleries, such as **The House of the Potter** (12391 East Main Street; 814–725–4791), which features watercolors and limited-edition prints as well as stoneware, porcelain, and wood. (Open Tuesday through Saturday 10:00 A.M.–5:00 P.M.)

A few blocks south of Gibson Park in the center of town is the **Lake Shore Railway Museum** (31 Wall Street; 814–725–2724). It's an easy walk, but the drive requires a loop past the Lake Street underpass. It's hard to miss the array of locomotives—four of them, among twenty-seven pieces of rolling stock like sleepers, refrigerator cars, and a tank car—sitting outside the former New York Central Depot. Stop inside to check out train memorabilia, or watch one of the sixty-some trains that pass daily. (Free admission. Open May, September, and October, Saturday and Sunday 1:00–5:00 P.M.; Memorial Day through Labor Day, Wednesday through Sunday, 1:00–5:00 P.M.; also by appointment.)

Return to Main Street and head west on U.S. 20. About 3.5 miles from town, on your right, is **Presque Isle Wine Cellars** (9440 West Main Road, North East; 814–725–1314 or 800–488–7492; www.piwine.com) in a lovely wooded area with a deck that overlooks a stream very popular with fisherfolk. (You'll see anglers all over the area this weekend.) This is Governor Ridge's favorite Lake Erie winery and, frankly, for us wine snobs it's as good as it gets in Erie, with some pretty drinkable dry reds like the unexpected Lemberger and Carmine, and a good-value Cabernet Sauvignon. There's also an array of sweet wines and, like most local wineries, home wine-making supplies, including various grape juices. (Open year-round, Monday through Friday 8:00 A.M.–5:00 P.M.; during pressing season, late September through October, Monday through Saturday 8:00 A.M.–6:00 P.M., Sunday 8:00 A.M.–2:30 P.M.)

Loop right to Catholic Cemetery Road and head north to PA 5, practically on the shore of Lake Erie. Head west for a few miles, and watch for the right turn to **LakeView on the Lake** (8696 East Lake Road, 15 miles east of Erie; 814–899–6948 or 888–558–VIEW; www.lakeviewerie.com).

LODGING: Check into the area's only lodgings with an actual view of the lake. You're high enough not to worry about flooding, and there's a sturdy staircase to take you right down to the shore. There's also an outdoor swimming pool, plus badminton, boccie, and that incredible view. Book a mini cottage for privacy. (Massages and wine-tasting weekends are available.)

DINNER: Follow East Lake Road (PA 5), also known as the Seaway Trail, all the way into downtown Erie to the Bayfront Parkway for another view of the lake. When you see the Commodore Perry Yacht Club and the Bay Harbor Marina, turn right for **Shakespier's Bar & Grill** (726 Bayfront Parkway; 814–452–6607) and a view of Presque Isle in a casual atmosphere.

Order the house specialty prime ribs with crabcakes, crab legs, shrimp, perch, or the catch of the day, although it is tempting to consider the Pittsburgh Poor Boy: a clam or oyster variation on the classic sandwich with french fries and coleslaw piled on. Or you can stick to the clam chowder, capped with caramel Granny Smith apple pie. (Open Tuesday through Saturday 11:30 A.M.–9:00 P.M., Friday and Saturday 11:30 A.M.–10:00 P.M.)

Evening

Return along the Bayfront Parkway to **Dobbins Landing**—it's where the big tower is sticking out. Enjoy the long sunset in summer on the **Bicentennial Tower** (814–455–6055), which opened in 1995 to commemorate Erie's 200th anniversary. Walk or take the elevator to two observation decks, the top one at 138 feet. (Admission $2.00, free on Tuesday, and from January through March. Open seven days a week, in April, 10:00 A.M.–6:00 P.M.; May, 10:00 A.M.–8:00 P.M.; Memorial Day through Labor Day, 9:30 A.M.–10:00 P.M.; the rest of September, 10:00 A.M.–9:00 P.M. in October, open only Tuesday, Saturday, and Sunday 10:00 A.M.–6:00 P.M.; January through March, only Saturday and Sunday 10:00 A.M.–6:00 P.M. Closed Easter.)

Bicentennial Tower gives you the eagle's-eye view of Lake Erie.

DAY 2

Morning

BREAKFAST: Your room or cottage includes a coffeemaker and coffee. That and a muffin from yesterday's picnic is enough to tide you over till a rather sumptuous brunch (reservations are a good idea, and local calls are free).

Take a drive through Lake Erie wine and fruit country. A few miles west on PA 5, you'll pass **Penn Shore Vineyards** (10225 East Lake Road; 814–725–8688; www.pennshore.com), with an attractive grape arbor that leads to a tasting room featuring native varieties. (Open July and August, Monday through Saturday 9:00 A.M.–8:00 P.M., Sunday 11:00 A.M.–5:00 P.M.; September through June, Monday through Saturday 9:00 A.M.–5:30 P.M., Sunday 11:00 A.M.–5:00 P.M.)

Turn right (south) onto PA 89 and then left onto Middle Road. After the intersection with Dill Park Road, Middle Road twists to the left. Look right to see the unusual **Octagon Barn** (11441 East Middle Road; not open to the public), the only one of its kind around here. Its century-plus-old brick walls are 8 inches thick. Middle Road twists to the right again. When it twists back left, you can follow it to **Mazza Vineyards** (11815 East Lake Road, North East; 814–725–8695; www.mazzawines.com) for fruit wines, flavored wines, and some varietals in the second-floor tasting room. (Open July and August, Monday through Saturday 9:00 A.M.–8:00 P.M., Sunday 11:00 A.M.–4:30 P.M.; September through June, Monday through Saturday 9:00 A.M.–5:00 P.M., Sunday 11:00 A.M.–4:30 P.M.)

Return south along Middle Road and follow the signs to U.S. 20 and **Arrowhead Wine Cellars** (12073 East Main Road; 814–725–5509; www.arrowheadwine.com) at Mobilia Fruit Farm, with fresh fruit, juices, and more. (Open Monday through Saturday 10:00 A.M.–6:00 P.M.; Sunday noon–5:00 P.M.)

Follow U.S. 20 west through farm country to the outskirts of Erie. Veer right onto PA 955 at Harborcreek, and continue west on PA 5 and PA 5A. French Street is 1 block east of State Street.

BRUNCH: Where's the fire? It's tempting not to rush to brunch at **The Pufferbelly** (414 French Street; 814–454–1557). The former fire station, built 1807–1808 and named for the steam pumpers of the late nineteenth century, features memorabilia and fire department patches from around Pennsylvania. It's a good idea to get reservations for the small but popular (and very inexpensive) buffet, which features a different specialty egg dish each week, plus omelettes, waffles, pastries, carved meats, and hot entrees. (Open Monday through Thursday 11:30 A.M.–9:00 P.M., Friday and Saturday 11:30 A.M.–11:00 P.M.; Sunday brunch, 11:00 A.M.–3:00 P.M., dinner 3:00–8:00 P.M.)

Afternoon

You're on the east side of the block known as **Discovery Square,** which includes three museums and specialty shops. You'll pass one as you circle around to the south. **Glass Growers Gallery** (10 East Fifth Street; 814–453–3758) showcases art glass, handmade jewelry and scarves, and other pieces. The **Erie Art Museum** (411 State Street; 814–459–5477; www. erieartmuseum.org), housed in the onetime Custom House, an 1839 Greek Revival landmark, has an eclectic collection of some 4,000 works, including an intricate fabric sculpture of a late, lamented local diner, complete with detailed denizens. Also check for traveling and special exhibits, and monthly performances. (Admission is $2.00; it's free on Wednesday. Open Tuesday through Saturday 11:00 A.M.–5:00 P.M., Sunday 1:00–5:00 P.M. **Erie Art Museum Frame Shop Gallery,** 423 State Street, free admission; open Tuesday through Friday 10:00 A.M.–5:00 P.M., Saturday 10:00 A.M.–3:00 P.M.)

Pick up the car and take a quick spin through downtown Erie, making sure you go past the historic **Warner Theatre** (814–452–4857) at 811 State Street, a 1931 landmark now undergoing a $10.3 million Benedum Center–like renovation. The only Warner Theatre left in its original form (there were about 800 built) is home to the **Erie Philharmonic** (814–455–1375; www.eriephil.org), the **Lake Erie Ballet Company** (814–864–1580), **Erie Civic Music Association** (814–459–1227; www.dnsllc.com/ecma), **Erie Broadway Series** (814–452–4857 or 814–456–7070; www.eriociviccenter.com), and others.

Continue north (downhill) on State Street toward Dobbins Landing, and turn right at the sign for the **Erie Maritime Museum** (150 East Front Street; 814–452–2744; www.brigniagara.org), which shares space with the county library's main branch, the Raymond M. Blasco Memorial Library, in the Bayview Commons Building. Museum exhibits focus on the Battle of Lake Erie and the details of life in the U.S. Navy at the time, with relatively little on the War of 1812 itself (perhaps just as well, since it was a silly land-grab war that primarily served to convince Canadians they did not want to be part of the United States, and eventually led to a sovereign Canada; see Northern Escape 4). The main attraction, when it's in port, is Pennsylvania's flagship, the brig *Niagara*. It's an accurate, though modernized reconstruction of Commodore Oliver Hazard Perry's flagship during the decisive battle on September 10, 1813. The seaworthy, working vessel includes several timbers from the original warship built in Erie in 1813, but with rigging of steel wire covered in polypropylene and two engines for times when the wind doesn't move the sails. Climb aboard (it's tight quarters if you're tall or otherwise large) for a guided tour and a taste of life aboard a tall ship. (Admission costs $6.00 when *Niagara* is in port, $4.00 when not. Open Monday through Saturday 9:00 A.M.–5:00 P.M., Sunday noon–5:00 P.M.)

DINNER: Dobbins Landing is only a few yards away, and right at the foot of the Bicentennial Tower is the **Waterfront** (4 State Street; 814–459–0606), as famous for its steaks and lobster bisque as for its romantic view of Lake Erie.

(Open for lunch, Monday through Friday 11:00 A.M.–2:30 P.M.; dinner, Monday through Thursday 4:00–9:00 P.M., Friday and Saturday 4:00–10:00 P.M., Sunday 3:00–8:00 P.M.)

Head west on the Bayfront Parkway until it curves southward and becomes—voilà!—I–79. It's about two hours back to Pittsburgh.

THERE'S MORE

Outdoor recreation includes boating, of course, and quite a lot of fishing, plus biking, hiking, and golf. Top-ranked courses (ratings from *Golf Digest*) include:

Riverside Golf Club, 4 stars, 24527 Highway 19, Cambridge Springs, Crawford County (814–398–4537).

North Hills Golf Course, 3½ stars, Corry. Designed by Edmond Ault (814–664–4477).

Downing Golf Course, 3 stars, Harborcreek. Designed by Garbin/Harrison (814–899–5827).

Culbertson Hills Golf Resort, 3 stars, Edinboro. Designed by Thomas Bendelow (814–734–1131).

The Firefighters Historical Museum. This small museum in a former 1903 fire station features two floors of fire-fighting equipment. Open May through October (814–456–5969).

Discovery Square. The cooperative expansion project includes the Erie History Center (814–454–1813) and the new expERIEnce Children's Museum (814–453–3743). Both the art and history museums are to be expanded, and a performance/lecture area added (814–452–1942).

Heritage Wine Cellars. This large winery near North East features many dessert, fruit, and spiced wines; grape juice and wine-making supplies; plus its own restaurant, the **Gathering** (closed Sunday and in winter). Heritage has outlets in Belle Vernon and McKeesport (814–725–8015 or 800–747–0083; www.heritagewine.com).

Erie SeaWolves. Catch a double-A baseball game in intimate (and fairly new) Jerry Uht Park in downtown Erie. The team is now affiliated with the Detroit Tigers, and not the Pirates anymore (814–456–1300 or 800–456–1304; www.seawolves.com).

PREVIEWS OF COMING ATTRACTIONS

The Presque Isle Center, still in the planning/land-acquisition phase, will include research as well as visitors facilities near but not in the park (www.goerie.com/greenway).

SPECIAL EVENTS

March. Erie Maritime Museum offers free admission on Charter Day, in honor of the signing of the Pennsylvania Charter between King Charles II and William Penn (814–452–2744; www.brigniagara.org).

August. We Love Erie Days in Perry Square (check out the heroic statue of the commodore) includes entertainment, food, and more (814–833–7343).

September. Wine Country USA's annual Wine Festival in North East includes tastings, entertainment, food (814–725–4262).

December. During Christmas at the Station, the Lake Shore Railway Museum features holiday decorations. Open Saturday and Sunday afternoon (814–725–2724).

OTHER RECOMMENDED RESTAURANTS AND LODGING

Stonehouse Inn. A fine-dining favorite (814–838–9296).

Matthew's Trattoria at Lovell Place. A popular new spot with a martini lounge (814–459–6458).

Hector's. Line up on 18th Street for pasta fagiole, homemade spaghetti, sausage, and antipasto (814–454–9130).

Chuck and Ginny's Place. Family Italian cooking at excellent prices (814–455–0000).

Baybreeze Restaurant. International fusion cuisine in an art-filled space near the entrance to Presque Isle State Park. Live jazz on Sunday, vocalists Tuesday and Thursday, piano during dinner (814–835–0808; www.eriebaybreeze.com).

Smuggler's Wharf. Right across from the Waterfront on Dobbins Landing (814–459–4273).

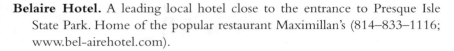
Belaire Hotel. A leading local hotel close to the entrance to Presque Isle State Park. Home of the popular restaurant Maximillan's (814–833–1116; www.bel-airehotel.com).

Glass House Inn. This third-generation-run motel 2 miles from Presque Isle includes a swimming pool, garden, and continental breakfast (814–833–7751 or 800–956–7222; www.glasshouseinn.com).

Spencer House B&B. A Victorian mansion along Erie's former "Millionaires' Row" (814–454–5984 or 800–890–7263).

FOR MORE INFORMATION

The Erie Area Convention and Visitors Bureau, 109 Boston Store Place, Erie, PA 16501; 814–454–7191; www.eriepa.com.

Niagara-on-the-Lake and Stratford, Ontario

CULTURE, VITICULTURE, EH?

3 NIGHTS

Theater • Wine • Art • Gardens • History • Romance

This is the longest and most ambitious trip in this book, but well worth it. Niagara-on-the-Lake makes an easy weekend destination but, once you're there, it would be a shame not to continue on to Stratford. Both of these very English-style towns not only are considered among the most beautiful in Canada but are also among the top one hundred small arts cities in North America, home to superb professional theater festivals. Close to the famous falls, Niagara-on-the-Lake enjoys a mild climate courtesy of the Niagara Escarpment's effect on air movement. Canadians refer to this rich land of orchards and vineyards as the Banana Belt, and while its blossoming wine industry doesn't exactly rival Napa Valley's or even the Finger Lakes' (see Northern Escape 6), it does indeed produce some very credible table wines. Relatively more isolated and laid-back, Stratford is less commercialized yet still cosmopolitan. You may want to strap your bicycles to the back of the car. (Remember that prices quoted are in Canadian dollars.)

DAY 1

Morning

Head north on I–79 to I–90 at Erie, then take the New York State Thruway to Buffalo and I–190—about three and a half hours. Take a break at exit 6

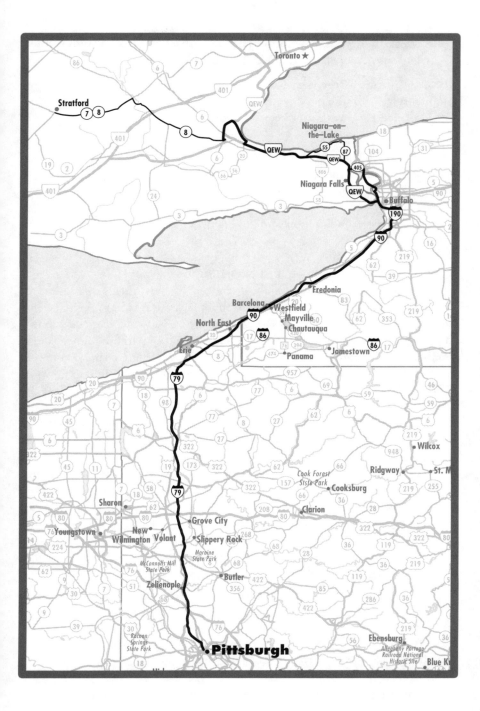

(Elm Street), following signs to the Theatre District and Information Center (Elm, left onto Goodell, right onto Main Street).

LUNCH: Empire Brewing Co. (623 Main Street; 716-840-2337; www. empirebrewco.com). The designated driver can wash down jambalaya or wood-grilled pizza with root beer brewed on the premises.

Afternoon

Continue through the Theatre District and follow the signs to the **Peace Bridge** just a few blocks away, passing a few gas stations (fill up before crossing the border). For customs, make sure you have proof of citizenship (such as a passport or voter registration card), though you probably won't have to show it. Switch the speedometer to metric and head 38 kilometers north on the QEW (Queen Elizabeth Way) to exit 38. Head east on York Road; where it ends, turn left to cruise along the Niagara Parkway.

Take your time. There are some lovely houses and gardens to admire on the drive, plus an occasional glimpse of the Niagara River (for a better view, stop at the Queenston Heights Park, site of the 165-foot-tall Brock's Monument) and innumerable farm markets. You can't take any fresh produce across the border, but you can enjoy it here or choose home-canned jams, chutneys, and relishes to take home. (Pick up a free guide from Tastes of Niagara, 905-357-6104.)

Catch up on Canadian history as you work your way toward town. The former capital of what was then called Upper Canada (now Ontario) was a highly contested area during the War of 1812. Right off the parkway is the **Laura Secord Homestead** (29 Queenston Street; 905–262–4851 or 877–NIA–PARK), an accurate reconstruction of the modest house of Canada's great heroine, who walked 20 miles through dangerous woods to warn British officers of an impending U.S. attack, leading to victory at the Battle of Beaver Dams. The description of "preserving Canada from the Republican menace to the south" alone is worth the $2.00 admission. (Open May 1 through June 19, Tuesday through Sunday 10:00 A.M.–4:00 P.M.; daily till 5:00 P.M. from June 20 through Labor Day.)

A brief hop down the parkway is the more socially prominent **McFarland House** (905–468–3322 or 877–NIA–PARK), badly damaged by those nasty Americans during the war, but now nicely restored. After a whiff of the herb garden and a tour ($2.00) of the Georgian house, you'll want to stop for tea on the terrace. (Afternoon tea, 1:00–4:00 P.M., includes finger sandwiches,

Niagara-on-the-Lake caters to the carriage trade.

fruit, sweets, and scones; tour hours are the same as the Secord Homestead.)

Just outside town on Queen's Parade is **Fort George** (905–468–4257). The only original building is the stone powder magazine from 1796, because the fort changed hands several times and our guys did some damage. The Canadians don't hold it against us, and you can tour the reconstructed fort with costumed guides who demonstrate the crafts and military maneuvers of the day. (Open 9:00 A.M.–5:00 P.M. Victoria Day [a week before our Memorial Day] through June 30; 10:00 A.M.–6:00 P.M. from July 1 through Labor Day; by appointment the rest of the year.)

Your first view of Niagara-on-the-Lake is likely to be an overwhelming vision of a lively street filled with shops, international visitors, and flowers, with the clock atop the war memorial standing sentinel in the center. It's a tempting stroll, but you probably want to check in to your B&B and freshen up for dinner and the theater.

LODGING: Country Side Bed and Breakfast (905–684–6218 or 905–704–9941) is not far from town on a working farm, at 102 Line One Road. Park near the pear orchard.

DINNER: The Shaw Cafe and Wine Bar (905–468–4772), serving lighter French fare and wines by the glass, provides a relaxed but quick repast. It's a short walk from all three theaters.

Evening

Figure on dressy resort wear for the theater. The **Shaw Festival** stages eleven plays in rotating repertory May through November in three theaters throughout town, generally at 2:00 and/or 8:00 P.M. daily (dark on Monday), so you could cram a lot of theater into a weekend. Joining plays by George Bernard Shaw are works by such contemporaries as Noel Coward and Thornton Wilder. It's a good idea to buy tickets ($15 to $75) well in advance (10 to 15 percent off for winter orders); or you can take a chance on rush seats at a 20 percent discount. The festival's season program is also a good visitors guide, and a voucher book entitles you to discounts and goodies at selected wineries (905–468–2172 or 800–511–7429; www.shawfest.sympatico.ca).

DAY 2

Morning

BREAKFAST: Stoke up for a day of wine tasting with truly fresh eggs, fruit, and homemade baked goods at Country Side B&B. The region is best known for ice wine, a lush dessert wine made from grapes frozen on the vine, but there's been successful experimentation with vinifera as well. There are ten wineries within a few miles, more than a dozen not much farther, free maps to help you explore, and road signs to guide the way. The one-ounce tastings generally cost from 50 cents for vin ordinaire to $3.00 to $4.00 for ice wine. U.S. customs will let each adult take home two bottles duty-free, but the duty is only 15 to 35 cents per bottle, and customs officers generally don't sweat the small change. Most wineries also have shops with a variety of related products (Wine Council of Ontario, 905–684–8070).

The nearest winery, **Stonechurch** (905–935–3535), on Irvine Road off Church Street (what Line One turns into heading west), features a not-too-oaky Chardonnay and wine-scented soap. The small winery opens Monday through Saturday at 10:00 A.M., Sunday at 11:00 A.M.; it's open till 6:00 P.M. May through October, 5:00 P.M. in the off season.

My favorite, the **Chateau des Charmes** (905–262–4219; www. chateaudecharmes.com), is in the French tradition and a grand manse on York Road, between Concession Six Road and Four Mile Creek Road. Take a guided tour (hourly, 10:00 A.M.–4:00 P.M.), and be sure to try the intricate Cabernet. Open 10:00 A.M.–6:00 P.M. daily.

Continue along York Road, turn left onto Concession Road One, and follow this to **Maryknissen** (905–468–3554), a small, serious, family-run winery with no froufrou gifts and several drinkable wines for less than $10 a bottle. It opens Monday through Saturday at 10:00 A.M., Sunday at 11:00 A.M.; till 6:00 P.M. in summer, 5:00 P.M. in the off season.

Inniskillin (905–468–3554; www.inniskillin.com), around the corner at Line Three Road, just off the Niagara Parkway, is the granddaddy of local vinifera with a showy wine boutique in a former barn; it's a tad pricey. Open 10:00 A.M.–6:00 P.M. daily May through October; till 5:00 P.M. in the off season.

LUNCH: Stay with the winery motif at **Hillebrand Estates** (905–468–7123 or 800–582–8412; www.hillebrand.com), where Line Two Road (a "block" north of Line Three) crosses Niagara Stone Road (Route 55). The Vineyard Cafe serves local produce (free-range meats as well as fruits and vegetables) as well as its own wines for an elegant lunch or dinner. The winery also hosts a series of concerts, both jazz and blues. (In summer the restaurant is open for lunch 11:30 A.M.–3:00 P.M., dinner 5:00–9:00 P.M.; in winter, lunch noon–3:00 P.M., dinner 6:00–9:00 P.M.)

Afternoon

Take your wine back to the B&B (don't let it sit in your trunk) and enjoy the views along Lakeshore Road. On land, the Victorian and Edwardian houses have gorgeous gardens to admire; look out over the lake and you can see the skyline of Toronto. Back in Old Town, it's usually easy to find a parking space on a side street. Stroll along Queen Street for window-shopping, and do stop and smell the flowers: The town is festooned with them, in window boxes, street planters, and hanging baskets. There are many galleries to explore, such as **Signature Works** (905–468–2880), which showcases only Canadian artworks, mostly fine crafts; **Angie Strauss Fashions** (905–468–2570), featuring Canadian-made art clothing and accessories, and **Angie Strauss Art**

Gallery (905–468–2255), with watercolors and oils; and the **Niagara Pumphouse Visual Arts Centre** (905–468–5455; www.pumphouse.on.ca), a nonprofit gallery with occasional Sunday artists' salons.

DINNER: The historic **Oban Inn** (905–468–2165) on Front Street has two seatings for dinner; the first one, at 5-ish, leaves you time to enjoy the roast duckling before the show. If you can't get reservations, you may be able to just grab a table in the bar.

Evening

Plays rotate throughout the festival, so there's bound to be something you haven't seen yet at the Festival, Court House, or Royal George Theater.

DAY 3

Morning

BREAKFAST: Pack in another farm breakfast, say good-bye to your hosts and to Max the dog, then head for Stratford. Return to the QEW and head north to Hamilton, switching to the 403 (west, toward London), exiting onto Kings Highway 8 in Dundas, which turns into Ontario Street, the main drag, in Stratford. The trip will only take about two hours, giving you time to stop in at **Gallery Stratford** (54 Romeo Street, a right turn off Ontario; 519–271–5271) on the way into town. This regional art museum features changing shows by Canadian artists (including national juried exhibitions) and a gift shop offering strictly Canadian-made crafts. (Open Tuesday through Friday and Sunday 1:00–4:00 P.M., Saturday 10:00 A.M.–4:00 P.M., until May 24; open daily in summer; admission up to $8.00 for special exhibits.)

Return to Ontario Street and continue a few kilometers into town. Follow the signs to the information center, turn right down York Street, pull into the lot, and cross the street for lunch.

LUNCH: The York Street Kitchen (41 York Street; 519–273–7041) is a tiny, funky place known for creative wraps, soups, and sandwiches (like the spicy Thai chicken salad). There's seating inside, but you may want to stop at the take-out window and enjoy lunch along the riverfront. (Open 8:00 A.M.–8:00 P.M. seven days a week.)

Stop at the information kiosk across the street for a 50-cent bag of bird munchies (to feed the swans)—you could even rent a paddleboat to cruise the

Avon. But make sure you pick up the free *Stratford Strolls* booklet for self-guided walking tours. At the least, cross Huron Street at the end of York and explore the Shakespearean Garden, part of more than 1,000 acres of public parks in this small city. Re-create your own Romeo and Juliet on the balcony overlooking the Avon, or relax in the gazebo.

Check into your B&B (there's another hundred-plus here) and leave the car (but not overnight on the street). Stratford is lovely to walk about.

LODGING: The **Heritage House** (169 Church Street; 519–272–1222) is a 120-year-old house furnished with antiques. Host Lloyd Halyk, a retired CBC foreign correspondent, can help make reservations as well as recommendations for dinner, and has available many books about the area and clippings about the season's plays. From the B&B, stroll along Saint Patrick Street in this historic neighborhood, then up Wellington toward that massive Queen Anne Revival landmark: Stratford's City Hall, the Queen of the Square. Free tours are available in July and August (519–271–5140).

Turn right onto Market Place, and 1 short block takes you to the Avon Theatre, one of the festival's smaller venues, and dinner.

DINNER: The **Bistro au Jardin** (111 Downie Street; 519–275–2929) offers casual but creative dining (consider ostrich carpaccio), including a good wine list, at moderate prices in a former storefront. (Open Tuesday through Sunday 11:30 A.M.–2:00 P.M. Open for dinner every day—till 8:00 P.M. on Sunday and Monday, till 9:00 P.M. Tuesday through Thursday, and till 10:00 P.M. on Friday and Saturday.)

Head up and over Ontario Street toward the Avon River and the Festival Theatre, a distinctive evocation of Shakespeare's original Globe Theatre. Let's hope you have time to visit the gardens: There's a naturalistic terraced garden near the main entrance, and a new formal garden featuring a stainless-steel statue of the Bard. Both are filled with the flowers and plants from Shakespeare's plays, and smell as glorious as they look.

Evening

Officially known as the **Stratford Festival of Canada** (519–273–1600 or 800–567–1600; www.stratford-festival.on.ca), this internationally renowned play fest mounts thirteen productions in rotating repertory from May to November in three theaters, generally at 2:00 and/or 8:00 P.M. (Monday is dark.) While the emphasis is on Shakespeare, the festival covers the entire spectrum from Euripides to recent Broadway and off-Broadway hits, starring top Canadian, British, and U.S. actors. As at the newer Shaw, the Stratford Festival features a variety of tours, talks, and other programs; offers various packages with accommodations and other attractions; and publishes the best visitors guide for the area. Regular ticket prices run from $35.50 to $72.50, but there are various discounts for early-season previews, autumn performances, seniors, students, rush seats, and Tuesday (the cheapest at half off).

After the show, take a moonlit walk along Lakeshore Drive. Folks here have no qualms about walking through the parks at night.

DAY 4

Morning

BREAKFAST: The entrees and homemade baked goods vary daily at Heritage House, and there's fresh fruit in season.

This is a great arts town, so check out the galleries in the relatively compact business district. The most famous is the home and studio of **Gerard Brender á Brandis** (249 Ontario Street; 519–565–2222), who makes books with his own woodcut engravings—typesetting them, printing them on an 1882 press, and then hand-binding them. Sometimes he makes the paper, too. On a smaller scale, he's also well known for botanical prints (see some in Carnegie Mellon University's Hunt Botanical Library). (Open Wednesday through Sunday 10:00 A.M.–6:00 P.M., from May 15 through October 31).

Also worth checking out are **Gallery Indigena** (519–271–7881) at 69 Ontario Street and **Village Studios** (519–271–7231) nearby at 75 Ontario Street. Both feature a range of artisan crafts, the former by traditional and modern Inuit, Cree, and other First Nations artists, the latter more contemporary works by a range of Canadian artists. Both are open every day in season.

LUNCH: Just a few steps away at 99 Ontario Street is **Bentley's Pub** (519–271–1121). There's pub food like shepherd's pie, but also quiche, grilled chicken salads (no, they don't put french fries on them), and blackboard specials. There's an inn upstairs as well. (Open 11:30 A.M.–2:00 A.M. daily.)

Afternoon

You could catch a 2:00 P.M. matinee at the Festival, Avon, or Tom Patterson Theatre, but it'll mean a late arrival at home. Don't forget to organize your receipts for customs (Canadian art purchases are duty-free); you can get a refund of the goods and service tax at the border as well. Take Kings Highway

8 to Dundas, 403 east to the QEW, and 405 east to the Queenston Lewiston Bridge, usually the least busy of the Niagara crossings. Then take I–190 south to I–90 (New York State Thruway) west. Switch to I–79 south at Erie, drive to the Grove City exit, turn right onto PA 208, and right again onto U.S. 19. It's about a five-hour trip.

DINNER: Even if you opted for a matinee, **Rachel's Roadhouse** (1553 Perry Highway [U.S. 19]; 724–748–3193) will have those baby back ribs and roasted sweet potato for you, serving till 11:30 P.M. Monday through Saturday, till 10:30 P.M. Sunday. And you're only about an hour from home.

THERE'S MORE

Niagara Falls. You're there. It's there. The easiest way to see this wonder of the world is to cross into the United States at the Queenston Lewiston Bridge and follow the Robert Moses Parkway into Niagara Falls, New York, where you can pull over and gaze.

Hamilton. The Royal Botanical Gardens with its fifty collections makes a tempting stop on your way to or from Stratford—yes, you could have lunch at the Gardens Cafe (905–527–1158; www.rbg.ca).

Bicycling. Winery tours include at least four wineries and a van to pick up your purchases; $4.00 to $5.00 discount if you have your own bike (905–468–1300 or 800–680–7006; www.niagaraworldwinetours.com).

Cycling Niagara. A free booklet describes several routes in the area (905–984–3626 or 800–263–2988; www.tourismniagara.com/cycling).

Stratford–Perth Museum. This local history museum in a former teachers' school across from the Festival Theatre includes changing exhibits in old-style classrooms (519–271–5311; www.cyn.net/~spmuseum).

SPECIAL EVENTS

March. Paddyfest in Listowel, near Stratford—nine days of North America's largest Irish festival.

July 1. Canada Day fireworks at Fort George and festivities at parks and many of the farm stores.

June–September. Art in the Park, an outdoor artists' market of Canadian work, open Wednesday, Saturday, and Sunday from noonish to 5-ish along Lakeside Drive in Stratford (519–225–2692).

September. Niagara Grape and Wine Festival includes concerts, foods, wine, and parades for ten days (905–688–0212; www.grapeandwine.com).

Stratford Fall Fair: Four-day celebration at Stratford Fairgrounds, plus harvest festivals at local farms.

October. Guild of Artists studio tour, Stratford.

OTHER RECOMMENDED RESTAURANTS AND LODGING

Niagara-on-the-Lake

There are nearly 150 B&Bs available through the local B&B association in many price ranges; figure the closer to the center of town, the more expensive (905–468–0123; www.notl.on.ca).

The Prince of Wales Hotel. Luxury accommodations and great food in both casual and fine-dining modes just steps from the Festival Theatre (905–468–3246 or 888–669–5566; www.vintageinns.com).

Moffat Restaurant and Pub. Traditional pub fare plus more adventurous dining, with local beer and wine (905–468–0755).

Carriage Inn. The specialty downstairs is chateaubriand cooked tableside, with accommodations upstairs (905–468–4038; www.carriageinnnnotl.com).

Stratford

The Stratford Festival Accommodations Bureau is a free service that will help you book one of the many B&Bs, inns, guest houses, or hotels in town or the countryside (800–567–1600).

Sun Room. Organic local produce as well as creative casual meat, poultry, and fish (519–273–0331).

The Queen's Inn. Henry's and the Boar's Head Pub offer more traditional and pub foods at this 150-plus-year-old landmark (519–271–1400).

Fellini's Italian Caffe and Grill offers a limited menu after theater as well as moderately priced entrees, pastas, and pizzas all day (519–271–3333).

Rundles. Forget the budget and make reservations for a multicourse prix-fixe feast, fabulous view, and fine dining (519–271–6442).

FOR MORE INFORMATION

Niagara-on-the-Lake Chamber of Commerce, Visitor and Convention Bureau, 153 King Street, Niagara-on-the-Lake, Ontario, Canada L0S 1J0; 905–468–4263; www.niagaraonthelake.com.

Tourism Stratford, 88 Wellington Street, Stratford, Ontario, Canada N5A 2L2; 519–271–5140 or 800–561–SWAN; www.city.stratford.on.ca.

Chautauqua

BRANSON WITH BRAINS

1 NIGHT

Arts • Rocks • Grapes • Lakes

For more than 140,000 people each year, Chautauqua means the 750-acre educational center that hosts a range of visual and performing arts, lectures, classes, and camps on a religious but ecumenical model. Many visitors are families that have been coming for generations, loving the Chautauqua concept as much as the place itself. "Typically American, in that it is typical of America at its best," said one visitor, Theodore Roosevelt. While the bulk of the crowds come for the nine-week "season," Chautauqua is a year-round community with charming architecture, great sports amenities, and an unhurried approach to life.

But Chautauqua is also a lake, and though it's neither a Great nor a Finger, it offers boating, swimming, and fishing, including ice fishing in winter. And Chautauqua is a county, primarily agricultural, growing grapes and a variety of fruits. It also seems to be a state of mind. Folks in western New York were among the most progressive in the nineteenth century—leaders in the abolition, suffrage, feminist, temperance, and civil rights movements. This was the spirit that led to the founding of the Chautauqua Institution in 1874. But generally the people seem to have held on to their favorite parts of the 1800s: town squares, rambling houses, a lack of television in many guest rooms, Sunday noontime dinner as the big meal of the day—though when they do put on a brunch, watch out. And there's a certain expectation of behavior. Dressing for dinner. Courtesy without intrusiveness. No unnecessary noise, but have fun.

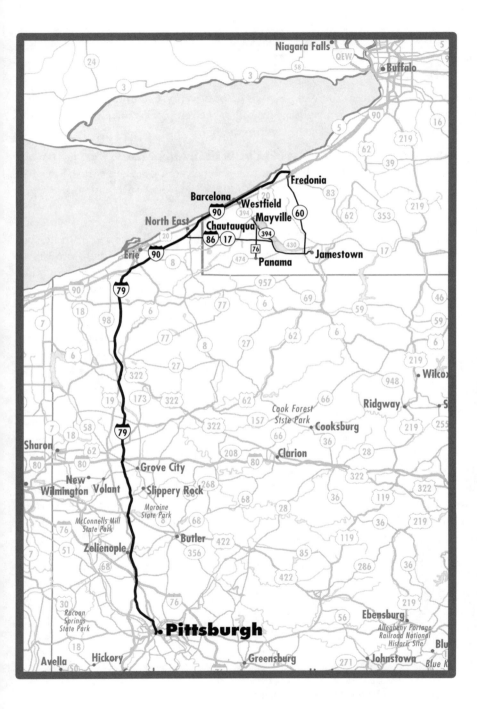

DAY 1

Morning

Take I–79 north to the Wexford exit (about twenty-five minutes from down-town Pittsburgh), turn right at the end of the ramp, then turn left at the light off PA 910 to the small strip mall up the hill.

BREAKFAST: At the Exxon station is **Oasis Express** (2619 Wexford Bayne Road; 724–940–2900), where you can grab take-out or eat-in coffee, Enrico's biscotti, breakfast wraps, and more from a variety of local restaurants. (Open seven days a week, 5:00 A.M.–midnight.)

Continue north on I–79; just before you reach Erie, turn onto I–90 east. About 14 miles later, take I–86 (formerly PA 17) east about 22 miles to County Road 33 south to Panama. Turn right at the flashing light onto NY 474, then left onto County Road 10 about a quarter mile later. Go up the hill and turn left into **Panama Rocks** (11 Rock Hill Road, Panama; 716–782–2845; www.panamarocks.com), an outcropping of glacier-carved conglomerate now surmounted by trees forcing their way into cracks to estab-lish a roothold. A 1-mile hiking trail leads around the formation and can be covered in twenty minutes but, for once, you are urged not to stay on the trail. Give in to the urge and explore the crevice alleyways and caves that lie off the main path. But please remember that the emphasis is on the natural here; there are no railings, and you'll sign a waiver of liability before you enter. If you're a photographer, bring your wide-angle lens. A picnic grove is available. Coin-operated shower facilities are available if you want to freshen up before con-tinuing. (Admission is $5.00. Open May through October, 10:00 A.M.–5:00 P.M. daily. Snack bar hours: noon–4:00 P.M. daily July and August, noon–4:00 P.M. weekends only in June and September.)

Return to Panama and retrace your route north on County Road 33, pass-ing under I–86. At the end of the road, turn left onto NY 394. Head north to Mayville, at the north end of Chautauqua Lake.

LUNCH: Webb's Captain's Table (West Lake Road [NY 394], Mayville; 716–753–3960; www.webbsworld.com) offers dining indoors or outdoors overlooking the lake. (Open for lunch, Monday through Saturday 11:30 A.M.–4:00 P.M.; for dinner, Monday through Thursday 4:00–9:00 P.M., Friday and Saturday 4:00–10:00 P.M., Sunday noon–9:00 P.M.)

Afternoon

Head south on NY 394. Just past the County Road 33 turnoff to Panama is the entrance to the **Chautauqua Institution** (716–357–6200 or 800–836–2787; www.chautauqua-inst.org). Parking is on your right; the visitors center is on your left. If you've arrived during the season (see "Special Events"), you'll want to pick up a copy of the schedule of events to see what lectures, concerts, dance or opera performances, theater events, or chamber-music concerts you want to attend. Note that it's a gated community; you'll need to get a pass at the visitors center. (Season fees can range from $7.00 for a single afternoon to $950.00 for the entire nine weeks. Sunday and off-season admission is always free. An extra fee is charged for classes, camp, and some entertainment.)

Once past the gate, you're inside someplace different. The Chautauqua is a mixture of small town, college campus, park, and summer camp. Brick pedestrian-only paths wind among the ornate Victorian-era cottages and carefully tended gardens. The streets belong to pedestrians and cyclists. Take a shuttle bus from the main gate to **Bestor Plaza,** the town square, or to the imposing **Athenaeum Hotel** on the lakefront. From the hotel, you can explore the shoreline with its beaches, moored sailboats, and recreation areas, then walk out to Miller Bell Tower for the best view of Chautauqua Lake. On your way there along South Lake Drive, you'll pass by Palestine Park, a relief map of the Holy Land, showing mountains, valleys, and cities at a scale of 1¾ feet per mile. Originally laid out for Bible history students, it still attracts a lot of adult interest and sparks interesting Bible discussions.

Or head uphill from the Athenaeum to the Amphitheater, roofed but unclosed by exterior walls, which seats 5,500. Stroll along the Brick Walk to Bestor Plaza, where you can relax, do some people-watching, and enjoy children interacting with the water spurting from the mouths of the four stone fish surrounding the fountain. Check out the specialty shops at the Colonnade, at the end of the Brick Walk. On Bestor Plaza you'll find the **Chautauqua Bookstore** (716–357–2151; bookstore.chautauqua-inst.org/index.html), which offers a wide range of books but specializes in those focusing on Chautauqua, its programs, and its themes, plus gifts like handmade jewelry. (Open daily 9:00 A.M.–5:30 P.M.; in summer, 7:00 A.M.–9:00 P.M.)

From the Colonnade, wind around Pratt Street and ramble down Ramble Street to take in an exhibition at the **Chautauqua Center for the Visual**

The fountain at Bestor Plaza features the four pillars upon which Chautauqua was founded: Education, Religion, Recreation, and the Arts.

Arts (716–357–2771; 716–673–9575 off season; www.ciweb.org) on Wythe Avenue. (Open Monday through Thursday and Saturday 10:00 A.M.–5:00 P.M., Friday 11:00 A.M.–7:00 P.M., Sunday noon–6:00 P.M.)

If you want to wander farther afield at a slightly faster rate, bicycle rentals are available at the Jamestown Cycle Shop's Chautauqua location (716–357–9032) next to the fire department, or you can bring your own—make sure it has a bell or other signaling device, and a headlight and reflectors for after dark. And remember to bike on the street, not the sidewalks. (Rentals Monday through Saturday 10:00 A.M.–6:00 P.M., Sunday noon–6:00 P.M.)

There are eight dining options on the institution grounds, some of them open only seasonally, but let's go exploring to **Jamestown.**

DINNER: Head south on NY 394 to I–86 east to Jamestown and **MacDuff's** (317 Pine Street, at the corner of Fourth; 716–664–9414). Signature dishes at this award-winning chef-owned restaurant are filet mignon with port and Stilton sauce, and veal with blackberry sauce. Choose from more than forty single-malt Scotches and an excellent wine selection. Reservations recommended. (Dinner served Monday through Saturday 5:30 P.M.–closing.)

LODGING: Head west from Jamestown on I–86 to the exit for NY 430 north and the **Lake Side Inn** (4696 Chautauqua Avenue, Maple Springs; 716–386–2500; www.mslsi.com), which occupies eleven wooded acres diagonally across the lake from the Chautauqua Institution. Enjoy the inn's private beach and dock.

Evening

If it's the season, you have a variety of events to choose from at the Chautauqua Institution. In winter, book a sleigh ride at the inn. Or just enjoy the solitude.

DAY 2

Morning

BREAKFAST: Have an early light munchie at the inn just to hold you for a bit.

From the Lake Side Inn, head south on NY 430 to I–86 east, then take NY 60 south through Jamestown to U.S. 62 and turn right. Take the first left turn after approximately 3 miles onto Riverside Road, then head left after about half a mile to the **Jamestown Audubon Nature Center** (1600 Riverside Road; 716–569–2345; www.jasny.org). The Roger Tory Peterson Nature Interpretive Building, which features a large collection of Peterson's bird prints, won't be open yet, but morning is the best time to see birds on the 600-acre wildlife sanctuary. More than 5 miles of trails, including boardwalks over wetlands, lead through the preserve—some may be a little much for the casual stroller. (Free. The building is open April through October, Monday through Saturday 10:00 A.M.–5:00 P.M., Sunday 1:00–5:00 P.M. November through March, open Tuesday through Saturday 10:00 A.M.–4:00 P.M., Sunday 1:00–4:00 P.M.)

That walk was good preparation for what's coming next. Return to I–86 and head west to NY 426 south. Drive about 5 miles, following the signs to **Peek'n Peak** (1405 Olde Road, Clymer; 716–355–4141, ext. 7155; www.pknpk.com).

BRUNCH: This is one of the most extravagant brunches you're likely to encounter anywhere. Each **Champagne Sunday Brunch** is on a different theme, from Europe or the Mediterranean to the Pacific to South America, with hot foods, cold salads, buffets, cooked or carved meats to order, mountains of desserts, and complimentary champagne and bloody marys. (Brunch seatings at 10:45 A.M. and 1:15 P.M., sometimes with hours extended. Reservations are recommended at least three weeks in advance. Four other restaurants are available at the resort for breakfast, lunch, and dinner, including seasonal dinner buffets. See "There's More.")

Return to Jamestown via I–86. From NY 60, heading south into town, turn left onto Buffalo Street, left onto Falconer Street, and left onto Curtis Street. The striking, neo-Arts-and-Crafts **Roger Tory Peterson Institute** (311 Curtis Street, Jamestown; 716–665–2473; www.rtpi.org) houses wildlife art and photography exhibitions and the collection of naturalist Dr. Roger Tory Peterson. Exhibitions focus on this famed Jamestown native's appreciation of the natural world. The twenty-seven-acre setting provides the opportunity for a short walk. (Admission: $3.00. Hours: Tuesday through Saturday 10:00 A.M.–4:00 P.M., Sunday 1:00–5:00 P.M.)

From Jamestown, NY 60 traverses farmlands and orchards as it heads north. In season, watch for signs to direct you to produce available at farm stands as well as card tables set up in front of farmhouses. Continue to, and turn right onto, U.S. 20. Turn right again after 1 mile onto South Roberts Road and follow it 3 miles south to **Woodbury Vineyards** (3230 South Roberts Road; 716–679–9463). Woodbury cultivates vinifera grapes; the Glacier Ridge Red was the winner of my taste test. (Summer hours: Monday through Saturday 9:00 A.M.–8:00 P.M., Sunday noon–8:00 P.M. Off season, Monday through Saturday 9:00 A.M.–5:00 P.M., Sunday noon–5:00 P.M.)

Return to U.S. 20 and head west to hail **Fredonia** (for Marx Brothers fans, this is Duck Soup). On the north side of the classic town square, with its ornate fountain, is the 1891 **Fredonia Opera House** (9–11 Church Street, Fredonia; 716–679–1891; www.fredopera.org). The restored building offers a full schedule of concerts, films, plays, and dance recitals. Guided tours are available. The tree-shaded streets around the square are inviting, and you may succumb to the lure of pedestrianism.

Continue west on U.S. 20 past row upon row of grapevines. For the most part these grapes are being grown for juice rather than for wine. Ahead is **Westfield,** Grape Juice Capital of the World and home to Welch's and Mogen David. In the park at the corner of Main (U.S. 20) and Portage Streets stands a statue of **Abraham Lincoln** and another of **Grace Bedell.** Miss Bedell was the young girl who wrote a letter to Mr. Lincoln suggesting that he might attract some votes if he grew some "whiskers." The two statues commemorate their meeting when Lincoln's inaugural train stopped in Westfield, and Bedell had the chance to see Lincoln's new beard in person. The town's historic district stretches south along Portage Street and east along East Main Street from the statues, and is worth a stroll for its lovely turn-of-the-twentieth-century houses.

Head north on North Portage Street (NY 394) to the intersection with NY 5 at Barcelona. The fieldstone **Barcelona Lighthouse** was the first, and only, lighthouse in the country to be fueled by its own source of natural gas. The idea didn't catch on, the gas well ran out, and the lighthouse was belatedly decommissioned. Today, the lighthouse—a private residence and popular postcard icon—is lit with a modern gas lamp. There is a parklet with picnic benches near the tower.

For a change of scenery, return to Fredonia via NY 5 east along the lakeshore, turning right onto Temple Road as the power-plant stacks of Dunkirk come into view, then left onto U.S. 20.

DINNER: The tall white columns of the **White Inn** (52 East Main Street, Fredonia; 716–672–5770; www.whiteinn.com), built in the style of a country manor, are just steps away from the town square. In the 1930s Duncan Hines (yes, he was a real person and the arbiter of taste then) included the White Inn on his fifty-member "Family of Fine Restaurants" list. (Breakfast, Monday through Saturday 7:00–10:00 A.M., Sunday 8:00–11:00 A.M. Lunch, Monday through Saturday 11:30 A.M.–2:00 P.M. Dinner, Monday through Thursday 5:00–8:30 P.M., Friday and Saturday 5:00–9:00 P.M., Sunday 12:30–8:00 P.M.)

Head a mile and a fraction east on U.S. 20 and north on NY 60 to the NY Thruway (I–90) entrance. Follow I–90 to Erie, then head south and home on I–79.

THERE'S MORE

Peek'n Peak Resort and Conference Center. This four-season resort features twenty-seven ski slopes and trails served by nine chairlifts, plus other winter sports. In warmer weather, reserve tee times well in advance at the two eighteen-hole golf courses: the Upper Course, designed by John Exley, is rated 4 stars by *Golf Digest;* the Lower Course, designed by Fred Garbin, 3½. Brush up on your skills at the **Roland Stafford Golf School**

(800–447–8894; www.staffordgolf.com). Accommodations are available in the main inn; also condos and suites (716–355–4141; www.pknpk.com).

Chautauqua Golf Club. The Chautauqua Institution has two courses, both rated 4 stars by *Golf Digest:* the Lake Course, designed by Donald Ross, and the Hill Course, designed by Xen Hassenplug (716–357–6211).

The Lucy-Desi Museum. Lucille Ball's hometown celebrates the memory and preserves the effects of the First Couple of Comedy. Open every day May through October, weekends only the rest of the year. (Admission is $5.00; 716–484–7070; www.lucy-desi.com).

Summer Wind Chautauqua Lake Cruises. Leave from Lucille Ball Memorial Park in Celoron (716–763–7447).

Merritt Estate Winery. The first of the modern farm wineries in Chautauqua County. Forestville (716–965–4800 or 888–965–4800; www. merrittestatewinery.com).

SPECIAL EVENTS

June–August. Chautauqua Institution hosts its own resident theater company, ballet, opera, and orchestra, not to mention its various arts, music, and dance schools, camps for young people, movie theater, and more. The nine-week season includes a variety of lectures, readings, and other events covered by the gate fee. Separate tickets are required for opera and theater, and those tickets serve as gate tickets. Amphitheater seating is first-come, first-served. Performers have ranged from the Beach Boys to *A Prairie Home Companion* to the Pittsburgh Symphony Orchestra (as featured on Chautauqua's own performance program on National Public Radio). The 2001 lecture themes are "The Abrahamic Initiative," focusing on building bridges among Jews, Muslims, and Christians; and "The Lincoln Program," exploring professional ethics. For tickets, call 716–357–6250. For the accommodation referral service, 716–357–6250. For general information, 716–357–6263 or 800–836–2787. The Web site is www.chautauqua-inst.org.

Free musical concerts in the Celebrate Jamestown series are held every Thursday evening and Friday afternoon at Potters Terrace in downtown Jamestown. Concerts include big-band, hip-hop, classic rock, and country offerings. Free admission. Thursday 7:00–9:00 P.M., Friday noon–2:00 P.M. (716–664–2477).

August. Two-day Nature Art Festival features eighty nature artists at work in festival studios at four locations in Jamestown (716–569–2345 or 800–758–6841).

September–October. See cider being pressed on an 1890-vintage cider press at the Busti Cider Mill Farm Market, Jamestown. Saturday and Sunday 1:00–4:00 P.M. (716–487–0177).

OTHER RECOMMENDED RESTAURANTS AND LODGING

Barker Brew Company. Big deli sandwiches and a selection of microbrews in a historic building on the Fredonia town square (716–679–3435).

Italian Fisherman. Casual bar food inside or on the deck, with frequent live music events, such as the Trombone Concert and rooftop Pops Symphony (www.bemusbaypops.com) performances. (Bemus Point; 716–386–7000; www.italianfisherman.com).

William Seward Inn. Historic bed-and-breakfast. A fixed-price dinner is available to nonguests but must be reserved, with the appetizer and entree selected in advance. One seating at 7:00 P.M. (Westfield; 716–326–4151 or 800–338–4151; www.williamsewardinn.com).

The Athenaeum Hotel. The grand hotel built in 1881 overlooks Chautauqua Lake on a tree-shaded hill on the grounds of the Chautauqua Institution. The high-ceilinged rooms contain authentic period furnishings with wicker chairs and lace curtains. American plan: three meals a day, including lunch buffet and a five-course "classic American" dinner. Dress code for dinner (716–357–4444 or 800–821–1881; www.athenaeum-hotel.com).

The Spencer Hotel. A remodeled historic Victorian hotel on the grounds of the Chautauqua Institution. Each room is painted by local artists or portrays a theme from a literary work (716–357–3785 or 800–398–1306; www.thespencer.com).

FOR MORE INFORMATION

Chautauqua County Visitors Bureau, P.O. Box 1441, Chautauqua Institution Welcome Center, Route 394, Chautauqua, NY 14722; 800–242–4569; www.tourchautauqua.com.

New York's Finger Lakes

WINING AND GORGING

3 NIGHTS

Glass • Wine • Farm Products • Grand Canyons

This trip is brought to you by: geology. Don't worry, I'm not going to get academic about it—much. But you might want to be thankful for the glaciers that made this trip possible, grinding up boulders into sand for glassmaking at Corning, carving out the Finger Lakes themselves to provide the microclimate that makes wine production in upstate New York possible, and creating the spectacular geographic features that bracket our trip: the Genessee Gorge of New York (billed as the Grand Canyon of the East) and Pine Creek Gorge (the Grand Canyon of Pennsylvania). While I feel that each has its high points, my opinions aren't carved in stone.

The Finger Lakes area is something like the Napa Valley—without the priciness or the attitude. The second largest wine-producing region in the United States also manages to make some of the very best wine in the U.S., perhaps even the world. There are more than sixty wineries on the eleven lakes; you'll have time to visit only a few of the ones along two lakes. And given the rich farming country around here—casual roadside farm stands abound—there's fabulous food as well, making for a "budget luxury" excursion, if an occasionally cheesy one.

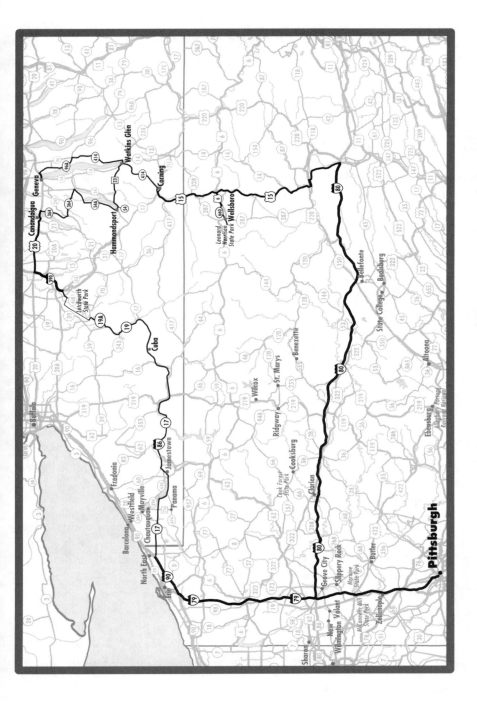

Head north on I–79 to I–90, then east to I–86 (it's what used to be PA/NY 17), to NY 305 and south on to **Cuba** in less than three hours. The **Cuba Cheese Shoppe** (53 Genessee Street; 716–968–3949 or 800–543–4938; www.cubacheese.com) features adult-flavored XXX-sharp, a-little-goes-a-long-way-in-flavor cheddar. Or try the milder-flavored cheddars and cheese spreads. Store legend holds that Cuba was once the center of a cheddar cartel that set prices each week throughout the land. Be that as it may, with some cheddar from the source, some fruit, crackers, or bread, and beverages (just across the road a piece are Giant Food supermarket, 716–968–2360, and the smaller Story Block Grocery, 716–968–1057, if you want to add to your fare), you have the makings for a picnic lunch. But don't eat just yet: Return to I–86 east and head toward the perfect spot for your picnic. (Open Monday through Friday 9:00 A.M.–6:00 P.M., Saturday and Sunday 9:00 A.M.–5:00 P.M.)

LUNCH: Continue 13 miles (two more exits) east on I–86 to Belvedere, and take NY 19 north to Portageville. Just north of town is the entrance to **Letchworth State Park** (716–493–3600) and the forested upper reaches of the Genessee Gorge. The 17-mile-long Grand Canyon of the East features 600-foot-high cliffs, and Inspiration Point provides a view of two of the park's three major waterfalls on a trail loop. One of the park's picnic areas provides the perfect setting for lunch. Or stick with a restaurant and overlook the falls at **Glen Iris Inn** (716–493–2622; www.glenirisinn.com), the former country estate of William Pryor Letchworth, donor of the original park property. (Park admission costs $4.00 per vehicle. It's open 6:00 A.M.–11:00 P.M. every day.)

Afternoon

Follow the park road to the north end of the park, turn right onto NY 36 to Mount Morris, then left onto NY 408 to the I–390 interchange. Take I–390 north to U.S. 20, head east to **Canandaigua,** and follow the signs to the **Sonnenberg Gardens** (151 Charlotte Street; 716–394–4222; www.sonnenberg.org). You can tour the forty-room Victorian mansion, replete with Queen Anne–style turret, balconies, verandas, arches, and niches, but it's the dozen theme gardens that attract me: the Sub Rosa "secret" garden planted solely in green and white, the fragrant Moonlight Garden, the Formal Garden with its cone-shaped trimmed yews and 15,000 hand-planted annuals, and the naturalistic Rock Garden with streams, pools, and a vine-covered Lookout Tower. (Admission is $8.50. Open mid-May through October 15, daily 9:30 A.M.–5:30 P.M. Open for special holiday programs till December 31, Tuesday through Friday 5:30–9:00 P.M., Saturday and Sunday 3:30–9:00 P.M.)

Head east briefly on U.S. 20; turn right onto NY 364 and head south to **Penn Yan,** which takes its name from the Pennsylvanians and Yankees who combined in its founding. Buckwheat is one of the major local crops, and you can pick up some of the local product (kitchen ready as flour, groats, and the like) in the small retail outlet in the office lobby of **Birkett Mills** (163 Main Street; 315–536–3111; www.thebirkettmills.com), famed for mixing the batter for the world's largest-ever buckwheat pancake in a cement truck for the area's onetime Buckwheat Festival. (Open Monday through Friday 8:00 A.M.–noon and 1:00–4:00 P.M. Mill tours are by appointment only.)

Take NY 54A south along the east branch of Y-shaped Keuka (pronounced KYOO-kuh) Lake, over the hill at Bluff Point, and south along the west branch of Keuka Lake on what the British Airways magazine *Highlife* proclaimed to be one of the fifteen most scenic drives in the world. The shaded, winding road, never far from the shore of the lake, leads to the picture-perfect town of **Hammondsport,** nestled at the south end of the lake.

DINNER: The **Village Tavern** (30 Mechanic Street; 607–569–2528), on the north end of Village Square, is the best place to get an early tasting of local wines; it has probably the widest array of local wine by the glass. Order several to wash down fresh fish and seafood, steaks, chicken, pasta, and vegetarian dishes in this aviation-decorated casual eatery. (Open seven days a week, Memorial Day through December 1; lunch, 11:30 A.M.–3:00 P.M., dinner, 5:00–9:00 P.M., till 10:00 P.M. Friday and Saturday; closed Monday and Tuesday the rest of the year.)

Evening

Cross the street into the Village Square; the gazebo bandstand hosts many a concert on summer Thursday evenings. Or just stroll around town before making your way east around the south end of Keuka Lake onto NY 54 north briefly. Veer right onto County Road 67, turn right onto County Road 96 just beyond North Urbana, and continue straight onto County Road 23 and into **Watkins Glen.** Take NY 414 for 7 miles north up the east shore of Seneca Lake (you'll pass a little waterfall) to the **Chateau LaFayette Reneau** (607–546–2602 or 800–469–9463; members.aol.com/clrwine).

LODGING: A winery as well as a B&B, the Chateau LaFayette Reneau offers spectacular views of Seneca Lake on its 140 acres.

DAY 2

Morning

BREAKFAST: Sit down to a massive country breakfast served family-style with eggs, fresh fruit, toast, potatoes, fresh baked goods, and sometimes two kinds of sausages as well as bacon.

Head south from Watkins Glen on NY 414. As you pass through the hamlet of Beaver Dam, watch for a farmhouse on your right displaying a sign advertising cheese for sale. Doris Roy at **Foxridge Jersey Farm** (607–962–5446) has been greeting prospective cheese purchasers at the farmhouse door for many years with three kinds of New York cheeses. (Hours? If you see the sign, it means she's at home, Sunday sales included.)

Continue south on NY 414 to **Corning,** a town twice reborn. Stripped bare of trees by logging in the mid-nineteenth century, the town lured a Brooklyn glassmaker to upstate New York with the promise of skilled labor, inexpensive coal, and deposits of glacial sand. The result: Corning Glass Works, now world-famous **Corning Inc.** The second rebirth followed a 1972 flood that submerged the town's main street, since then simultaneously rebuilt and historically restored to a lively shopping district.

The main attraction is the newly renovated and expanded **Corning Museum of Glass** (1 Museum Way, off NY 414; 607–974–8274 or 877–733–2664; www.cmog.org). Glass fanciers can spend a full day and then some appreciating works like the new *Glass Wall,* a secular stained-glass-and-steel-cable monument, 65 by 14 feet, dedicated to the late Linda McCartney and featuring her favorite flower, the lily, as a motif. Your tour of the 35,000-square-foot museum starts at the new Glass Innovation Center, which provides a look at optics, materials, and discovery: the science behind the making of telescopes, televisions, windshields, lighthouse lenses, and casserole dishes. Visit the Hot Glass Show for a live, narrated demonstration of glassblowing; overhead monitors let you see the details without feeling (too much of) the heat. And walk through 35 Centuries of Glassmaking in the larger redesigned (and reopened in fall 2000) art and history galleries, the most comprehensive glass collection in the world—including the largest selection of glass from the upper Ohio Valley around Pittsburgh, from workaday bottles from the early

1800s to elaborate pieces made for the White House. Some of my favorites include George Woodall's delicately carved cameo glass (1890), an extravagant cut-glass table made by Baccarat for the 1878 Paris Exposition Universelle, and an ancient Roman vessel whose ribbon-glass design still looks hip and attractive after a couple of millennia. More recent works by today's glass artists (including Oakdale resident Kathleen Mulcahy) are featured in other galleries. And set to open in May 2001 is the final piece of the museum's expansion, the Special Exhibition Gallery, making its debut with Glass of the Sultans, a major overview of Islamic glass work, through September 3. (Admission $10.00, or $12.50 for a joint ticket with the Rockwell Museum. Open seven days a week, 9:00 A.M.–5:00 P.M.; July through the Labor Day weekend, till 8:00 P.M. Closed Thanksgiving, December 24–25, and January 1.)

Your path ends—surprise!—in the shops area, a veritable mall of glass, and it's not just, or even mostly, Corning products. Over here, find fine crystal from around the world, there a gallery of work from today's noted glass artists, here a selection of glass jewelry and beads, over there a variety of scientific toys, then a wallful of Christmas ornaments, and even more. Of course there's a Steuben Glass Gallery, and the largest shop is for Corning products (stock up on those two-quart Pyrex measuring cups while you have the chance). Yes, the shops will ship if you don't want to carry everything home.

LUNCH: The **Windows Cafe,** near the museum's admissions lobby, offers sandwiches, hot entrees, and a chance to rest your feet. (Open 9:30 A.M.–5:30 P.M.)

Afternoon

Head south across the Chemung River to downtown Corning. It's a short walk via the pedestrian bridge into Riverfront Centennial Park (look for kiosks and peddler wagons), or you can check in the museum lobby for that day's schedule of the museum's shuttle bus, which runs very frequently on summer weekends. Right past Market Street, on Cedar Street and Denison Parkway (NY 352), the **Rockwell Museum** (111 Cedar Street; 607–937–5386; www.stny.com/RockwellMuseum), housed in Corning's former city hall, has also caught the renovation spirit. The museum, which closed temporarily in September 2000, is to reopen in May 2001 with a new focus on its American western art and artifact collection—the largest in the eastern United States—with works by Frederic S. Remington, Thomas Moran, C. M. Russell, and N. C. Wyeth, among others. The new Rockwell is also expected to have its own cafe, space for special exhibitions, and an entirely new look. The museum's second major collection, Carder Steuben Glass, is to be relocated to another site, not yet determined at press time. (Admission costs $5.00, or $12.50 for a joint ticket with the Corning Museum of Glass. Open Monday through Saturday 9:00 A.M.–5:00 P.M.; Sunday noon–5:00 P.M. Closed January 1, Thanksgiving, and December 24–25.)

Stroll along Market Street and peek down the side streets for treasures, especially for the variety of some one hundred galleries, antiques shops, and other interesting outlets, including **Cool Arts at The Gallery** (607–962–1212), **Vitrix Hot Glass Studio** (607–936–8707), **Van Etten Antiques & Collectibles** (607–936–3560), and **18th & 19th Century Antiques** (607–962–0876). My favorite is the **Glass Menagerie** (37 East Market Street; 607–962–6300), which has an assortment of glass gifts and antique children's books but is most notable for one of the nation's largest selection of artist-made, often limited-edition kaleidoscopes. Ask Dick or Jackie Pope for the newest offerings. (Open Monday through Friday 10:00 A.M.–8:00 P.M., Saturday 9:30 A.M.–8:00 P.M., Sunday noon–5:00 P.M.)

DINNER: It's not far down Market to the **London Underground** (69 East Market Street; 607–962–2345), with dining areas on three floors to enjoy creative and nouvelle pairings of local produce with local wine. (Open Monday through Saturday 11:30 A.M.–11:00 P.M.; seating until 9:00 P.M.)

Evening

Return north on NY 414 to your B&B. Enjoy an evening under the stars.

DAY 3

Morning

BREAKFAST: Fuel up for a day of winery-hopping with another country breakfast.

Brace (and pace) yourself. It wasn't too many years ago that most of the wine production of the Finger Lakes was pink and sweet and came in varieties that shared names with local geographic features. Now dozens of Finger Lakes vineyards are planted in vinifera varieties whose wines compete (and win awards) on an international level. You'll have the chance to visit the region's vinifera pioneers, as well as newcomers bent on establishing reputations. There are advantages to visiting the new kids on the oenological block:

You'll find a warm welcome and an openness to discussion missing from their California counterparts. Be prepared to pay a tasting fee of $1.00 or $2.00, generally refunded if you buy something. Just watch for the purple signs with a bunch of grapes, marking the way to the many wineries. And be on the lookout for roadside farm stands.

Most of the wineries here do best with Pinot Noirs and Chardonnays. Also, if you're used to, and tend to avoid, Riesling with a high sugar content, you may be pleasantly surprised by the dry Rieslings produced by a few of the wineries. Our starting point is right here: the **Chateau Lafayette Reneau** itself. Stroll down to the antique barn and enjoy the view of the lake and vineyards from the tasting deck.

Next, head north on NY 414 along the east side of Seneca Lake. Just south of Lodi is **Lamoreaux Landing Wine Cellars** (9224 Route 414; 607–582–6011; www.fingerlakes.net/lamoreaux), offering estate-bottled vinifera wines. A window in the tasting room in the striking Greek Revival winery lets you watch the wine-making process. Competition judges like the Rieslings. (Open Monday through Saturday 10:00 A.M.–5:00 P.M., Sunday noon–5:00 P.M.)

Continue north on NY 414, and turn left in Ovid onto NY 96A north. The fenced-in area on your right is the former Seneca Army Depot, fallen prey to a round of military base closures. Not far before Geneva, you'll see a sign indicating a left turn to **New Land Vineyard** (577 Lerch Road; 315–585–4432). The wines are much better than the unprepossessing sales cabin in the middle of a field might indicate. The vineyard grows only vinifera grapes. My choice is the Pinot Noir—then play with the resident dog, who's good at training humans to throw sticks. (Open May 1 through November 15, Monday through Friday noon–5:00 P.M., Saturday 11:00 A.M.–6:00 P.M., Sunday 11:00 A.M.–5:00 P.M.)

Continue north on NY 96A, then turn left onto U.S. 20 through Geneva. Beyond the center of town, watch for the cloverleaf turnoff to the right onto NY 14 along the west shore of Seneca Lake.

LUNCH: Belhurst Castle (2 miles south of Geneva on NY 14; 315–781–0201; www.belhurstcastle.com), an 1890 private-home-turned-casino-turned-speakeasy-turned-restaurant-inn, overlooks Seneca Lake, with a small garden in between. Dine in one of the six carved-wood rooms or on the veranda, if the weather cooperates. Guest rooms also available, and B&B guests have access to wine on tap on the second floor. (Open for lunch, Monday

Belhurst Castle is a great place to relax.

through Saturday 11:00 A.M.–2:00 P.M.; dinner, Monday through Saturday 5:00–9:30 P.M., Sunday 3:30–9:00 P.M.; brunch, Sunday 11:00 A.M.–2:00 P.M.)

Afternoon

Farther south on NY 14 is the **Anthony Road Wine Co.** (1225 Anthony Road, Penn Yan; 315–536–2182). I've enjoyed tracking the progress of this relative newcomer to the Finger Lakes wine scene. (Open Monday through Saturday 10:00 A.M.–5:00 P.M., Sunday noon–5:00 P.M.)

Continue on NY 14 through Dresden, and in a few miles you'll see on your right the modest sign for one of the area's stars. The namesake of the **Hermann J. Wiemer Vineyard** (3962 Route 14, Dundee; 607–243–7971 or 800–243–7971; www.wiemer.com), born into a family with 300 years of wine-making experience in Germany's Mosel Valley, was one of the leaders in bringing vinifera to the Finger Lakes. The winery, installed in the shell of a barn, is notable for its austere, almost ecclesiastical white interior. You may see Mr. Wiemer himself in the wine-production area; please don't disturb him, but leave him to his craft (that's more wine for the rest of us). The helpful sales staff will provide samples of Chardonnay, Pinot Noir, and dry Riesling; all are can't-go-wrong choices. (Open Monday through Friday 10:00 A.M.–5:00 P.M.; from April through November open only Saturday 10:00 A.M.–5:00 P.M., Sunday 11:00 A.M.–5:00 P.M.)

Just a few more miles south on NY 14 is **Wixson's Honey Stand** (4937 Lakemont-Himrod Road, Dundee; 607–243–8493), which sells honey and beeswax candles. Inside the store you'll find a glass-enclosed hive in action; see if you can spot the queen bee. I like the fruit-honey spreads, and occasionally indulge in an ice cream cone. (Open May 15 through October 15, seven days a week, depending upon traffic and the bees' production.)

Retrace your route north on NY 14 to Dresden, and take NY 54 south to Penn Yan. Leave Penn Yan on NY 54A south along the west shore of Keuka Lake. Just after the west branch of Keuka Lake joins the main body of the lake (as you pass the tip of Bluff Point), look for a turnoff to your right onto Gallagher Road at Gibson Landing. Follow this up a very steep hill, then turn right onto Middle Road, then left to the area's most highly respected winery, **Dr. Konstantin Frank Vinifera Wine Cellars** (9749 Middle Road; 607–868–4884 or 800–320–0735; www.drfrankwines.com). The late Dr. Frank's pioneering work in establishing vinifera in the eastern United States is carried on by his grandsons Frederick Frank and Eric Volz. My favorites here are the Pinot Noir and the Fleur de Pinot Noir. The Rieslings and Chardonnays comport themselves well in competitions, and Fred boosts his very dry sparkling wine. For something different, listen to the story of, and try a taste of, the available-nowhere-else-I-know-of Rkatsiteli (yes, that's the spelling), a red wine with Eastern European roots. (Open Monday through Saturday 9:00 A.M.–5:00 P.M., Sunday noon–5:00 P.M.)

Continue south on Middle Road, turn right onto Wright Road, then turn left onto County Road 76 to the **Heron Hill Winery** (9249 County Road 76; 607–868–4241 or 800–441–4241; www.heronhill.com), whose recent expansion project included a new tasting room adjacent to a patio with a spectacular view of Keuka Lake. The Chardonnays represent a good value. Check out the wine spreads and sauces in the gift shop. (Open Monday through Saturday 10:00 A.M.–5:00 P.M., Sunday noon–5:00 P.M.)

Retrace your route to NY 14 and head south to Watkins Glen at the south end of Seneca Lake. With a spectacular gorge in the center of the village and many farms and orchards nearby, Watkins Glen is a tourist base for the lake district. The downtown scene offers a variety of shops, including the Seneca Earthworks Cooperative Market on Thursday and Saturday, and of course plenty of wine and great food.

DINNER: Traveling south on NY 14, just as you're easing into downtown Watkins Glen, take the sharp right up the hill on NY 409. Follow the signs to a right turn onto NY 28, and then follow the signs to **Castel Grisch Estate Winery** (3380 Country Route 28, Watkins Glen; 607–535–9614; www. fingerlakes-ny.com/castlegrisch/). If the weather is nice, opt for a table on the porch for a spectacular view of Seneca Lake. Or snuggle up inside the Swiss-German rustic restaurant and enjoy the cheese fondue, a house specialty. Note that the wines tend to be on the sweet side, the better to pair with a very generous duck a l'orange and hearty schnitzels. (The restaurant is open daily from 11:00 A.M. to 9:00 P.M. from May through October, weekends only the rest of the year.)

Evening

It's a short drive south on Franklin Street (NY 14) to **Watkins Glen State Park** (607–535–4511). Walk up eighty-three steps into the gorge for **Time-spell** (607–535–8888), which uses the stone cliffs of a natural amphitheater in the gorge, carved out over the millennia by water, as the backdrop for a light, sound, and laser presentation of geologic and local history. Visitors stand for the forty-five-minute show. (The park is open year-round, though the trails to the falls are closed in winter. Timespell admission is $6.50 for adults, $5.50 for children six to twelve. There are shows every day, June 28 through Labor Day, at 9:15 P.M.; Labor Day through October 15, 8:00 P.M.)

DAY 4

Morning

BREAKFAST: Don't overlook the pancakes that come with your eggs and meat and fruit and everything else at the Chateau Lafayette Reneau.

Bid farewell to Watkins Glen and head south on NY 14, then west on I–86 at Horseheads. At Painted Post, take U.S. 15 south. Soon after crossing into

Pennsylvania, U.S. 15 widens and winds downhill with a spectacular view of the Tioga Reservoir and Hammond Lake. Continue south to Mansfield, exiting at U.S. 6 to head west and join up with PA 660. Stay with PA 660 through Wellsboro, then another 10 miles to the 585-acre **Leonard Harrison State Park** (570–724–3061). Part of the 160,000-acre Tioga State Forest (570–724–2868), Leonard Harrison offers spectacular vistas along the eastern rim of Pine Creek Gorge, the Grand Canyon of Pennsylvania: 47 miles long and 800 feet deep in some locations. The Pine Creek Trail, constructed on an abandoned railroad right-of-way at the bottom of the canyon, offers 22 miles of biking, hiking, and (in winter) cross-country skiing. The much shorter 0.6-mile Overlook Trail provides a gorgeous view to the south. Across the canyon, along its western rim, is the more rustic companion park, Colton Point. A small environmental interpretive center at the Leonard Harrison main overlook entrance is open in summer and through the fall foliage season.

Return via PA 660 to the county seat, **Wellsboro** (www.wellsboropa. com), a lovely small town set around a nineteenth-century village square. Take a stroll along Main Street (U.S. 6/PA 660), head southwest on Central Avenue for 1 block, and turn right onto Pearl Street.

LUNCH: You'll find **Harland's Family Style Restaurant** (17 Pearl Street; 570–724–3111; harlands.tripod.com) rustic on the outside, homey on the inside. Who can pass up the charbroiled burger 21-Bun Salute? (Open daily, 6:00 A.M.–10:00 P.M. Serves breakfast all day.)

Afternoon

Rejoin U.S. 15 for the long descent to Williamsport, and connect with U.S. 220. Long stretches are divided highway as you head west and south. Connect with I–80 and continue west. I sometimes detour to State College (see Heartland Escape 3) via PA 26, but it's faster to continue west on I–80 to I–79, then south.

DINNER: Exit at Grove City and turn right (west) onto PA 208, then left (south) onto U.S. 19 to the **Iron Bridge Inn** (1438 Perry Highway, Mercer; 724–748–3626; www.springfields.com) for three-mushroom veal, pecan pork medallions, or chicken Wellington. (Open Monday through Thursday 11:00 A.M.–10:30 P.M.; Friday and Saturday 11:00 A.M.–11:30 P.M.; Sunday 10:30 A.M.–10:30 P.M.)

You're less than an hour from Pittsburgh via I–79.

THERE'S MORE

Golf. The Finger Lakes area prides itself on the wealth and quality of its outdoor activities, from biking to hot-air ballooning, and including such top-ranked (ratings from *Golf Digest*) courses as:

Bristol Harbour Golf and Resort, 4 stars. Designed by Robert Trent Jones. Canandaigua (716–396–2460).

Soaring Eagles Golf Club, 4 stars. Designed by Archibald Craig. Mark Twain State Park, Horseheads (607–739–0551).

Centerpointe Country Club, 3½ stars. Designed by John Thornton and Elmer Michaels. Canandaigua (716–924–5346).

Glenora Wine Cellars. Dine with your wine in a lakefront setting or cruise the gift shop at this fun winery. Guest rooms are now available, too. On Seneca Lake (800–243–5513; www.glenora.com).

Bully Hill Vineyards. The second largest winery in New York State includes a restaurant and gift shop. On Keuka Lake (607–868–3610; www.bullyhill.com).

McGregor Vineyard Winery. Friendly people really know how to set up a tasting; also features local cheese (607–292–3999 or 800–272–0192).

Watkins Glen International Race Track. NASCAR racing on weekends from May through September. Southeast of Watkins Glen on County Road 16. Tickets can be ordered online (607–535–2481; www.theglen.com).

The Clemens Center for the Performing Arts. Newly renovated and expanded; hosts performing artists from Bill Cosby to the touring company of Chicago to modern dance groups, in Elmira, south of Corning (607–734–8191; www.clemenscenter.com).

Aviation museums. The winds make this a great place for kite flying, parasailing, and the like, and there's a celebration of local flying at:

The Glenn H. Curtiss Museum focuses on early aviation and the life and times of aviation pioneer (and motorcycle man) Glenn H. Curtiss (607–569–2160; www.linkny.com/curtissmuseum).

National Warplane Museum. Military aviation history with twenty-seven vintage planes at the Elmira-Corning Regional Airport (607–739–8200; www.warplane.org).

National Soaring Museum. The world's largest glider collection, plus a sailplane simulator in Elmira (607–734–3128; www.soaringmuseum. org).

Keuka Maid. See the lake along with lunch, Sunday brunch, and dinner. Cruises leave from the south end of the lake off NY 54 in Hammondsport (607–569–2628).

Tioga Central Railroad. Operates excursion trains, dinner trains, theater trains, and charter trains on a 34-mile railroad extending north from Wellsboro, Pennsylvania, to about 3 miles south of Corning, New York (570–724–0990).

SPECIAL EVENTS

June. Fisherfolk generally need a license, except during Free Fishing Days, the last full weekend in June. For one-day fishing licenses, call 518–457–8862.

July. Finger Lakes Wine Festival features about fifty local wineries offering free tastings, plus wine and other merchandise for sale, which you can stash at the Welcome Tent until you're ready to leave. Discount tickets for designated drivers. Food, entertainment at Watkins Glen International Race Track (607–535–2481; www.theglen.com/winefest).

July–August. Corning Summer Song presents free community concerts on Thursday in Centerway Square, Market Street, Corning (607–936–4686).

August. Seneca Lake Whale Watch features two stages of music, food, wine, cheese, arts, and more in Geneva's Lakeshore Park (315–781–0820; www.whalewatch.org).

OTHER RECOMMENDED RESTAURANTS AND LODGING

Genessee Falls Inn. A Victorian inn with a chef-operated restaurant near Letchworth State Park in Portageville (716–493–2484).

Kelloggs Pan Tree Inn. Great homemade biscuits to match the great view of Canadaigua Lake (716–394–3909).

Pelham's Upstate Tuna Company. Choose from a variety of steak and seafood offerings, and, if you like, cook it yourself. In downtown Corning (607–936–8662).

Snug Harbor Marina & Restaurant. This popular waterfront restaurant in Hammondsport also bottles and sells its own salad dressings (607–868–3488).

Waterfront Restaurant. Come by boat or car to the south shore of Keuka Lake in Hammondsport (607–868–3455).

Laurel Cafe. Spectacular breakfasts and a bowling alley. In Wellsboro (570–723–2233).

Antlers Inn. Great prime ribs, steaks, and corn bread amid the trophies of many hunting trips. In Gaines, off U.S. 6. Dinner only (814–435–6300).

Penn Wells Hotel. A grand old hotel with a dining room and guest rooms on Main Street of Wellsboro (570–724–2111).

Finger Lakes B&B Association (800–695–5590).

FOR MORE INFORMATION

Finger Lakes Association, 309 Lake Street, Penn Yan, NY 14527; 315–536–7488 or 800–KIT–4–FUN; www.FingerLakes.org.

Steuben County Conference and Visitors Bureau, 21 West Market Street, Suite 201, Corning, NY 14830; 607–974–2066; http://corningsteuben.com.

Tioga County Visitors Bureau, 114 Main Street, Suite B, Wellsboro, PA 16901; 570–724–0635 or 888–TIOGA–28; www.visittiogapa.com/.

WESTERN
ESCAPES

Washington Count(r)y

THE BRIDGES OF
WASHINGTON COUNTY

1 NIGHT

Covered Bridges • Trolleys • Old Stuff • Farm Life

Madison who? Pittsburgh's southwest neighbor has more than twenty covered bridges, most of them of the queenpost type, found off winding township roads in this largely rural area. Yes, although less than an hour from Pittsburgh and convenient to the international airport, Washington County still holds on to much of its country character. Named for its first surveyor and major landowner, not to mention war hero and U.S. president—same guy—Washington can trace its history much farther back, even before Columbus, very possibly to the earliest human footsteps on this continent.

This trip takes in mainly the western portion of Washington County, which is still rich in farm life, plus slivers of West Virginia's skinny northern panhandle and Pennsylvania's Beaver County. A large chunk concentrates on ten of the classic "kissing bridges" clustered in the southwest corner of the county, plus one bonus bridge. Unfortunately, the map from the county is less than pinpoint accurate, but I'll take you to three bridges north of I–70, and seven south of the interstate that bisects the county—all within an easy drive of downtown Pittsburgh. Maybe *easy* isn't quite the word. While most of the bridges are still in use, the roads they serve are often single-lane gravel, some with steep grades, sharp curves, missing guardrails, and occasionally slow-moving farm equipment or farm animals. The scenery and solitude are worth it. Bring plenty of film.

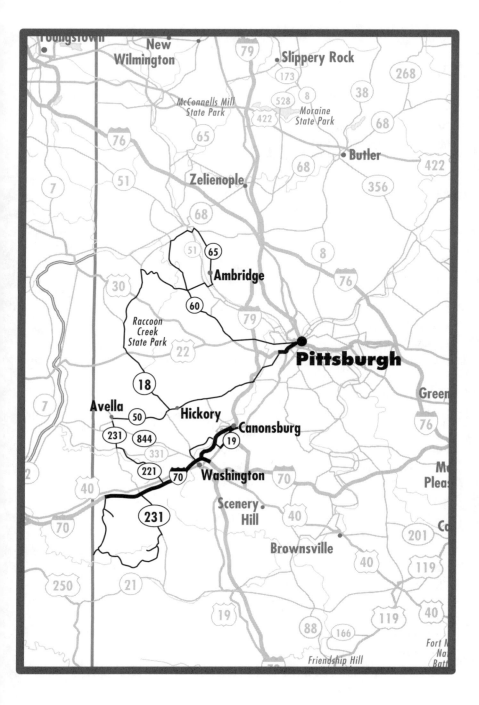

DAY 1

Morning

Head south on I–79 to exit 11 (Bridgeville), and turn left to head west on PA 50. Within minutes, suburbia fades away. Before you cross the border into **Washington County,** you'll see on your left the current home of the region's oldest and largest farm market, which began on Pittsburgh's North Side more than seventy years ago. (Hours are very weather dependent, but figure Monday, Wednesday, and Friday 5:30 to about 8:00 or 9:00 P.M., from April or May till—if you're lucky—the day before Thanksgiving.)

Continue on PA 50 through small towns with smatterings of development. This area was part of the major holdings of one George Washington in his land-speculating days, and after you pass the Geo. Cowden Farm (cows on your left, barn with sign on your right), you'll see on the next hill a historical marker on the right about George dealing with squatters on his land. Soon you're in the small town of **Hickory.** Let's check out a covered bridge before breakfast. Just past the old post office on your right, turn right (check your odometer) onto Wabash Avenue (also marked with a CHERRY VALLEY sign). Follow Wabash downhill, under a railroad bridge, and after 0.4 mile veer to the right at the fork in the road onto SR 4015. About 3.7 more miles on your left is **Krepps Bridge** (look for the blue COVERED BRIDGE sign). At 24 feet long, it's the shortest bridge on the tour.

Retrace your route to Hickory and turn right onto PA 50. Continue through Hickory to PA 18, then turn south to the Village Green Golf Course.

BREAKFAST: The public course's **Village Grille** (724–356–4653) gets folks onto the greens early, fortified with raspberry or blueberry pancakes, and a lunch buffet for the nineteenth hole. (Serves Monday through Friday 7:00 A.M.–9:00 P.M., Saturday and Sunday 6:00 A.M.–9:00 P.M.)

Return to PA 50 and continue west. In about a mile Woodrow is on your right; turn left onto SR 4035. In 1.9 miles, at the T-intersection, turn right, then after another 0.2 mile (mile 2.1) turn left to **Wilson's Mill Bridge,** two small parking lots, and a picnic table. West of the bridge you'll find Cross Creek Lake and a county park. Though the bridge was built in 1889, it was only in 1978 that it was moved to its present location as part of a flood-control project.

Continue over the bridge on single-lane gravel Oakleaf Road (T 486), which becomes Willow Road (SR 4045) after 1.5 miles. After another mile,

Visit many of Washington County's twenty-some covered bridges.

turn right onto PA 844, which passes through West Middletown. Turn left onto the aptly named Scenic Drive (PA 231) at mile 5.4, just beyond a driving range; watch for the CLAYSVILLE sign. A few miles down this ridgetop road with its striking views, three state highways converge in a sparsely populated wooded glen for no apparent reason. Turn left at mile 9.6 where PA 331 joins PA 231. Turn right at mile 9.8 and follow PA 331. Turn left at mile 9.9, following PA 221 (Buffalo Creek Road). You can see **Sawhill Bridge** on the right of PA 221 at mile 12.6, on Camp Buffalo Road. The 49-foot-long bridge was built in 1915 of wood, a result of wartime steel shortages.

Continue south on PA 221 through Taylorstown. On your right, just before PA 221 intersects U.S. 40 (5.6 miles beyond Sawhill Bridge), is a stone **S bridge** (it bends twice), which carried traffic along the National Road, the progenitor of U.S. 40. There's a replica mile marker nearby. Some of the original mile markers remain on U.S. 40; missing ones have been replaced with replicas.

Continue south on PA 221 and go west on I–70 for the second segment of the bridge tour. Take the exit at West Alexander, turn right, then turn right again after 0.2 mile to T 903, then turn right onto Lynn Street (T 423, Waynesburg Road) just past the I–70 overpass. At mile 1.6, the road passes over the **Mays** (aka **Blaney**) **Bridge,** over Middle Wheeling Creek. Retrace your route to the West Alexander I–70 interchange, and head south on SR 3023. After 2.4 miles, turn right onto SR 3018, Middle Creek Road, and in another half mile turn left at T 321 to see one of the oldest covered bridges left, the **Erskine Bridge,** built in 1845 over Middle Wheeling Creek.

Return to SR 3018 (Middle Creek Road) and turn right. After half a mile, veer right onto SR 3021 (McGuffey Road). At mile 2.9, make a sharp left turn onto SR 3019 (Beham Ridge Road), then turn right onto SR 3037 (West Finley Road) at mile 3.3, just before McDonald Road. After a few miles, the tin-roofed Crawford Bridge is visible to your right; a right turn onto T 316 (Crawford Road) at mile 7.2 will take you directly to it.

Continue on SR 3037 through two exceedingly tight switchbacks. Turn left onto SR 3037 after 0.9 mile to West Finley, then in another 0.2 mile turn left onto SR 3029 (Burnsville Ridge Road). At mile 1.8, just beyond the Windy Gap Presbyterian Church, turn right onto SR 3035 (Rocky Run Road), a winding, one-lane asphalt road leading down to, and across, a valley. On your right at mile 5.2, T 451 (Newland School Road) leads up to the blocked-off **Sprowl's Bridge,** built in 1875.

Continue on SR 3035 and in 0.2 mile turn left onto T 450 (Fairmount Church Road). Veer left after 0.1 mile onto one-lane gravel Skyview Road. The reason for the name becomes evident at the top of a rise, where it is nearly impossible to see the road in front of you because of the sharp crest, but soon you'll cross **Plants Bridge,** a kingpost bridge. Turn right onto T 414 (Templeton Run Road), a one-lane gravel road that makes sharp right turns at miles 0.5 and 1.5. Pass East Finley Park on your right at mile 1.8; at mile 2.1 you'll cross the **Brownlee Bridge,** with its rough, vertical plank siding. (To cut the tour short, continue across the bridge and turn left onto PA 231.)

Retrace your path 0.3 mile southwest on Templeton Run Road and turn right onto T 412 (Park Road). At the end of Park Road, turn left onto SR 3029 (Burnsville Ridge Road), which turns to the left at the crest of a hill at mile 2.5. Continue straight ahead onto T 379 (Dogwood Hill Road), and at the fork a few hundred feet later, veer right onto **Danley Bridge** at mile 3.4. Thus endeth the tour.

Retrace your route on Dogwood Hill Road, then left onto SR 3029, then make another left at PA 231 to reach Claysville and U.S. 40. A left turn onto U.S. 40 brings you to the I–70 interchange of Claysville and, as far as anybody knows, one of the world's largest selections of hubcaps. Take I–70 east to Washington.

LUNCH: Leave I–70 at Washington's U.S. 40 exit and head east to **Angelo's Ristorante** (955 West Chestnut Street; 724–222–7120), an Italian restaurant opened in 1939 and now run by the third generation, featuring classic Italian as well as more innovative dishes. (Open Monday through Thursday 11:00 A.M.–10:00 P.M., Friday and Saturday 11:00 A.M.–11:00 P.M., Sunday noon–8:00 P.M.)

Afternoon

Head north on PA 18 and turn right onto SR 4020 to the **Pennsylvania Trolley Museum** (724–228–9256 or 877–728–7655; www.pa-trolley.org)— formerly the Arden Trolley Museum. The only museum of its type, it offers not just displays and videos but also an actual ride—more than a mile—on streetcars, on the once-common 5-foot-2½-inch gauge. Although it began as a venue to preserve local trolleys, the indoor-outdoor museum now houses more than thirty from all over the country, including a real "streetcar named Desire" from New Orleans. Generally speaking, not all of the trolleys may be on display when you go; the best time is during the Trolley Fair on the last weekend in June. (Admission $6.00. Open weekends April 1 through December 30; open Memorial Day through Labor Day, seven days a week, 11:00 A.M.–5:00 P.M. The last ride is at 4:05 P.M.)

There are many antiques shops in the area, mostly of the "collectibles" variety, but an ulterior motive leads us north. U.S. 19 hosts thirty dealers at **Antique Junction** (724–746–5119), twenty-three at the **Route 19 Antique Mall** (724–746–3277), and more at **Whiskey Run Antiques Southpointe** (724–745–5808). You're also close to **The Meadowlands,** home of the area's largest flea market on the last Sunday of every month, February through November (Antiques Fair at the Meadows, 724–228–3045; admission $3.00; 8:00 A.M.–3:00 P.M.)

Follow the signs west to I–79, but go underneath the overpass and cross the railroad tracks to Canonsburg and a break: **Sarris Chocolates** (511 Adams Avenue; 724–745–4042 or 888–SARRIS–1; www.sarriscandies.com).

Treat yourself to a cone or sundae (especially with a hardcap milk or dark chocolate topping), stock up on the best chocolate-covered pretzels, and explore the aisles of penny candy. (Open Monday through Saturday 9:00 A.M.–9:00 P.M., Sunday 11:00 A.M.–9:00 P.M.)

Head south on Adams, the main business street, into downtown and **Canonsburg Antique Mall I** (724–745–1333). Make sure you check out side streets and head to **Where the Toys Are** (724–745–5808), **Annabelle's Antiques and Curios** (724–746–5950), **Stone Bridge Antiques** (724–745–7414; www.stonebridgeantiques.com), and **Tri-State Antique Center** (724–745–9116), all on West Pike Street. Swing by the municipal building on Adams to check out the statue of Canonsburg's favorite son, **Perry Como;** before you get back on I–79, near the interchange is the **Canonsburg Antique Mall II** (724–745–1050). Head back south to Washington.

DINNER: Treat yourself to Washington's hottest restaurant, **Barry's on the Avenue** (939 Jefferson Avenue; 724–222–6688) for blackened tuna, swordfish, and fabulous desserts. (Open Monday through Saturday 11:00 A.M.–10:00 P.M., Sunday 11:00 A.M.–9:00 P.M. Reservations suggested.)

Evening

Game? **Ladbroke at The Meadows** (412–563–1224 or 724–225–9300; www.latm.com) features live harness racing year-round, plus simulcasts from Pocono Downs, Philadelphia Park, and Penn National Raceway, as well as dinner, drinks, and snacks. Admission and parking are free. Post time is 6:30 P.M., except for the Adios Day Doubleheader (in August) at 1:00 and 8:00 P.M. (Live racing October through January on Tuesday, Thursday, Friday, and Saturday; February and March on Tuesday, Friday, and Saturday; April through September on Tuesday, Thursday, Friday, Saturday, and Sunday.)

LODGING: Head back to farm country along PA 844 and get away from the madding crowd at **Weatherbury Farm** (724–587–3763; www.weatherburyfarm.com).

DAY 2

Morning

BREAKFAST: Stoke up on a farm breakfast of fresh eggs, baked goods, and more, served buffet-style at 8:30 A.M.

Weatherbury is a real working farm—it has been at least since 1860, and possibly much earlier, though the buildings are mainly from the 1920s—primarily raising cattle and sheep. And to turn a profit, the farm grows its own feed: timothy grass, alfalfa, and clover. Folks wanting a full farm stay can pitch right in and get at least a taste of the modern farm experience with the Tudor family, who even provide a booklet about Weatherbury Farm, which includes farm lingo.

After breakfast, start with the daily tour. Yes, you can feed the animals— the shaggy-coated Scottish Highland cattle like carrots and apples. All the animals have literary names (Weatherbury itself is named for Thomas Hardy's *Far from the Madding Crowd*): The Hereford cattle are Shakespearean characters, the Southdown sheep Dickensian, bantam chickens from Lewis Carroll, guinea fowl for Tudor royalty, Indian runner ducks for Native Americans, and the billy goat, of course, is Gruff. And while most farms don't have a resident blacksmith, this one does, operated by son Nigel (stop by and visit the forge).

If you're strictly on vacation, just lounge by the pool (in season, of course), play lawn games, put together puzzles in the music room, learn more about farming from the variety of videos and books on hand, or just hang out and check out the farm (do observe the safety rules, though; this is a real farm, not a theme park).

When you're ready, head east on PA 844 to PA 231 and the Breezy Heights Golf Driving Range and Miniature Golf Course.

LUNCH: The **Breezy Heights Tavern** (724-587-3461) retains some of its 1928 look with its original mural of local life. The prices and portions also seem to be from that era. Be prepared for the taxidermy display from the owner's hunting trips. If the weather's nice, eat outside on the patio overlooking the golf course. (Open Monday through Thursday noon–9:30 P.M., Friday and Saturday noon–10:30 P.M., Sunday noon–7:30 P.M.)

Afternoon

Now get a different view of rural life at the **Meadowcroft Museum of Rural Life** (724–587–3412; www.cobweb.net/~mcroft/). Follow PA 231 north and PA 50 east back to Avella, then follow the signs to Meadowcroft. On the one hand, this is a re-created nineteenth-century village—a "living museum"— using actual historic buildings that have been moved here. But more significantly, it's also the home of **Meadowcroft Rockshelter,** the oldest known site

of human habitation (and in the longest continual use) in eastern North America. It dates to 12,000 B.C. and maybe as far back as 17,000 B.C.

The village is the home of our trip's eleventh covered bridge, which leads to a one-room schoolhouse ("classes" are regularly led by a volunteer "school-marm" in costume), a blacksmith shop (with a working forge), a sheep pen, a farmhouse where there's likely to be something baking, and more. Elsewhere you can explore an old general store, peek inside an old-fashioned barbershop, and climb aboard a train. This still relatively young museum is developing more buildings and exhibits, most notably for the Rockshelter. The visitors center includes displays about local life at the end of the last glaciation; outdoors are regular demonstrations of the atlatl, a spear thrower used by prehistoric hunters. The Rockshelter itself (an official state "treasure") is off limits to the public except for occasional tours led by the archaeologists in charge of the dig (reservations a must), but there are plans for a permanent structure to protect the archaeological deposits and allow visitors an opportunity to see the site. (Admission is $6.50. Open Memorial Day through Labor Day, Saturday noon–5:00 P.M., Sunday 1:00–5:00 P.M., plus special-event weekend programs till mid-December, weather permitting.)

Return to Avella, head east on PA 50, then turn north onto PA 18, across the Beaver County line. Watch for the sign (on your left) to Frankfort Mineral Springs, a partly restored mineral springs spa building almost 200 years old, accessible only by foot now but a tourist magnet for more than a century. Watch for the right turn into **Raccoon Creek State Park** (724–899–2200). Follow the road through the park (maybe take a "detour" for a look at the lake) to U.S. 30. Turn right and then a quick left into the park's **Wildflower Reserve** (nature center, 724–899–3611). You can see just about all of western Pennsylvania's wildflowers—more than 500 species—along the trails of these 314 acres. Peak season is spring, with skunk cabbage, trout lily, jack-in-the-pulpit, trillium, geranium, and many more through May and into June. The "second wave" is August and September. Several well-marked trails roam through various habitats, from open fields to stands of oak, hickory, and pine. Watch for frogs, turtles, owls, deer, and other wildlife. (The park is open dawn to dusk.)

Maybe there's still time to capture another very unusual piece of the past. Head north on PA 18, turn east onto PA 151 to the Ohio River, head north briefly on PA 51, and cross the Ohio River at Ambridge. Head south briefly on PA 65. Turn left at Eighth Street (PA 989); at the second traffic light, turn left onto Merchant Street. Follow Merchant for 5 blocks, then turn left onto

13th Street. Go 1 block and turn right onto Church Street. **Old Economy Village** (724–266–4500; www.oldeconomyvillage.org) is the final and communal home of the Harmony Society (for the first home, see Northern Escape 1), a nineteenth-century utopian society somewhat similar to the better-known Shakers in their industriousness, ingenuity, and outlook. The six-acre historic site includes seventeen restored historic structures and garden built 1824–30. The most popular tour stop in summer is the wine cellar, where it's always cool. (Admission is $5.00. Open Tuesday through Saturday 9:00 A.M.–5:00 P.M., Sunday noon–5:00 P.M.)

DINNER: Head north on PA 65, cross the Beaver River at Beaver, and head west on PA 68. Relax riverside at **Lock 6 Landing** (610 Midland-Beaver Road; 724–728–6767; www.lock6.com), a former lock and dam powerhouse (built 1904) on the Ohio, now sensitively restored and serving great seafood. (Open Monday through Thursday 11:00 A.M.–10:00 P.M., Friday 11:00 A.M.–11:00 P.M., Saturday 5:00–11:00 P.M., Sunday 4;00–8:00 P.M.)

The restaurant is a little over a mile from PA 60, the Airport Expressway; or you can head back to town via PA 65 (Ohio River Boulevard).

THERE'S MORE

Homer Laughlin Co. Factory Outlet. The home of Fiestaware, off WV 2 at the top of the West Virginia panhandle in Newell, sells all colors and styles. Open Monday through Saturday 9:30 A.M.–5:00 P.M., Sunday noon–5:00 P.M.; the factory seconds warehouse is open Monday and Thursday 11:00 A.M.–4:45 P.M., Tuesday, Wednesday, Friday, and Saturday 9:30 A.M.–4:45 P.M., Sunday noon–4:45 P.M. Factory tours are by reservation (800–452–4462; www.hlchina.com).

Downtown Washington offers three small but notable museums. The **David Bradford House** (724–222–3604; www.bradfordhouse.org) at 175 South Main Street was the home of the leader of the Whiskey Rebellion of 1794. The **LeMoyne House** (724–225–6740; www.wchspa.org) at 49 East Maiden Street, Pennsylvania's first National Historic Landmark of the Underground Railroad, honors a man ahead of his time: Dr. F. Julius LeMoyne worked for the abolition of slavery, promoted education for women and for African Americans (he founded LeMoyne College, now LeMoyne-Owen College), and founded a free public library in 1869, among other accomplishments. The **Duncan & Miller Glass Museum**

(724–225–9950; www.duncan-glass.com) at 525 Jefferson Avenue is home to the history and artifacts of one of America's greatest makers of tableware and decorative glass, 1872–1955.

Washington and Jefferson College. Founded in 1781, this is the oldest college west of the Allegheny Mountains and eleventh oldest in the United States. It's home to the Olin Fine Arts Center and a lovely campus to visit (60 South Lincoln Street; 724–223–6074 or 888–W–AND–JAY; www. washjeff.edu).

Montour Trail. Several sections of this 47-mile rail-trail are open to bikers, walkers, and, in some areas, horseback riders (412–831–2030; www. montourtrail.org).

SPECIAL EVENTS

June, December. Canonsburg-based All-Clad Metalcrafters Inc.'s semiannual factory sale (at the Meadowlands) of first-quality and seconds of professional cookware at discounts of up to 70 percent attracts home cooks from across the mid-Atlantic (724–745–8300 or 800–255–2523; www.allclad.com).

September. The Annual Covered Bridge Festival features food and entertainment at nine sites in Washington and Greene Counties (724–228–5520 or 800–531–4114; www.washpatourism.org/cbfestival.html).

October. Harvest events include the Hickory Apple Festival (724–356–3378; www.wpcd.com/mtpvfd) and Houston Pumpkin Festival (724–745–0266; hvfd@sgi.net), with entertainment, arts and crafts, and many foods featuring local produce.

November. Fiestaware fanciers throng to the annual warehouse sale at the Homer Laughlin Co. Limit four crates per person (800–452–4462; www. hlchina.com).

OTHER RECOMMENDED RESTAURANTS AND LODGING

Drovers Inn. On WV 27 (what PA 844 turns into) in Wellsburg, the old stopover for cattle drovers is more interesting for its historical ambience than its buffet, but the wings are good (304–737–0188).

Trax. A former railroad station in the historic part of Wellsburg serves a range of sandwiches and salads above a disco (304–737–3205).

Capi's Pizza Plus. Find big sandwiches and breakfasts just outside Hickory on PA 50 (724–356–4663).

Hungry Jose's. Unique Mecican food and friendly service in downtown Washington (724–228–1311).

Country Road Bed & Breakfast. For total privacy, stay in the log cabin at this country B&B near the Pittsburgh International Airport and Raccoon Creek State Park (724–899–2528; www.pittsburghbnb.com/country.html).

Rush House. A B&B close to downtown Washington in a century-old house at 810 East Maiden Street (724–223–1890).

FOR MORE INFORMATION

Washington County Tourism Promotion Agency, Franklin Mall, 1500 West Chestnut Street, Washington, PA 15301; 800–531–4114 or 724–228–5520; www.washpatourism.org).

WESTERN

Columbus, Ohio

DISCOVERING COLUMBUS

2 NIGHTS

Art • Historic Renewal • Nightlife • Zoo • Science

Those who haven't been through Ohio's capital for a few years will be surprised at how much the area has grown. Ohio State University, one of the nation's largest campuses, and the state government are certainly dominant factors, though neither dominates the Columbus area. The city itself has expanded while sprucing up and adding attractions: cherished landmarks, new museums, varied concepts in shopping, and nightlife. And with the inaugural season of the NHL Blue Jackets, Columbus has truly hit the major leagues.

DAY 1

Morning

Head south on I–79 to I–70, and follow the western route. Less than an hour from Columbus, you'll pass by Zanesville, home of **Eaglesticks Golf Club** (614–454–4900), rated 4½ stars by *Golf Digest*. Continue to **Columbus** and take the Front/High Street exit to downtown. You may want to stash the car and depend on public transit, or some healthy walking, after the three-hour drive.

BREAKFAST: J&G Diner (733 North High Street; 614–294–1850) is a classic Greek-based eatery (the killer Greek omelette packs olives, gyro meat, and loads of feta cheese and onion) with Cajun overtones. (Open Monday through Friday 10:30 A.M.–10:00 P.M., Saturday 9:00 A.M.–10:00 P.M., Sunday 9:00 A.M.–9:00 P.M.)

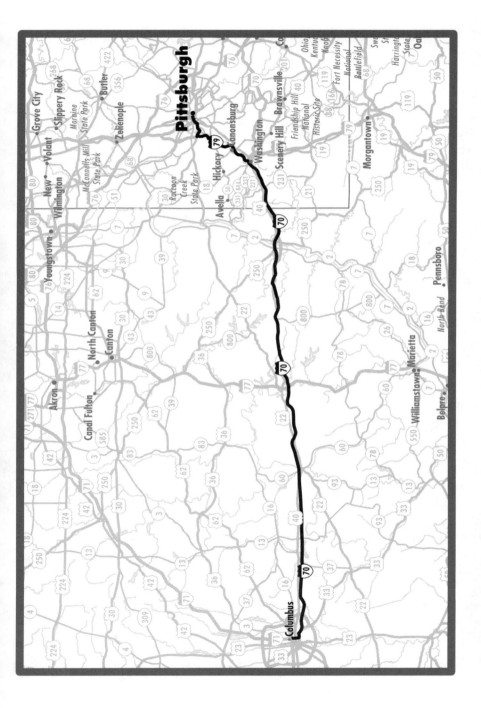

This is the **Short North** arts district between downtown and the Ohio State campus. You'll find plenty of interesting shops, including **An Open Book** (614–291–0080), a neat bookstore (check out the cards) practically next door at 761 North High Street. If this is the first week of the month, make plans to be back, then hop onto the High Street **COTA Link** trolley for a 25-cent ride to the State Street stop and the **Ohio Statehouse.** (Transit information, 614–228–1776; www.cota.com.)

One of the oldest and grandest capitol buildings in the United States, the Ohio Statehouse underwent a $126 million renovation in 1990–96 to return it to its pre–Civil War splendor. The massive marble Grand Staircase was scrubbed to its original white, the stained-glass skylight representing the state seal was uncovered, and 317 rooms were unchopped up and returned to the original 53 stately rooms. Built between 1839 and 1861, the Greek Revival building twice provided a forum for Abraham Lincoln and once a viewing spot for his casket—and it's now a popular place to visit. Free tours (614–728–2695 or 888–644–6123) are available seven days a week, for walk-ins as well as for individuals and groups with reservations. (Tours start at the Third Street entrance, 9:30 A.M. weekdays, 11:15 A.M. weekends; the last tour is at 3:00 P.M. About forty-five to sixty minutes.)

LUNCH: On the lower level, just outside the **Statehouse Museum Shop** (614–728–9234; www.statehouse.com) is the Crypt, featuring historical exhibits. And right next to that is the **Capitol Cafe** (614–728–9231), where you can get basic soups and sandwiches, capped by bread pudding with whiskey sauce. (Open Monday through Friday 7:30 A.M.–3:00 P.M.)

Afternoon

Outside the Statehouse, do stop to take a closer look at the **Ohio Veterans Plaza,** and get your hanky ready. Two limestone walls inscribed with the words from 250 actual letters from service members to their loved ones tell the stories of Ohio veterans from World War II to the present. Catch the COTA Link trolley again, or just hoof the 6 blocks to the **German Village.** (Look on the side streets for glimpses of Columbus's restored historic theaters, including the grand State Theater.)

Starting in 1840, German immigrants settled in this neighborhood just south of central Columbus, adjacent to the **Brewery District** where many of them worked. They built small but very sturdy houses out of brick, while grander houses for the brewery owners and managers surrounded the tidy, flower-filled **Schiller Park.** Anti-German sentiment in two world wars, Prohibition, and urban flight almost sent German Village the way of so many ethnic neighborhoods. But an ambitious restoration movement began in 1960, and the result is the largest privately funded restored historic landmark neighborhood in the United States, comprising 233 acres with more than 1,600 buildings, primarily private homes. Various group-only tours are available ($5.00 to $12.00 per person), but you can stroll on your own with the help of a map and brochure from the German Village Society (614–221–8888; www. germanvillage.org) at the **German Village Meeting Haus,** 588 South Third Street. Notice the brickwork on the sidewalks, and make sure you check out Frederich Schiller's poetry (in German, of course) in the park named for him.

DINNER: Ready for the wurst? **Schmidt's** (240 East Kossuth Street; 614–444–6808) is a bit touristy, but its sausages are worth the kitsch factor. Now operated by the fifth generation, Schmidt's started as a meatpacking company in 1886 and still uses some of its original sausage recipes, from a traditional bratwurst to a modern hickory-smoked beef-pork "Bahama Mama." (Open Sunday and Monday 11:00 A.M.–9:00 P.M., Tuesday through Thursday 11:00 A.M.–10:00 P.M., Friday and Saturday 11:00 A.M.–11:00 P.M.)

Evening

By detouring ever so slightly to the west on your way back to downtown Columbus, you run right into the Brewery District. While it's not a restoration of the nineteenth-century district, it does indeed have places to hoist a brew, like **Columbus Brewing Co.** at 525 Short Street (614–224–3626); or have some fun, like at **Howl at the Moon** at 450 South Front Street (614–224–5990), which features dueling pianos and sing-alongs. (Columbus Brewing serves till 10:00 P.M. Monday through Thursday, 11:00 P.M. Friday and Saturday; Howl at the Moon is open till 2:00 A.M. Tuesday through Saturday.)

LODGING: Time to head back downtown. Go north on Front Street then turn right to reach 55 Nationwide Boulevard. **The Lofts** (614–461–2663 or 800–73–LOFTS; www.55lofts.com) features a new and probably unique concept for a hotel. The former plumbing supply warehouse has been divided into loftlike, spacious rooms, each one different because of the configuration of the space. Before you drag yourself into bed, do remember to jot down your breakfast preferences, including time, and hang the form on the doorknob.

DAY 2

Morning

BREAKFAST: A "butler" delivers your preferences of a European-style breakfast: hot coffee or tea, juice, fruit, pastries, and/or cold cereal.

Public transit from downtown to the **Columbus Zoo and Aquarium** (9990 Riverside Drive, Powell; 614–645–3550 or 800–MONKEYS; www. colszoo.org) is available during summer, or take I–70 west to I–270 north, exit at U.S. 33 east, and turn left onto OH 257 after crossing the Scioto River. Gene, Hurricane, and Dundee, among the 2,500 known manatees in the world, are the main attraction in the conservation-minded **Manatee Coast,** one of only three places outside Florida to showcase these friendly sea mammals. Or explore the new African Forest: Stroll through a central African rain forest that combines cultural artifacts and environmental information with habitats for different species of apes, birds, big cats, red river hogs, and more. Another recent addition is the completely restored 1914 **Mangels-Illions Carousel**—thirteen years older than the zoo and with all fifty-two of its original horses. There's plenty more to explore, from the koalas of Australasia to amphibians of Ohio wetlands, and one of the largest reptile collections in captivity. The 534-acre zoo along the Scioto River, open 365 days a year, is home to more than 6,000 animals representing nearly 600 species. (Open 9:00 A.M.–5:00 P.M. daily, till 6:00 P.M. Memorial Day through Labor Day. Admission is $7.00 per adult; $2.00 parking.)

Head back to town, retracing your route on I–270 and I–70, exiting north at South Front Street. Then turn left to cross the Scioto River and reach the block between Broad and Town Streets on the west bank of the Scioto, across from downtown. From the riverside, it presents the beaux arts facade of the old Central High School, built in 1924 and an official National Historic Landmark, but now remodeled and expanded into the new Center of Science and Industry, better known simply as **COSI** (614–228–COSI).

LUNCH: Make your first landing into the **Atomic Cafe.** The COSI food court offers nutritional information as well as Pizza Hut pizza, soups, sandwiches, salads, and fruit, plus a view of the river and outdoor dining in season. Work it off at the "high-wire unicycle" suspended above the entrance area.

Afternoon

COSI's 320,000 square feet feature seven "learning areas," grouping exhibits (mostly interactive) by theme. **Life** is definitely geared for grown-ups, with videos of surgeries and decomposition, and birth and death stories. On the lighter side, you also get to play with visual and aural perspectives. Have some fun with **Gadgets,** seeing how things work, including just what will happen if you stick a magnet in front of a computer monitor (don't try this at home). Make a reservation for the **Gadgets Cafe,** at which you can take things apart and put the pieces back together in whatever configuration you can manage. Or try problem solving with **Adventure in the Valley of the Unknown,** underwater fantasy and fact in **Ocean,** and more. COSI exhibits are included in the basic $12 TechPass; the various dome theater and ultralarge-screen films, and other recorded and live shows, are covered by the $21 SuperPass (otherwise there's a separate fee for each). It's free to go into the **i/o** entrance area—home of Technostalgia, a curated museum of video games from pre-Pong to today. (The entire center is open 9:00 A.M.–5:00 P.M. every day; on Friday and Saturday the movie theaters and other electronic shows, plus the gift shop, operate till 9:00 P.M.; the Atomic Cafe stays open till 7:00 P.M. on those days.)

Head across the river (east on U.S. 40, West Broad Street, then left, or north, onto U.S. 23, North High Street for dinner and more entertainment in Short North.

DINNER: **Lemongrass—An Asian Bistro** (641 North High Street; 614–224–1414), regularly voted among the top restaurants in Columbus, scores as much for its feng shui as its food. Sit back and relax among the paintings and piano music, or in the courtyard. Try anything with the signature peanut satay sauce; the pad Thai is excellent. (Open Monday through Thursday 11:00 A.M.–10:00 P.M., Friday 11:00 A.M.–midnight; Saturday 3:00 P.M.–midnight.)

Evening

If it's the first Saturday of the month, you'll notice that the streets are pretty crowded for the **Gallery Hop.** Most of the action is along North High Street, but check out the side streets as well, especially the corner of Pearl and Warren (to the east) for the giant mural on the side of the **Reality Theater:** It's the Mona Lisa, Columbus-style, and an icon of the local arts district. In this mile-long area, you can stroll into nine galleries, five antiques shops, three the-

aters, twenty-seven pubs and eateries, and lots more. Just about everyone stays open late—the more folks having fun, the later they stay open. (A free map and directory is available from the Short North Business Association, 614–421–1030; www.shortnorth.org.)

Continue to paint the town red in the new **Nationwide Arena District,** just a short stroll south and west from Short North (and little more than a block from the Lofts). The ninety-five-acre "village" around the brand-new Nationwide Arena (open fall 2000) already includes a brewpub, Irish pub, movie theater, and more, with a lot still to come. Hey, maybe the Blue Jackets will be playing at home tonight in the NHL's newest arena (614–232–5900 or 800–645–2657; www.columbusbluejackets.com).

DAY 3

Morning

BREAKFAST: Your choice of pastries, fruit, et cetera, delivered right to your room.

Okay, so Columbus isn't Paris, but you can still spend **A Sunday Afternoon on the Island of la Grand Jatte.** Get right into Georges Seurat's famous painting—or, rather, a rendition in topiary—to start a day of art exploration in the **Discovery District,** a few blocks east of downtown. Old Deaf School Park, at East Town Street and Washington Avenue, is open every day, sunset to sundown, for free. The best viewing is April through November, from the Gatehouse (Town Street), also the site of the park's visitors center and museum store, Yewtopia (614–645–0197).

Just a few blocks north along Washington is the **Columbus Museum of Art** (480 Broad Street; 614–221–6801; www.columbusart.mus.oh.us). Traveling exhibits at the two-story museum augment the collection of primarily mid-nineteenth-century to twentieth-century American modernism, French impressionism, and German expressionism, plus the world's largest collection of Columbus native George Bellows. Also find some monumental glass pieces in the indoor Derby Court, an occasional installation, and a fun, informative, long-running introduction to art, Eye Spy. In residence at least through 2001, "Eye Spy" is allegedly for kids, but grown-ups have fun exploring perspective, sketching still lifes, and studying symbolism in ancient Mexican art. (Open 10:00 A.M.–5:30 P.M. Tuesday through Sunday; till 8:30 P.M. Thursday. Admission is $4.00 per adult; parking costs $2.00.)

The Franklin Park Conservatory blooms inside and out.

LUNCH: Take a break and head to the museum's lower level for the cozy **Palette Cafe,** featuring a limited but artistic menu of soup, sandwiches, and salads 11:30 A.M.–1:30 P.M., with prepackaged snacks and beverages until 4:30 P.M.

Afternoon

One block east on Broad and a left turn left onto Jefferson brings you to a once-fashionable street divided by a park down the middle. Most of the former homes now house nonprofit groups, including the **Thurber House** (77 Jefferson Avenue; 614–464–1032; www.thurberhouse.org), the childhood home of writer-cartoonist James Thurber and now a literary center. You can walk through the house (noon–4:00 P.M. daily) to see literary and personal memorabilia, or just stop into the "reading garden" to see five sculptural depictions of Thurber's famous cartoon dogs.

Head east for more than a mile on Broad Street to the **Franklin Park Conservatory & Botanical Garden** (1777 East Broad Street; 614–645–

TREE or 800–214–PARK; www.fpconservatory.org). A winding walking tour through the conservatory takes you through about a dozen habitats—from the Himalayan Mountains to Desert to a Bonsai Courtyard to a Tropical Cloud Forest—to see thousands of plants. And you end up in the grand Victoria Palm House, actually the original conservatory, built in 1895. (Open Tuesday through Sunday 10:00 A.M.–5:00 P.M., till 8:00 P.M. on Wednesday. Closed Monday except Monday holidays. Regular admission is $4.00 per adult, $5.00 during the Fall, Winter, and Spring Flower Shows.)

Head east on U.S. 62 and north on I–270 to the Morse Road exit and **Easton Town Center** (www.eastontowncenter.com), a development of seventy retail, restaurant, and entertainment spots (including the thirty-screen Planet Movies by AMC, 614–416–7000) arranged to resemble an old-fashioned small-town business district. While specific hours at shops and eateries may vary, mall hours are Monday through Thursday 11:00 A.M.–9:00 P.M.; till 11:00 P.M. Friday and Saturday; Sunday noon–8:00 P.M.

DINNER: The **Ocean Club** (4002 Easton Station; 614–416–CLUB) specializes, of course, in seafood. Take your choice from among East Coast, West Coast, and Gulf Coast dishes including pan-seared swordfish, char-grilled Pacific mahi mahi, and Cajun blackened catfish, not to mention a mean Maryland crabcake with mango chutney. Yep, there are midwestern dishes, too, with twists like truffle mashed potatoes and balsamic onion relish to top off that grilled beef filet. (Open Monday through Thursday 11:30 A.M.–10:00 P.M., Friday and Saturday 11:30 A.M.– 11:00 P.M., Sunday noon–9:00 P.M.)

Hop back onto I–270 south, then I–70 east, for the trip back to Pittsburgh.

THERE'S MORE

Guide to Outdoor Sculpture in Columbus. This booklet and map ($6.95) outlines three easy downtown walking tours to dozens of sculptures, and pinpoints the locations of dozens more (614–224–2606; www.gcac.org).

Wexner Center for the Arts. More cutting-edge fine and performing arts at Ohio State (614–292–3535).

North Market. Near Short North, Columbus's version of the Strip District with more than thirty vendors (614–463–9664).

Battelle Riverfront Park. Features a full-scale replica of Columbus's flagship, the *Santa Maria* (614–645–8760).

Golf. Champions Golf Course, 3½ stars (614–645–7111); Airport Golf Course, 3 stars (614–645–3127).

SPECIAL EVENTS

June. Get a peek inside some of spectacularly restored homes in the German Village Haus und Garten Tour (614–221–8888; www.germanvillage.com).

June–August. Thurber House holds literary picnics with visiting authors (614–464–1032; ThCountry@thurberhouse.org; www.thurberhouse.org).

September. German Village Oktoberfest with food, beer, and music (614–221–8888).

OTHER RECOMMENDED RESTAURANTS AND LODGING

Martini Italian Bistro. An upscale Italian and martini menu in Short North (614–224–8259).

Tony's Italian Ristorante. Take a break from *gemütlichkeit* in German Village (614–224–8669).

Hoster Brewing Co. Cajun, Texan, and southwestern flavors in a Brewery District brewpub (614–228–6066).

Le Metropolitian Restaurant. Enjoy French munchies in the Brewery District. Look for the Eiffel Tower (614–621–8020).

GameWorks. Play video games till 2:00 A.M. (midnight on Sunday) and munch on creative pizzas and bar food in Easton Center (614–428–7529).

157 on the Park. This German Village B&B fronts Schiller Park (614–443–6935).

50 Lincoln Inn. Short North's only B&B (614–299–5050 or 888–299–5051).

FOR MORE INFORMATION

Greater Columbus Convention and Visitors Bureau, 90 North High Street, Columbus, OH 43215; 614–221–6623 or 800–354–2657; www.columbuscvb.org.

Summit and Stark Counties, Ohio

WHERE THE ROAD MEETS THE RUBBER

1 NIGHT

Science • House & Garden • Historic Canal • Football

It's tempting to refer to Akron bouncing back, but the wealth and scientific research that helped make this Ohio town the rubber capital—with Goodyear leading the pack—also built its major attractions of the postindustrial era: luxurious house museums and one of the best interactive science centers in what I hate to call the Rust Belt. And while so much of America's canal system has been ignored, abandoned, or filled in, there's enough left in this area for you to get a real feel for the "interstates" of the early nineteenth century.

One word of warning: This is not an outing for the cholesterol challenged. You can't venture into Akron, Canton, and environs without being tempted by specialty foods, gooey doughnuts, chocolates, and comfort food that doesn't stint on cheeses and sauces.

DAY 1

Morning

Head west on the Pennsylvania Turnpike and stay on I–76 even after it leaves the Ohio Turnpike, to **Akron:** two hours or less. Take exit 25 (Martha Avenue to Kelly Avenue), turn right onto Martha Avenue, then turn left onto East Market Street (OH 18) for about 6 miles. Watch for the garish HOT DOUGH-NUTS NOW sign on your right.

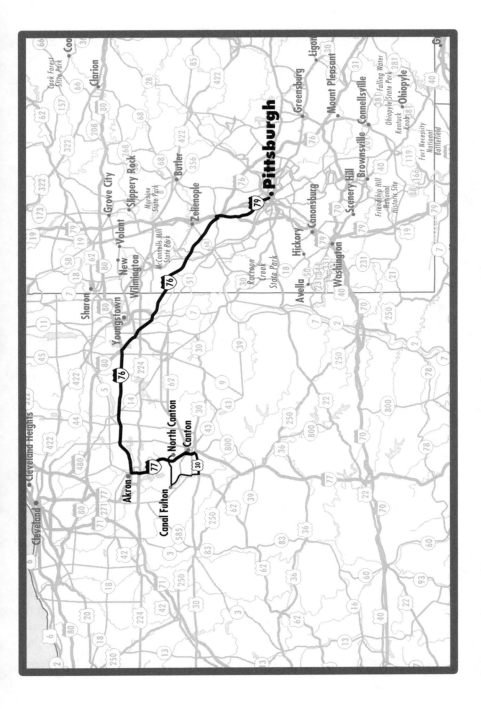

BREAKFAST: Though they've been around more than sixty years in their native North Carolina, **Krispy Kreme Doughnut Shops** (1699 West Market Street; 330–864–9955) are suddenly trendy and moving north. Dunk a glazed into coffee. (Open 6:00 A.M.–10:30 P.M. seven days a week.)

You just want to make sure you're not on an empty stomach when you step into **West Point Market** (330–864–2151 or 800–838–2156; www.westpointmarket.com) up the street at 1711 West Market, although you may want to stop by the market's **Beside the Point Cafe** and get a sandwich, hot potpie, or other goodie from the deli. The famed independent grocery story features a great variety of top-of-the-line cheeses, sausages, condiments, wines, and more, but regulars gush most about the bakery, which makes everything from its fabulous breads to trademark killer brownies from scratch. (Open Monday through Friday 8:00 A.M.–8:00 P.M., Saturday 8:00 A.M.–7:00 P.M.; closed Sunday.)

Head back downtown on OH 18 (southeast on Market Street), turn right onto OH 261 (South High Street), then left onto East Cedar Street, and left again at the next corner. You'll pass your destination (it's a one-way street) at 221 South Broadway and park in the Morley Health Center parking garage at Broadway and Bowery Street. The **National Inventors Hall of Fame** at **Inventure Place** (330–762–4463 or 800–968–4332; www.invent.org) features five floors of an atrium devoted to America's greatest inventors, plus displays of historic patent models. But the real attraction is down below in the Inventors Workshop, where you can play with lasers, water currents, air pressure, and more in the morning, before the place gets overrun by kids in the afternoon. (Admission is $7.50; parking validation at the ticket desk. Open Tuesday through Saturday 9:00 A.M.–5:00 P.M., Sunday noon–5:00 P.M.)

Continue on South Broadway for a couple of blocks, then turn right onto Mill Street, which becomes South Forge Street. Turn right again to 60 Fir Hill. Tucked into a tiny residential part of the University of Akron is the **Hower House** (330–972–6909), an eccentric but attractive house museum. The 1871 Victorian Italianate mansion, from the early days of the city's prominence, is built on the "Akron Sunday School" floor plan, meaning that the rooms radiate from a center hall and are filled with light. Nearly all the furnishings are original to the Hower family, who collected some major-league antiques. (Guided tours cost $5.00 and are offered Wednesday through Saturday noon–3:30 P.M., Sunday 1:00–4:00 P.M. Closed January.)

The Hower widows clung to their family manse in the heart of the city even as fashionable Akron moved to the "country" west of town, where **Stan**

Hywet Hall and Gardens (330–836–5533; www.stanhywet.org) presides as one of the most elegant and popular house museums in the United States. Head west on Market Street, turn right onto North Portage, and follow the signs.

LUNCH: Make your first stop the **Carriage House Store and Cafe** for light sandwiches and salads, or afternoon tea with scones. Some of the baked goods will look familiar from the West Point Market; the cafe features foods from throughout northeastern Ohio.

Afternoon

Stan Hywet (pronounced stan HEE-wit), Old English for the stone quarry on the original grounds, was built 1912–15 as much for comfort as for looks by a cofounder of the Goodyear Tire and Rubber Company. No expense was spared to make the sixty-five-room Tudor Revival mansion a welcome place for family and guests that ranged from President Taft to the Von Trapp family to Polish president and composer Ignace Paderewski, who played on the organ (it still works) in the vast music room. Start with a guided tour of the mansion (reservations suggested), and note how the modern conveniences (like a then-state-of-the-art telephone system) are disguised. Then explore the sixty-five acres of grounds and gardens at your leisure later in the day. There's almost always something in bloom, from the tulips and wildflowers of April to rhododendrons in June to a range of annuals in October, in more than half a dozen gardens. The museum hosts a variety of special tours, concerts, classes, monthly wine tastings, and more. (Admission is $8.00, or $4.00 for the gardens only. April 1 through December 31, house tours are offered 10:00 A.M.–4:30 P.M.; the grounds are open 9:00 A.M.–6:00 P.M. seven days a week. From the end of January through March, open Tuesday through Saturday 10:00 A.M.–4:00 P.M., Sunday 1:00–4:00 P.M. Photography is restricted.)

Return to West Market Street, turn right, and head past the West Point Market to 1970 West Market Street on your left. Park in front.

DINNER: Ken Stewart's Grille (330–867–2555), a popular spot for several counties around, features a regularly changing menu of aged prime beef, massive lobsters, and artful vegetarian dishes. It's not cheap, but it's worth it. There's a great selection of wines by the glass, or cruise the extensive list. (Lunch, Monday through Saturday 11:00 A.M.–2:00 P.M.; dinner, Monday through Thursday 5:00–10:00 P.M., Friday and Saturday 5:00–11:00 P.M. Closed Sunday.)

Turn right onto West Market for about a mile, then bear right onto South Hawkins Avenue. Make a quick left onto West Exchange Street and look for the Tudor mansion.

LODGING: The **O'Neil House** (330–867–2650) at 1290 West Exchange Street, built in 1923 for a mogul at General Tire Company, is now a quietly elegant B&B with four rooms to choose from.

Evening

Cozy up on the leather sofa in the library with a good book before the fire, play the grand piano in the formal living room, or stroll in one of the restored gardens.

DAY 2

Morning

Breakfast will be cooked to order while you look at the garden and the early birds in the breakfast room at the O'Neil House.

Return downtown via Market Street to the **Akron Art Museum** (70 East Market Street; 330–376–9185; www.akronartmuseum.org), an intimate, family-oriented museum with a small collection of paintings and large sculptures in a fun outdoor sculpture garden, augmented by traveling exhibits. (Open seven days a week, 11:00 A.M.–5:00 P.M., plus some Thursday-evening concerts. Admission is free, but parking costs $2.00.)

Head south on I–77 to exit 113 (Akron/Canton Airport), go right onto Lauby Road, and turn right into the lot for **Harry London Candies** (330–494–0833 or 800–321–0444; www.harrylondon.com). On the forty-five-minute chocolate factory tour ($2.00; reservations recommended), you get to see folks making the chocolates as well as some history, the Chocolate Hall of Fame, and, at the end, a packet of Harry London's signature mint meltaways. The large gift store will attract you even more with a range of truffles, dipped chocolates, candy bars, and gift items. (Tours are offered Monday through Saturday 9:00 A.M.–4:00 P.M., Sunday noon–3:30 P.M. The store is open Monday through Saturday 9:00 A.M.–6:00 P.M., Sunday noon–5:00 P.M.)

Don't fill up on candy. Head south on Lauby Road and turn right where it ends at Mount Pleasant Road. Pretty soon you'll see what looks like a World War II air base in Scotland.

LUNCH: Entering the **356th Fighter Group** (4919 Mount Pleasant Road; 330–494–5509; www.356th.com) feels like climbing into the screen during an old war movie, from the bunkerlike walls at the entrance to the vintage-radio music and piped-in commentary. The food is more modern, as are the planes you can watch taking off from the Akron-Canton Regional Airport. (Open Monday through Thursday 11:00 A.M.–midnight, Friday and Saturday 11:00 A.M.–2 A.M., Sunday 10:00 A.M.–midnight, with brunch 10:00 A.M.–2:30 P.M.)

Afternoon

Continue west on Mount Pleasant Road, which becomes Lake O'Springs Avenue as it veers south. Turn right onto Portage Street, and follow it to **Canal Fulton.** Turn left at Cherry Street (OH 93), then left onto Tuscarawas Street. You may want to explore some of the shops there, then visit the Canal Fulton Heritage Society's **Heritage House & Old Canal Days Museum** (330–854–3808 or 800–HELENA–3) for a look at the days when canals were the state-of-the-art transportation mode that greatly speeded up travel and made commerce to the West possible. Then go into Village Park and the society-operated *Saint Helena III,* an authentically built replica of an early-nineteenth-century canal boat. A horse-drawn cruise along an original section of the Ohio & Erie Canal includes a still-working lock (make sure you slather on insect repellent). The **Oberlin House,** also operated by the society, is a living-history museum in an 1847 house open sporadically. (The museum is generally open daily 12:30–4:30 P.M.; boat rides, weather permitting, are offered at 1:00, 2:00, and 3:00 P.M.)

Head south on Canal Street, which becomes Erie Avenue and joins OH 236 (which is also First Street) as you get into **Massillon.** Turn left before you reach Lincoln Way (the main street of town) and detour through the town's historic district for a gander at the massive **Five Oaks Historic Home** (330–833–8153) at 210 Fourth Street Northeast (open for tours by appointment and for special events). On the main drag you'll pass the **Massillon Museum** (121 Lincoln Way East; 330–833–4061), a former store now housing an eclectic collection of art, history, sports, and circus memorabilia. (Open Tuesday through Saturday 9:30 A.M.–5:00 P.M., Sunday 2:00–5:00 P.M.)

Head south on OH 21, east on U.S. 30 into **Canton,** and north on I–77 to the OH 687 exit and the recently expanded **Pro Football Hall of Fame**

Relive the Steeler championship years at the Football Hall of Fame.

(2121 George Halas Drive Northwest; 330–456–8207; www.profootballhof. com). Pittsburgh fans can feel some vindication at the extensive exhibit on William "Pudge" Heffelfinger, the first authenticated pro football player (actually, the first seven pros all played in the Pittsburgh area); the many Steelers and the Pittsburgh-heroes-who-got-away in the Enshrinement Galleries; and the various shoes, jerseys, and other mementos of local football greats. Totally new for visitors are the GameDay Stadium, a rotating theater of virtual football, plus a call-the-play theater and a photo gallery. (Admission is $10. Open every day but Christmas: Memorial Day through Labor Day, 9:00 A.M.–8:00 P.M.; the rest of the year, 9:00 A.M.–5:00 P.M.)

From the hall, it's a short one-exit hop south on I–77 to **The Stables Restaurant & Hall of Fame Grille** (2317 13th Street Northwest; 330–452–1230 or 888–GO–STABLES; www.thestables.com).

DINNER: Score a grilled steak or ribs in this remodeled horse barn that emphasizes its football theme. (Serves lunch Monday through Friday 11:00 A.M.–4:00 P.M., Saturday 11:30 A.M.–4:00 P.M.; dinner Monday through Thursday 4:00–10:00 P.M., Friday and Saturday 4:00 P.M.–midnight, Sunday 2:00–9:00 P.M.; Sunday brunch 10:00 A.M.–2:00 P.M.)

U.S. 30 looks tempting, but it's actually much quicker to retrace your steps on the interstates: I–77 north to I–76 east to home in around two hours.

THERE'S MORE

Base Ball. Yes, two words, referring to the game as it was played in the 1860s, with rather different rules, equipment, and terminology. Stan Hywet sponsors two clubs, the Akron Black Stockings and the Akron Lady Locks, April through October (330–836–5533; www.stanhywet.org).

Golf. Akron's 4-star-rated public courses are **J. E. Good Park Golf Club** (330–864–0020) and **Turkeyfoot Lake Golf Links** (330–644–5971 or 800–281–4484). Ranked 3½ stars is **Valley View Golf Club** (330–928–9034), Akron. To the south, **Legends of Massillon** also has 4 stars. (330–830–4653 or 888–839–7277).

Quaker Square. This former Quaker Oats silo and mills turned into a hotel/entertainment/shopping complex is located a few blocks from Inventure Place at 135 South Broadway (330–253–5970; www.akronbanquets.com).

Hoover Historical Center. Resist the usual jokes about the world's only vacuum cleaner museum. It's in the restored Victorian boyhood home of W. H. Hoover, founder of The Hoover Company, North Canton (330–499–0287).

Canton Classic Car Museum. Cars and memorabilia 1904–81 (330–455–3603).

Canton Museum of Art. This small art collection features watercolors, ceramics, and traveling exhibits (330–453–7666).

National First Ladies' Library. The restored home of Ida Saxton McKinley, the twenty-fifth first lady, in Canton (330–452–0876; www.firstladies.org).

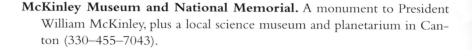
McKinley Museum and National Memorial. A monument to President William McKinley, plus a local science museum and planetarium in Canton (330–455–7043).

SPECIAL EVENTS

July. Enshrinement Day at the Pro Football Hall of Fame is the peak of an eleven-day festival capped by the AFC-NFC Hall of Fame Game (330–456–7253).

August. Tour of Gracious Living includes private, exclusive Akron residences and Stan Hywet (330–836–5533; www.stanhywet.org).

October. Stan Hywet hosts the Wonderful World of Ohio Mart, a top-rated crafts show with exhibitors and strolling performers in Tudor and Renaissance clothing (330–836–5533; www.stanhywet.org).

OTHER RECOMMENDED RESTAURANTS AND LODGING

Treva Restaurant & Market. Contemporary fusion before the game, near Akron's Canal Park (330–253–0340).

Piatto Italian Restaurant. In the heart of downtown Akron (330–255–1140).

The Inn at Brandywine Falls. Enjoy the country life outside Akron (330–467–1812 or 330–650–4965).

Hilton Akron at Quaker Square. Within walking distance of Inventure Place (330–253–5970 or 800–HILTONS).

Canal House Bed & Breakfast. Two suites available in the Canal Fulton B&B (330–854–6229).

FOR MORE INFORMATION

Akron/Summit Convention and Visitors Bureau, 77 East Mill Street, Akron, OH 44308; 330–374–7560 or 800–245–4254; www.visitakronsummit.org.

Canton/Stark County Convention and Visitors Bureau, 229 Wells Avenue Northwest, Canton, OH 44703; 330–454–1439 or 800–533–4302; www.visitcantonohio.com.

WESTERN

South Bend, Indiana
WHEN THE IRISH AREN'T FIGHTING

2 NIGHTS

Sports • Classic Cars • Art and Architecture • Tradition

You can hear that song in your head already, right? Given its historic prominence in football as well as movies like *Knute Rockne, All-American* and, more
recently, *Rudy,* Notre Dame is probably America's most famous and beloved
university, with devoted students ("Domers") from all over the United States.
The campus is a magnet for Domers, former Domers, wannabe Domers, and
friends of Domers. This is especially true on football weekends, when the
town swells to accommodate the capacity crowds (only one nonsellout since
1966) at the recently enlarged stadium: 80,012. That's bigger than all but a few
municipalities in Pennsylvania—heck, bigger than almost half the counties
here.

But there's plenty to do here besides or even (blasphemy!) instead of Notre
Dame football. The campus itself offers many possibilities, and the city of
South Bend is also famous as the home of the Studebaker. The area has built
on those legacies in the new College Football Hall of Fame, attractive history
museums, and more.

DAY 1

Morning

It's turnpike all the way: Pennsylvania, flattening out to Ohio to Indiana—less
than six hours easy at the 70-mile-per-hour speed limit.

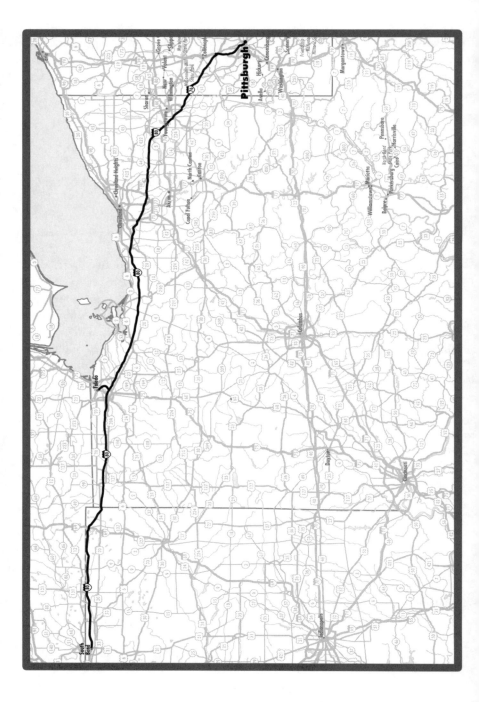

BREAKFAST/LUNCH: Take a break from the road at the midpoint on Plaza 3 in Ohio at **Charlie's General Store** (419–825–1843) between exits 39 (3B) and 52 (3A). A bit of a break from typical pike fast food, Charlie's sit-down eatery offers homemade soups, sandwiches, and breakfast 24/7.

Afternoon

Take exit 77 for **South Bend,** and at the traffic light at the end of the exit ramp, turn right to head downtown to what made South Bend famous before anybody started throwing footballs around. Henry and Clem Studebaker set up shop here in 1852. They soon turned their blacksmithing talents to wagons and carriages, and their family business was the only one to successfully make the transition to automobiles. The **Studebaker National Museum** (525 South Main Street; 219–235–9479; www.studebakermuseum.org) traces the company's 114-year history with seventy-five vehicles from an early conestoga wagon to four presidential carriages to the last Studebaker to roll off the South Bend assembly line in 1966. You don't have to be a car nut to appreciate the lines of the Packard Predictor (a prototype still in pristine shape), the first of only forty-one Golden Eagles, and many other classic cars. The current space, a Studebaker dealership built in 1919, offers less than ideal conditions, but it's scheduled to be replaced on February 16, 2002 (the 150th anniversary of the company's founding), with a state-of-the-art 95,000-square-foot museum. (Admission is $4.50; open Monday through Saturday 9:00 A.M.–5:00 P.M., Sunday noon–5:00 P.M.)

From the museum parking lot, head 1 block east to Michigan Street, then go north to the Century Center on South Saint Joseph Street. The convention facility is the new home of the **South Bend Regional Museum of Art** (120 South Saint Joseph Street; 219–235–9102; www.sbt.infi.net~sbrma), which has grown to more than 40,000 square feet with five galleries showcasing the permanent collection of nineteenth- and twentieth-century works in traditional media, plus quirky temporary exhibits. Make sure you explore the galleries beyond the sculpture court (a wide hallway in the Century Center); you could easily miss them. (A donation of $3.00 suggested; open Tuesday through Friday 11:00 A.M.–5:00 P.M., Saturday and Sunday noon–5:00 P.M.)

DINNER: The Vine (122 South Michigan Street; 219–234–9563) is right across the street, or perhaps you've already parked in front of it. If it's warm outside, you can dine out on the plaza across from the College Football Hall of Fame (we'll get there later, don't worry), but the name of this game is to

Drive through 114 years of automotive style at the Studebaker National Museum.

relax with wines by the glass. There are light entrees available, but you may prefer to graze on several appetizers (especially the hot crab dip) and a gourmet pizza. (Open Monday through Wednesday 11:00 A.M.–10:00 P.M., Thursday till 11:00 P.M., Friday till 1:00 A.M., and Saturday noon–1:00 A.M.)

Evening

Cross Saint Joseph Street and then the Saint Joseph River on Colfax Street or LaSalle Street to see what may be the only downtown-based white-water rafting in the country. The 2,000-foot-long **East Race Waterway** (The Waterway, 126 North Niles Avenue; 219–233–6121), a former millrace on the Saint Joseph River, was the first artificial white-water course in North America when it opened in 1984, with waves up to 6 feet high. The banks of the race include more than 5 miles of paved, lighted walkways for an evening stroll. (Operates June through August. Rental packages for rafts, kayaks, and "funyaks" range from $2.00 to $10.00. Watching is free.)

Before you get into your car, check out the **Chocolate Café** of the South Bend Chocolate Company (219–287–0725 or 800–301–4961; www. sbchocolate.com) in the same building as The Vine. Maybe you enjoyed one of the homemade desserts at The Vine and just want a coffee to cap the night, or maybe you need some serious ice cream. Desserts bear names like The Gipper (a hot fudge sundae with chocolate-covered peanuts) and the Four Horseman (a four-scoop banana split). House-specialty chocolates include Rocknes (a nut-coconut haystack) and Domers (truffles). Or choose one of the coffee or chocolate drinks (Chocolate LaSalle is made with local mint oil). (Open Monday through Thursday 7:00 A.M.–10:00 P.M., Friday and Saturday 7:00 A.M.–midnight, Sunday 10:00 A.M.–5:00 P.M.)

LODGING: Just a few blocks from the heart of downtown at 116 South Taylor Street is the **English Rose Inn** (219–289–2114; www.bbonline.com/in/englishrose/), part B&B, part antiques shop. Your room will be decorated with antiques, all of them for sale. Before you turn in, discuss what time you want breakfast with proprietor Susan Kessler.

DAY 2

Morning

BREAKFAST: You need only be presentable enough to accept a tray of coffee or tea, juice, and a variety of freshly baked sweet and/or savory pastries. Enjoy them in your room.

Time for The Pilgrimage (don't try this on a home football game day). Drive north on Michigan Street to Angela Boulevard, turn left onto Notre Dame Avenue, then left into the marked visitors lot. **The University of Notre Dame du Lac** (219–631–5000; www.nd.edu) is comprised of some 1,250 tradition-filled acres with two lakes, woods, a designer golf course, several of the most famous college landmarks in the nation, and a carefully designed central campus in a collegiate Gothic style. One alum describes it as going to school in a theme park. In its late-1990s building boom, the school answered the demand for more tourism facilities with the **Eck Visitors Center** (219–631–5726), where you begin. The center itself features displays of school memorabilia (including footballs and news clippings of memorable games), along with an orientation video outlining the history and prominence of the university since its founding in 1842. Tours are offered at 11:00 A.M. and 3:00 P.M., but pick up a campus map and visitors guide for your own. (The

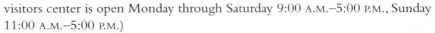
visitors center is open Monday through Saturday 9:00 A.M.–5:00 P.M., Sunday 11:00 A.M.–5:00 P.M.)

Walk north—straight toward the **Golden Dome**—through Notre Dame Circle and on to where the South Quad meets the Main Quad. The gentleman on the pedestal there is **Father Edward Sorin,** the French missionary from the Congregation of the Holy Cross who founded the school in what was then wilderness. Continue toward the Dome, but stop first at the **Basilica of the Sacred Heart,** built 1870–92 and a treasure trove of ecclesiastical art. Look up as well as on the walls for the stunning murals (recently cleaned) by Vatican artist Luigi Gregori, who worked for seventeen years under Father Sorin himself (he and other priests, brothers, and laymen posed for figures in some of the Stations of the Cross and murals). Walk around the seven Apsidal Chapels for a better view of the stained-glass windows. Tours (219–631–7329) are available, and an attached museum includes such artifacts as a papal tiara. (The museum is open Monday through Friday 9:00–11:00 A.M. and 1:00–4:00 P.M.; Saturday call for information; Sunday 1:00–4:00 P.M.)

If you leave by the southern door near the basilica museum, you're a short stroll from Corby Hall and the statue of Father William J. Corby with his arm raised in blessing, a gesture that earned this piece the nickname *Fair Catch Corby.* (It's actually a copy of a statue in Gettysburg National Battlefield; see Eastern Escape 3.) Continue southwest past the small **Log Chapel,** a replica of the original home of the frontier university, down the walkway and across Holy Cross Drive to **Saint Mary's Lake.** Stroll northward along the edge of the lake, noting the healthy ducks fed by generations of Domers, to the grotto across the street on your right. The **Grotto of Our Lady of Lourdes,** a one-seventh-sized version of the shrine in Lourdes, France, is probably the most popular spot on campus to pray and light a candle (daily rosary at 6:45 P.M.).

Take the left walkway up the hill, behind the basilica, to the **Main Building,** topped by the Golden Dome, covered in twenty-three-karat gold leaf and probably the best-known college landmark in the world (and a guidepost for passing pilots). A $58 million renovation has spruced up and literally brightened up the 144,000-square-foot structure considerably. You can appreciate the woodwork and ornate lighting fixtures, and get a much better look at the inner-dome mural and the famed **Columbus murals** (also done by Gregori; and, again, models purportedly included on-campus priests). Outside, the rear entrance now has an attractive portico. Head southeast past Washington Hall, which is supposedly haunted by the spirit of George "The Gipper" Gipp, to the **LaFortune Student Center** and a break.

LUNCH: Choose from the fast-food offerings of the **Huddle** food court on the first floor of the student center, or the **Allegro** on the lower level for subs and sandwiches. (During the academic year, open 7:30 A.M.–3:00 A.M.; summer session, 7:30 A.M.–10:00 P.M.)

Afternoon

Head east, through the Stonehenge-looking **War Memorial Fountain** toward the largest (fourteen-story) college library in the country, the **Hesburgh Library,** big enough to accommodate half the 10,000-strong student body at any given time. At its base is a rather florid-looking statue of Moses, one finger pointing upward. This, of course, is *We're-Number-One Moses.* Turn right (south) toward the stadium, and after 100 yards or so, turn around to look at the south face of the library and Notre Dame's second most famous landmark. It's a ten-story-high mosaic, *Word of Life,* depicting Christ surrounded by saints and scholars, composed of more than 7,000 naturally colored stones, but known to football fans around the world as *Touchdown Jesus.* Continue on course, but rather than heading across Moose Krause Circle to an empty stadium (unless you really want to pay homage to the House That Rockne Built), let's stop at the **Snite Museum of Art** (219–631–5466; www.nd.edu/~sniteart). The two-story museum rotates its 18,000-piece permanent collection to showcase about 800 works at any given time, ranging from Meso-American and Native American works to Rembrandt etchings to nineteenth-century photographs and, of course, ecclesiastical art. (Free admission; open Tuesday and Wednesday 10:00 A.M.–4:00 P.M., Thursday through Saturday 10:00 A.M.–5:00 P.M., Sunday 1:00–5:00 P.M.)

A short stroll west brings you back to Notre Dame Circle, then south to the Eck Building, also home to the new **Hammes Bookstore** (219–631–6316). Work your way through two floors of Notre Dame–licensed clothing from caps to socks—ND dog collars are the "in" gift for one's significant other—jewelry, memorabilia, foods (ND BBQ sauce?), and just weird stuff. Need a refrigerator magnet that plays the Notre Dame fight song? Oh, yeah, there are books, too, including one of the best selections of popular theology books around. (Open Monday through Saturday 9:00 A.M.–10:00 P.M., Sunday 11:00 A.M.–10:00 P.M.)

Head back to town for the **Northern Indiana Center for History** (808 West Washington Street; 219–235–9664; www.centerforhistory.org), which includes four museums on ten acres. If you're still up for walking, make sure you book a house tour (the last one's at 3:30 P.M.) for **Copshaholm** or **Dom Robotnika.** The former is the grand thirty-eight-room national landmark mansion of the Oliver family (they built their fortune on farm implements in the nineteenth and twentieth centuries), furnished with antiques dating to the seventeenth century. The latter is a "typical" worker's home from a 1930s Polish neighborhood, reflecting South Bend's ethnic heritage though perhaps not the hardships of the times. Take a stroll through the two-and-a-half-acre **Oliver Gardens,** and visit the center's museum (which includes the **kidsfirst Children's Museum**). Galleries showcase the history of the Midwest, of Notre Dame, and of the **All American Girls Professional Baseball League** (remember *A League of Their Own?*). The South Bend Blue Sox, one of fourteen teams in the nation's only professional women's baseball league, played during the entire lifetime of the AAGPBL, 1943–54. And South Bend is the national repository of the league's records and artifacts, some of which—gloves, programs, trophies—are on regular display. (Basic admission $5.00, up to $8.00 to include both house tours. Open Tuesday through Saturday 10:00 A.M.–5:00 P.M., Sunday, noon–5:00 P.M.)

DINNER: Just a short walk from your B&B, **LaSalle Grill** (115 West Colfax Avenue; 219–288–1155 or 800–382–9323; www.lasallegrill.com) offers relaxed fine dining in the 1868 vintage Saint Joseph Hotel, the oldest commercial building in South Bend, restored and remodeled to a stylish modern version of neoclassic. The food is definitely today's, with a daily changing menu and, often, local produce. (Open Monday through Thursday 5:00–10:00 P.M., Friday and Saturday 5:00–11:00 P.M. Reservations are recommended and can be placed up to three months in advance, including online.)

Evening

Linger over such LaSalle after-dinner bar specialties as the Full Moon (Grand Marnier and B&B) and enjoy live jazz by a variety of local artists. (Every Friday and Saturday 9:30 P.M.–12:30 A.M.; $3.00 cover.)

DAY 3

Morning

BREAKFAST: You won't need anything heavy on your tray this morning at the English Rose Inn—your brunch will be fairly substantial.

But first head back downtown to what looks like a small football field, probably with a few kids tossing around a ball. That's the entrance to the **College Football Hall of Fame** (111 South Saint Joseph Street; 219–235–9999 or 800–444–3263; www.collegefootball.org). Though only a few years old, the hall honors more than 840 players and coaches of the past century. Their plaques are arranged chronologically according to active playing time, in a multimedia exhibit that traces the evolution of football in the context of American history. You'll find plenty of local stars, from the original Iron Dukes of the 1930s to Pitt's Tony Dorsett, who's also represented in the three-story-high *Pursuit of a Dream* sculpture that marks the entrance to the Stadium Theater and Hall of Champions. Interactive exhibits also lets fans kick, throw, announce games, and more. (Admission $9.00. Open daily 10:00 A.M.–7:00 P.M.)

BRUNCH: Relive the luxury of the Studebakers in their 1886–89 mansion, **Tippecanoe Place** (630 West Washington Street; 219–234–9077), now a popular restaurant with a very reasonably priced brunch (especially considering the seafood omelettes). The various dining rooms preserve the charm of South Bend's most famous hosts of the nineteenth century. (Open for Sunday brunch 9:00 A.M.–2:00 P.M.; lunch, Monday through Friday 11:30 A.M.–2:00 P.M.; dinner, Monday through Friday 5:00–10:00 P.M., Saturday 4:30–10:30 P.M., Sunday 4:00–9:00 P.M. Reservations recommended.)

Take it easy on the way home, back along the Indiana and Ohio Turnpikes, maybe with a quick swing to I–75 and the **Toledo Museum of Art** (2445 Monroe Street at Scottwood Avenue; 419–255–8000 or 800–374–0667). Admission is free (except for special events) to this world-class home of masters from Rembrandt to Picasso. (Open Tuesday through Saturday 10:00 A.M.–4:00 P.M., Sunday 1:00–5:00 P.M.) While you're there in the historic Old West End, take a self-guided tour (free brochure available from The Women of the Old West End, 419–246–7779). The home of the Toledo Mud Hens is worth a revisit and a closer look.

DINNER: Exit the Pennsylvania Turnpike at Mars for a panoply of national chain restaurants, or stick to the old neighborhood standby **Marty's** (20700 Perry Highway, U.S. 19; 724–776–9902) for comfort food and sandwiches. (The dining room is open Sunday through Thursday 7:00 A.M.–9:30 P.M., Friday and Saturday till 11:00 P.M.)

THERE'S MORE

The South Bend Chocolate Company offers free factory tours at its West Sample Street headquarters (800–301–4961).

Saint Mary's College. The traditional "sister school" to Notre Dame is likewise a scenic campus, with the artistically significant Church of Loretto and the Moreau Center for the Arts, a venue for nationally touring performing arts (219–284–4626).

Golf. Two on-campus choices: **The Notre Dame Golf Course,** nine-hole golf; and the new eighteen-hole **Warren Golf Course** designed by Coore & Crenshaw (219–631–6425). Also, **Blackthorn Golf Course** rated tops in Indiana (219–232–4653).

Warren Dunes State Park. A favorite end-of-the-school-year trek for Domers are the giant sand dunes and beaches on Lake Michigan, north along Michigan's antiques-shop-lined Red Arrow Highway (616–426–4013).

Rutherford B. Hayes Presidential Center. The president might have been forgettable, but his thirty-three-room mansion in the residential neighborhood of Fremont, twenty minutes south of the Ohio Turnpike, is among the finest presidential libraries and museums (and was the first) (800–998–7737).

SPECIAL EVENTS

April. Notre Dame Bookstore Basketball, the largest 5-on-5 basketball event in the world, involves thousands of students, faculty, and staff in a single-elimination tournament as famous for its often unprintable but hilarious team names (www.nd.edu/~bkstr/favteam.htm) as its quality of play (219–631–6028).

June. Ethnic Festival at the East Race Waterway includes food, entertainment, carnival rides, more (219–235–9952).

July–August. Free concerts every Sunday in Seitz Park at the mouth of the East Race Waterway (219–233–6121; www.ci.south-bend.us/PARKS/index.htm).

August. Enshrinement festivities at the College Football Hall of Fame include a golf tournament and fanfest (219–235–9999 or 800–444–3263; www.collegefootball.org).

Notre Dame's still-young Summer Shakespeare includes plays in Washington Hall and outdoor community events (219–631–6556).

OTHER RECOMMENDED RESTAURANTS AND LODGING

Notre Dame has more than half a dozen eateries, from coffee and smoothies in **Reckers** (219-631–8638) to sit-down dining in **Sorins** (219–631–2020; www.sorinsnd.com). ND food services is at 219–631–7253.

Mishawaka Brewing Company, the area's only brewpub, in nearby Mishawaka (219–256–9993).

Morris Inn. Stay right on the Notre Dame campus (219–631–2000).

The Inn at Saint Mary's. Or stay on the campus next door (219–232–4000).

FOR MORE INFORMATION

South Bend–Mishawaka Convention and Visitors Bureau, 401 East Colfax Street, Suite 310, P.O. Box 1677, South Bend, IN 46634-1677; 219–234–0051 or 888–242–9906; www.livethelegends.org.

Cleveland

OTHER SIGNS OF LIFE

1 NIGHT

Markets • Music • Art

You've seen the T-shirt, right? A picture of a road sign: PITTSBURGH, 143 MILES. Underneath, the words: THE ONLY SIGN OF LIFE IN CLEVELAND. Pittsburgh and Cleveland squabble like kid cousins at a family picnic, trading insults and maintaining legendary rivalries, especially (but not exclusively) in football. Yet all but the most ardent anti-Brown Steeler fans have taken note of the lakefront town's recent renaissance and its age-old treasures in art and music.

There's plenty to do in our neighbor to the north before, after or instead of the game. *(Warning:* If you're in town when the Browns play, the postgame traffic pretty much wipes out access to the lakefront.) There are world-class cultural institutions (no jokes, please), a wealth of nightspots and the sort of marketplace that Pittsburgh lost in its own renaissance.

DAY 1

Morning

Head west on the Pennsylvania Turnpike, then the Ohio Turnpike to exit 13 (I–480/OH 14). Head northwest on I–480 to exit 20B (I–77 N/I–77 S to Cleveland/Akron); northwest on I–77 to exit 161B (I–490 W to Toledo/East 55th Street); and west on I–490, then I–90, to exit 170A (25th Street/U.S. 42). Head north on U.S. 42 (West 25th Street). As the city becomes more evident in the **Cleveland** neighborhood of **Ohio City,** you'll see a 137-foot clock tower atop an old-fashioned markethouse, probably with a lot of people flock-

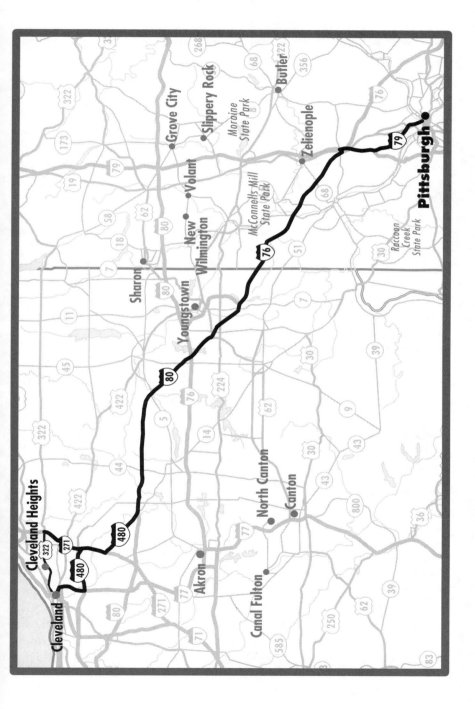

ing inside. Park on the street or nearby lots, but there's plenty of parking at Saint Ignatius High School (West 32nd Street and Lorain Avenue).

BREAKFAST: There are more than one hundred independent vendors at the **West Side Market** (Lorain Avenue at West 25th Street, Ohio City; 216–664–3386; www.westsidemarket.com) with a variety of meats, fish, produce, imported foods, teas, coffees, et cetera, from a United Nations of cuisines. Along the Lorain Avenue side of the 1912-era markethouse are most of the bakery stands, with breads and pastries (an Irish one, Reilly's, even has savory pasties) for breakfast (there's hot coffee near the West 25th Street entrance), or quick eateries with bagels, hot dogs, gyros, and the like to nosh while you appreciate the terra-cotta ornamentation. You'll see dozens of varieties of sausages made from pork, beef, turkey, and chicken, more than one hundred varieties of pierogi, and some cheeses you hadn't thought about (goat's milk Brie?). If you packed a cooler and want to do some real shopping, remember that there are no shopping carts, and you'll curse the folks who clog the aisles with their own wheeled contraptions during the peak (10:00 A.M.–3:00 P.M.) crowds. Bring sturdy canvas bags, and try not to go overboard. (Open Monday and Wednesday 7:00 A.M.–4:00 P.M., Friday and Saturday 7:00 A.M.–6:00 P.M.)

Cross the Hope Memorial Bridge (named for Clevelander Bob Hope; check out those art deco 43-foot-tall "Guardians of Traffic") into downtown, onto Carnegie Avenue, left onto East Ninth Street, then left onto Prospect Avenue, and go just past the hotel into the parking garage at 527 Prospect Avenue to stash the car and check your stuff.

LODGING: The **Residence Inn by Marriott** (527 Prospect Avenue, downtown; 216–443–9043 or 800–331–3131) provides apartmentlike suites in a classic building that's part of the Colonial Marketplace complex, combining the historic Colonial and Euclid Arcades. And it's a short walk to Jacobs Field, Gund Arena, and other downtown attractions. There's a fridge to store any perishables you might have been tempted to buy at the West Side Market. Elevators permit access to the parking garage without having to brave the outdoors.

Stroll down Prospect to that art-deco-looking building dead ahead at **Public Square** (take time to look at some of the monumental artworks outside). **Tower City Center** (216–771–0033; www.towercitycenter.com) includes a shopping-dining-hotel complex atop a transit center, the current incarnation of the nation's first. The original Terminal Tower complex over Union Station not only was the first underground station, but at the time was also the

Get a taste of Cleveland at the West Side Market.

world's largest integrated group of buildings under one management. Stop by the visitors center (216–621–7981) and ask about getting the full view of Cleveland from the Terminal Tower's forty-second-floor Observation Deck (open Saturday and Sunday 11:00 A.M.–3:30 P.M.). There are also dozens of shops to explore in **The Avenue at Tower City Center** (230 West Huron Road), including department store Dillard's (216–579–2580) and many nationally known names. (Open Monday through Saturday 10:00 A.M.–8:00 P.M., Sunday noon–6:00 P.M.)

LUNCH: For a quick bite, there's the Team Diner food court with more than a dozen fast-food possibilities; or have a seat at **Century at the Ritz Carlton** (1515 West Third Street, next to The Avenue; 216–902–5255), inspired by the dining car of the *Twentieth-Century Limited.* Admire the train memorabilia over a "lunch box" of soup, salad, entree and dessert, or enjoy sushi from the Orient Express. (Serves seven days a week: breakfast, 6:30–11:00 A.M.; lunch,

11:30 A.M.–2:30 P.M.; dinner, Sunday through Thursday 5:30–10:00 P.M., Friday and Saturday 5:30–11:00 P.M.; sushi bar, 11:30 A.M.–10:30 P.M. Live entertainment 5:30–11:00 P.M.)

Afternoon

Take the escalator down to the Tower City rapid transit station for the **Waterfront Line** (Greater Cleveland Regional Transit Authority RTA Answerline, 216–621–9500; www.gcrta.org). On this line only, the $1.50 fare is good for four hours of travel, so you'll probably be able to return on the same electronic ticket; you could also get an all-day pass for $4.00 and go on any line. Rapids (that's what Cleveland calls its light-rail vehicles) run every twelve to fifteen minutes from about 7:00 A.M. to 11:48 P.M. on the Waterfront Line to the North Coast Harbor Station.

You can see the distinctive I. M. Pei–designed tentlike building from the station itself, and it's a short stroll to the **Rock and Roll Hall of Fame and Museum** (1 Key Plaza, East Ninth Street at Lake Erie; 216–781–ROCK or 888–764–ROCK; www.rockhall.com). There's more than 55,000 square feet of exhibit space—more than fifty-five constantly changing exhibits—and a variety of short videos, long films, the world's biggest jukebox (more than 27,000 songs) and artifacts of the greats, from Jim Morrison's Cub Scout uniform to Leadbelly's Stella twelve-string to Phish's giant flying hot dog from its 1994 tour and millennium concert. It's probably the first thing you notice when you head down to the ground level, where the Phish fries and soda are found. My fave, though, is the tribute to One-Hit Wonders. (Admission $15.00; $3.00 off if you show a Waterfront Line pass. Open every day but Thanksgiving and Christmas, 10:00 A.M.–5:30 P.M., till 9:00 P.M. on Wednesday.)

It's a short stroll along the lakefront to the **Great Lakes Science Center** (601 Erieside Avenue; 216–694–2000; www.greatscience.com). Your hair will literally stand on end with a static electricity generator. More than 300 interactive exhibits let you have fun with light and optics, sound and resonance, motion and mechanics, electricity and magnetism, and weather. You also get to play with materials, pick up a car (though you don't get to keep it), and get up close and personal with an MRI before your doctor ever tells you to. (Admission $7.95 for exhibits only or Omnimax only, or $10.95 for both. Open Sunday through Friday 9:30 A.M.–5:30 P.M., Saturday 9:30 A.M.–6:45 P.M.)

If you have time when you're heading back to the transit station, stroll a little farther south on East Ninth Street, past the transit station, to Willard Park on

Lakeside Avenue for a look at **Free Stamp.** Making a heavy pop-art statement at 75,000 pounds, the sculpture by Claes Oldenburg and Coosje van Bruggen is supposed to be a "contemporary paraphrase" of the soldiers and sailors monument on nearby government buildings (although actually it was designed for another location entirely). Return downtown via the Waterfront Line and get ready to visit the **Warehouse District,** Cleveland's first neighborhood, between Public Square and the Flats, and an official National Historic Landmark. Downtown Cleveland's oldest business district is lined with late-Victorian warehouses and commercial buildings, many of them now fashionable lofts and trendy restaurants. You can take a self-guided history and architecture tour with the help of a $5.00 booklet from the Historic Warehouse District Development Corporation (216–344–3937; www.warehousedistrict.org).

DINNER: The **Cleveland ChopHouse & Brewery** (824 West Saint Clair Street; 216–623–0909) specializes, not surprisingly, in steaks, with the occasional veal or pork chop and rack of lamb. Top yours with bourbon whiskey sauce or roasted garlic or—for real excessiveness—crab and lobster sauce. Start with a sampler of the house-made brews to test them all for dinner. (Open Monday through Thursday 11:30 A.M.–10:00 P.M., Friday and Saturday 11:30 A.M.–11:00 P.M., Sunday 10:00 A.M.–2:00 P.M. for brunch, 4:00–10:00 P.M. for dinner.)

Evening

The ChopHouse features live jazz at night. Or you might cruise around the Warehouse District, the Gateway District, or the more youth-oriented **Flats** for your choice of dozens of nightspots, like the grinding pop dancing at **Heaven** (216–621–0440) or even more popular **Basement** (216–344–0287); jazz at **Bop Stop** (216–664–6610) or the **6 Street Under Jazz Club** (216–589–9313); or a variety of top acts at that famed concert club the **Odeon** (216–574–2525).

DAY 2

Morning

BREAKFAST: A full breakfast buffet in a historic clubroom is part of the package at the Residence Inn, but you may just want a muffin and coffee to tide you over till brunch.

Head straight out Euclid Avenue (U.S. 20) for about 4 miles to the **University Circle** area, home of Case Western Reserve University and of Cleveland's leading museums. You'll make a left turn (watch for the signs) just before **Severance Hall,** the newly remodeled home of the Cleveland Orchestra, which you'll see on a rise to your left. You can't help but notice the spectacular setting (even with ongoing restoration) of the **Cleveland Museum of Art** (11150 East Boulevard; 216–421–7340; www.clevelandart.org) on Wade Lagoon in a park. It's one of the best art museums in the United States and, amazingly enough, it's free (though there is an hourly fee for parking). Particularly notable are the collections of Mayan and Asian art; Western holdings range from medieval armor to Marie Antoinette's bed to a delightful indoor sculpture court and garden. The museum also hosts many major traveling exhibits; among those in 2001 are French Master Drawings from the Collection of Muriel Butkin and a companion show, Inventive Impressions: 18th- and 19th-Century French Prints (August 26 through October 28, 2001). (Admission is charged only for certain traveling exhibits. Open Tuesday through Sunday 10:00 A.M.–5:00 P.M., till 9:00 P.M. Wednesday and Friday.)

BRUNCH: The museum's lower level is home to **Oasis Restaurant** (216–229–6216), which hosts an exquisite Sunday brunch. Though small, the buffet includes a variety of smoked fish, seafood salads, carved meats, breads, a cheese table, and, of course, artfully crafted desserts. (Reservations necessary. Brunch is served 11:00 A.M.–2:30 P.M., with the last seating at 2:00 P.M.)

Afternoon

Wait for the free University Circle **CircleLink** (216–791–6226; www.universitycircle.org) shuttle bus at the museum entrance, or stroll along East Boulevard to the **Cleveland Botanical Garden** (11030 East Boulevard; 216–721–1600; www.cbgarden.org). Ten acres of gardens include six permanent gardens (including Ohio's first public garden especially for children) and several changing "living exhibit" gardens. Visitors can stroll from dusk to dawn in a formal rose garden, a classic Japanese garden, a soothing reading garden, a shrub garden, and a formal English knot garden with more than 300 herb species. A major part of this establishment, though, is education, with a library ("Hort Line," 216–721–0400) and, under construction, a new garden under glass that's not a conservatory but a "biome," an entire ecosystem. The new Glasshouse will ultimately feature two biomes: a Costa Rican cloud forest and a Madagascar spiny desert. (The buildings are open Monday through Saturday 9:00 A.M.–5:00 P.M., Sunday noon–5:00 P.M.)

Once you've finished inhaling the garden, hop on the shuttle or walk to the **Western Reserve Historical Society** (10825 East Boulevard; 216–721–5722; www.wrhs.org), which operates two museums at its headquarters here, and four others off site. Car buffs can check out more than one hundred vehicles at the **Crawford Auto–Aviation Museum.** The focus is on cars made in Cleveland (more than eighty marques actually originated in the area), with aircraft, bikes, Model Ts, and race cars. The **History Museum** features the Hay-McKinney Mansion designed and built in 1911 by the son of President James Garfield. There's a kind of *Upstairs Downstairs* feel to the range of exhibits from family to servants. Don't miss the Chisholm Halle Costume Wing, one of the tops in the country, with rugged clothing from the late eighteenth century to fancy Victorian gowns to today's garb. (Admission is $7.50. Open Monday through Saturday 10:00 A.M.–5:00 P.M., Sunday noon–5:00 P.M.)

Head southeast on East Boulevard, turn left at Ford Drive, and, in about a quarter mile, turn left onto Mayfield Road (U.S. 322), through Little Italy to Cleveland Heights. In about 1.5 miles turn right on Coventry Road into the small but very hip **Coventry Village** business district. There's a public parking garage on your left, or you can try to find street parking (good luck).

DINNER: You'll feel healthy ordering hearty soups and heartier salads at **Tommy's** (1824 Coventry Road; 216–321–7757; www.tommyscoventry. com), with lots of vegetarian offerings on a Greek-inspired menu. Check out some of the local art while waiting for your potato-escarole pie or tempeh burger. If you need to wait for a table, there's a doorway into a used-book store. Afterward, window-shop at Coventry Village boutiques. (Open Monday through Thursday 7:30 A.M.–10:00 P.M., Friday and Saturday 7:30 A.M.–11:00 P.M., Sunday 9:00 A.M.–10:00 P.M.)

Continue east on U.S. 322 until it joins up with I–271; head south and join up with I–480; follow I–480 southeast back to the Ohio and then Pennsylvania Turnpike.

THERE'S MORE

Cleveland Play House. The nation's oldest regional theater, founded in 1915, produces classic, new, and children's plays on four stages (University Circle; 216–795–7000; www.clevelandplayhouse.org).

Playhouse Square Center. Five refurbished 1920s-era movie palaces form the heart of downtown's Theater District. This is the home of the **Great Lakes Theater Festival** (216–241–5490; www.greatlakestheater.org) and the **Cleveland Opera** (216–575–0903; www.clevelandopera.org), and the Cleveland home of the **Ohio Ballet** (330–972–7900; www.ohioballet.com), as well as the venue for a variety of touring performances by a number of presenters (for ticket information call 216–241–6000 or 800–766–6048). Free tours are generally offered on the first Saturday and Sunday of the month, 10:00–11:30 A.M., from the State Theatre lobby (216–771–4444; www.playhousesquare.com).

Severance Hall. Home of the **Cleveland Orchestra** (216–231–7300 or 800–686–1141; www.clevelandorchestra.com), which performs September through May. Tours are available one Friday per month by appointment. The aluminum leaf patterns were inspired by Mrs. Severance's wedding dress (216–231–7463).

Cleveland Museum of Natural History. This small museum in University Circle is home to Lucy, the world's oldest and most complete skeleton of a human ancestor, plus the world's only mounted skeleton of the plant-eating dinosaur *Haplocanthosaurus* and a new gallery of minerals and gems (216–231–4600; www.cmnh.org).

Jacobs Field. Tours are available of the home of the **Cleveland Indians** (www.indians.com), even if you can't get a ticket for the game itself (216–241–8888; www.ticketmaster.com).

Steamer *William G. Mathers* Museum. This retired Great Lakes bulk freighter, built in 1925, is now a museum docked at East Ninth Street Pier, near the Rock and Roll Hall of Fame and Museum (216–574–6262; http://little.nhlink.net/wgm/).

National Cleveland-Style Polka Hall of Fame. Rock? Let's get down with the music Cleveland is really famous for (216–261–FAME [3263]; http://clevelandstyle.com).

SPECIAL EVENTS

June. Parade the Circle celebrates the visual and performing arts in many venues in University Circle in a grand free event (216–791–3900; www.universitycircle.org).

The Cleveland Botanical Garden Flower Show—the North American counterpart to the Royal Horticultural Society's Chelsea Flower Show—features twenty gardens (216–721–1600 or 800–766–6048; www.cbgarden.org).

July–Labor Day weekend. Blossom Music Festival features the Cleveland Orchestra in symphonic and popular works in outdoor setting in Cuyahoga Falls; a popular performance series with other groups starts in May (216–231–1111 or 800–686–1141; www.clevelandorchestra.com).

September. The Rock and Roll Hall of Fame and Museum celebrates its birthday with music, contests, and free admission on Monday (216–781–ROCK or 888–764–ROCK; www.rockhall.com).

October. Free Day of Music at Severance Hall (216–231–7300; www. clevelandorchestra.com).

December. Holiday CircleFest, a museum open house with seasonal entertainment at many venues in University Circle (216–791–3900; www. universitycircle.org).

OTHER RECOMMENDED RESTAURANTS AND LODGING

Watermark Restaurant. Upscale seafood in the Flats (216–241–1600).

The Flat Iron Cafe. A pub/restaurant in the Flats (216–696–6968).

Blue Point Grille. Creative American dishes in the Warehouse District (216–875–STAR).

Frank and Paulys. Popular Italian in downtown's Public Square area (216–575–1000).

Hunan Coventry. An attractive Chinese eatery in Coventry Village (216–371–0777).

Ohio City Bed & Breakfast Association. A network of accommodations in an up-and-coming area around the West Side Market (216–589–0121).

Private Lodgings Inc. Beyond the B&B (216–321–3213).

The Brownstone Inn. A downtown B&B with amenities for business travelers (216–426–1753).

Glidden House. A mansion-turned-B&B right in the heart of University Circle (216–231–8900).

FOR MORE INFORMATION

Convention and Visitors Bureau of Greater Cleveland, 50 Public Square, Suite 3100, Terminal Tower, Cleveland, Ohio 44113 (216–621–4110 or 800–321–1004; www.travelcleveland.com).

EASTERN

ESCAPES

Fayette County and National Road

HOUSE HUNTING

1 NIGHT

Homes of History • Scenery • Fabulous Food

There's no shortage of house museums available for today's tourist, but this region—barely an hour from Pittsburgh—has an incredible wealth of them, from the very earliest days of the nation to the most famous home of the twentieth century. That's not hyperbole. Fallingwater, Frank Lloyd Wright's masterpiece, is the building of the century according to the American Institute of Architects. But there's much more to see in this chunk of Fayette County (with slices of Washington and Somerset Counties) along U.S. 40, the original Gateway to the West. You can enjoy sites from America's early days, another Wright creation, great scenery, and food.

DAY 1

Morning

Take the Pennsylvania Turnpike east to exit 9 (Donegal); ask at the tollbooth for a list of the area's attractions, which includes directions. Turn left and drive 1 mile on PA 31 to the Old General Store (724–593–7112 or 877–593–7112; www.oldgeneralstore.com) and the **Country Pie Shoppe** (724–593–7105).

BREAKFAST: Choose from the freshly baked pastries and the best coffee in the area at the Country Pie Shoppe. In the same building the Old General Store

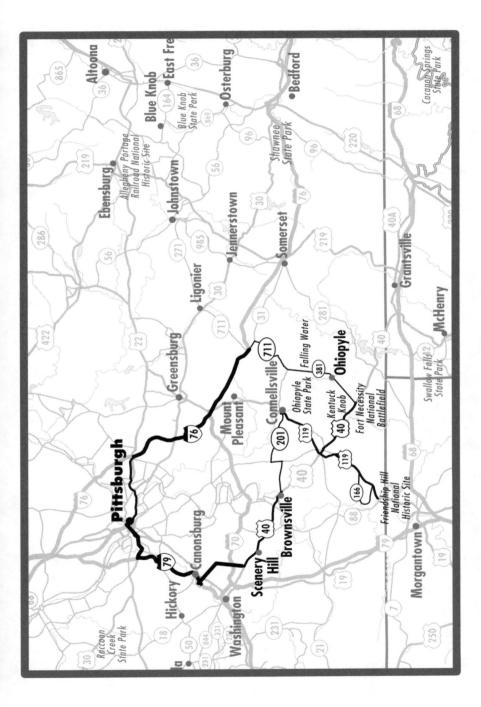

sells a variety of teas, coffees, preserves, and other gourmet foods. (Open 6:00 A.M.–8:00 P.M. every day.)

Continue on PA 31; turn right where PA 711 splits off, heading south through open farmland and wooded hillsides. Watch for the turnoff on your right for **Fallingwater** (724–329–8501; www.paconserve.org) in the Bear Run Nature Preserve, which offers hiking and nature trails. The parking area is a little distance from the famous house cantilevered over a waterfall, so that you can appreciate the approach and the view. The guided tour (you must have reservations) takes you throughout the main house, which still looks very much the way Wright designed and built it in the 1930s. Since opening for tours in 1964, the attraction has grown to include a very trendy gift shop and a cafe, discreetly out of sight of the house, plus occasional concerts. (Tours are offered mid-March through November, Tuesday through Sunday 10:00 A.M.–4:00 P.M.; also Memorial Day, July 4, Labor Day, Columbus Day, Thanksgiving Friday, and—weather permitting—December weekends to early January, the week between Christmas and New Year's Day, and the first two weekends in March. The cafe is open with a seasonally changing menu mid-April through mid-November, 8:30 A.M.–5:00 P.M. In winter it serves beverages and snacks only.)

Continue south on PA 381 for a few miles to **Ohiopyle State Park** (724–329–8591; www.dcnr.state.pa.us/stateparks/parks/ohio.htm), 19,052 acres of thickly wooded mountains and more than 14 miles of the Youghiogheny River Gorge, a favorite spot for white-water rafting and more tranquil boating. (There are plenty of outfitters in the town of **Ohiopyle**.) After passing under the bridge for the 28-mile **Youghiogheny River Trail,** watch for the turnoff to your right for the Falls Day Use Area lots. Stroll out to the observation deck for the best view of Ohiopyle Falls. The park's many hiking trails include Cucumber Falls and the wildflower-filled Cucumber Run Ravine, along with the Ferncliff Peninsula, a National Natural Landmark formed by a great horseshoe bend in the river that's an unusual habitat for southern wildflowers.

Continue south on PA 381 for about 6 miles to U.S. 40, turn right, and shortly you'll see one of the original inns (opened 1822) along the National Road.

LUNCH: The **Stone House Restaurant and Inn** (724–329–8876 or 800–274–7138; www.stonehouseinn.com) is now a posh but cozy inn with Victorian rooms and suites. The antiques-filled dining rooms serve dishes like the chicken and dumplings favored in the old days by nearby Uniontown native George C. Marshall (of Marshall Plan fame), plus newer specialties like Black and Bleu Salad—blackened strip steak and blue cheese on greens with seasoned fries. (Open January through March, Wednesday and Thursday 4:30–8:00 P.M., Friday and Saturday 11:30 A.M.–10:00 P.M., Sunday 11:30 A.M.–9:00 P.M. April, November, and December, Tuesday through Sunday 11:30 A.M.– 9:00 P.M., till 10:00 P.M. Friday and Saturday. May through October, Sunday through Thursday 11:30 A.M.–9:00 P.M., Friday and Saturday 11:30 A.M.–10:00 P.M.)

Afternoon

Continue west on U.S. 40 to Chalk Hill, turn right onto SR 2010 (Chalk Hill/Ohiopyle Road), and, in 6 miles, watch for the right turn to a lesser-known Wright creation, **Kentuck Knob** (724–329–1901; www.kentuckknob.com). Smaller than Fallingwater, Kentuck Knob generally strikes visitors as more homey and livable (indeed, the Hagan family of Hagan Ice Cream fame lived here year-round from 1956 to 1986; Fallingwater was strictly a summer home). Built in Wright's later Usonian style, the hexagonal-grid home of tidewater red cypress and native fieldstone is perched on a hilltop surrounded by woodland and a sculpture garden, which visitors can stroll through on their own after (or instead of) a guided tour of the house (reservations recommended). The gift center—actually the original greenhouse at Fallingwater—sells a variety of plants and gardening tools. (Regular tours are offered Tuesday through Sunday and holiday Mondays, 10:00 A.M.–4:00 P.M.; times vary depending on the weather from December through March. In-depth tours are conducted daily at 8:30 A.M. by reservation only. The tour fee is $10 on weekdays, $15 on weekends.)

Return to U.S. 40 and turn left down the hill, then right into **Fort Necessity National Battlefield** (724–329–5512; www.nps.gov/fone), where a young and reckless George Washington started the French and Indian War. Okay, historians quibble that if George hadn't been handy, somebody else would have ignited the powder keg of French-British relations in 1754, but the facts remain that it was under George's command that a skirmish resulted in the death of a French diplomat, and it was George's signature on the surrender of Fort Necessity that "admitted" the "assassination"—but only in the French version that he couldn't read. The stories of the war and frontier life are told in the visitors center, and you can visit the re-created fort itself (the

French burned down the original). Also take the time to climb the hill for a guided tour of **Mount Washington Tavern,** a stopover for the stagecoach trade 1828–55. (Admission is $2.00; a $15.00 pass covers twelve months at all National Historic Sites in southwest Pennsylvania. Open every day but Christmas, 9:00 A.M.–5:00 P.M.)

Continue up the hill on U.S. 40, and shortly on the right you'll pass **Braddock's Grave,** a monument to General Edward Braddock, who led the disastrous attempt to take Fort Duquesne in 1755 (Washington saved the company from massacre; his wartime experience was the training ground upon which the future Revolutionary War hero honed his skills). The general was originally buried in the road he and his troops had earlier built; the soldiers then marched over the grave to tamp down the ground and thus hide the body. At the top of the hill, you'll see the sign for a right turn to **Jumonville Glen,** the actual site of that original clash between Washington and the diplomat Sieur de Jumonville.

Back on U.S. 40, take it easy on the 2.5-mile hill down Chestnut Ridge. Near the bottom is the turnoff for Hopwood.

DINNER: Drive just a few blocks to the old Hopwood House, a stopping point for travelers since 1790 (including several presidents). Now it hosts **Chez Gérard** (724–438–0809; www.chezgerard.net), home of legendary authentic French cuisine (but no dress code), including a very affordable fixed-price six-course dinner. (Open Monday and Wednesday through Sunday; lunch, 11:30 A.M.–2:00 P.M.; dinner, 5:30–9:00 P.M. Reservations are strongly recommended.)

LODGING: Back up the hill is the appropriately named **Summit Inn** (724–438–8594 or 800–433–8594; www.hhs.net/summit) on Skyline Drive. Opened in 1907, the inn's guests have included Henry Ford and Thomas Edison (you can see their signatures in an old guest book), and after nearly a century the place retains the charm of polished wood and rich carpeting. Note, however, that there is no elevator, though rooms on the ground floor are accessible for people with impaired mobility.

Evening

Watch the sunset from the veranda. On a very clear day, you can just see the top of the USX Tower in downtown Pittsburgh.

Return to the earliest days of the republic at Friendship Hill.

DAY 2

Morning

BREAKFAST: Packages at the Summit Inn can include breakfast, breakfast and dinner, or both with golf. Order from the menu in the dining room. (Breakfast, 7:00–11:00 A.M.; lunch, 11:00 A.M.–5:00 P.M.; dinner, 5:00–9:00 P.M.)

Return to the earliest days of the republic by heading west on U.S. 40 to Uniontown, then south on U.S. 119 to Smithfield; turn right at the stop sign and take SR 3006 west, then head south on PA 166 through the small town of New Geneva, through the woods and the entrance to **Friendship Hill National Historic Site** (724–725–9190; www.nps.gov/frhi). This is the home of Albert Gallatin, one of the most fascinating (if now practically unknown) of our Founding Fathers. Best known as the secretary of the treasury under Presidents Jefferson and Madison, Gallatin was a financial whiz who reduced the national debt, arranged financing for both the Louisiana Purchase and the Lewis and Clark expedition, and set up a system of fiscal accountability to Congress. He also sought, only partially successfully, to build an industrial town in the wilderness and name it for his native Geneva, Switzerland. The house, built in 1789 and added to in 1798 for the growing Gallatin family, includes historical exhibits but, as yet, almost no furniture. As a house museum, it's a work in progress. Still, the grounds include more than 9 miles of trails for hiking and cross-country skiing, and a lovely overlook above the Monongahela River. (Free admission. Open 8:30 A.M.–5:00 P.M. every day but Christmas. House tours are offered from the Memorial Day weekend through the Labor Day weekend at 11:00 A.M. and 12:30, 2:00, and 3:30 P.M.)

Retrace your steps to U.S. 119. Head north to Connellsville, then west on PA 201 and north briefly on PA 819 to Dawson, an old-fashioned railroad town along the Youghiogheny. Follow the signs to **Linden Hall** (724–529–7543 or 800–944–3238; www.lindenhallpa.com). Now part of a private golf resort (724–529–2366), the original Tudor mansion, a National Historic Site, is open for tours. The lavish home cost $2 million when it was built in 1913, with thirty-five rooms, twenty-seven fireplaces, and thirteen baths decorated with baroque wood carving, marble, crystal, and gold leaf. The crown jewels are the signed Tiffany windows and an aeolian pipe organ, one of only three in the world. The grounds include a hiking trail with spectacular river views on the way to Dawson. (House tours cost $8.00 per adult and are offered March through October, Monday through Friday, 11:00 A.M.–3:00 P.M. on the hour; weekend tour hours vary and are by reservation only.)

Return to PA 201 and drive west from Dawson to the interchange at PA 51. Head south for 2 miles, then turn right onto SR 4028, which leads to U.S. 40 and to **Brownsville,** a historic town in its own right, and the grand old Thompson House, built 1906.

LUNCH: Now it's the home of **Caileigh's** (815 Water Street; 724–785–4744), with dining rooms on the first floor and gift shops on the second. Try the signature onion soup made with port wine and topped with french-fried onion rings. (Open Tuesday through Thursday 11:00 A.M.–9:00 P.M., Friday and Saturday 11:00 A.M.–10:00 P.M., Sunday 11:00 A.M.–6:00 P.M. Reservations suggested.)

Afternoon

Walk off some of Caileigh's apple pie along Front Street, originally the Nemacolin Trail, named for a literally trailblazing Seneca scout and chief. The street is lined with classic Federal, Greek, and Colonial Revival buildings. And do take a look at the **Church of Saint Peter,** built in 1845 of hand-hewn local stone in the Gothic Revival style, with striking stained-glass windows (tours available, 724–785–7781) at Shaffner and Church Streets.

Brownsville is blessed with not one but two national historic districts: downtown and North Side (upper Market Street), comprised of 315 structures in less than 2 square miles, including what are believed to be the oldest, most intact commercial buildings west of the Alleghenies. Chief among these is the **Flatiron Building** (69 Market Street; 724–785–9331; www.hhs. net/itforce/flatiron), built in 1830 and now being developed as the home of a local-history museum and the Frank L. Melega Art Museum. (Donations requested. Open Monday through Saturday 11:00 A.M.–8:00 P.M., Sunday noon–6:00 P.M.)

Take a quick stroll over **Dunlap's Creek Bridge,** the first cast-iron bridge built (1839) in the United States over what was then the National Road. It's still in use.

Between Front and Brashear Streets overlooking the Monongahela River is **Nemacolin Castle** (724–785–6882), which indeed looks like a castle from the outside. The original part of the house, built in 1789, was a frontier trading post and home to the Jacob Bowman family. As they prospered, they added to the house. Its current incarnation keeps every part of the house true to its original period in terms of decor and furniture, so that you start in pioneer days, move through antebellum America into Victoriana, and end up in the early twentieth century. (Admission is $5.00. Memorial Day through Labor Day, open Tuesday through Sunday 11:00 A.M.–5:00 P.M., plus weekends from Easter to mid-October. Candlelight tours are offered for ten days after Thanksgiving, 4:00–9:00 P.M.)

Continue west on U.S. 40 to the coyly named **Scenery Hill,** site of many country-style antiques shops and a picturesque view of perfectly rolling farmland and woods.

DINNER: Century Inn (724–945–6600; www.centuryinn.com), housed in a stone inn that has served travelers continuously since 1794, serves quail, duck, steaks, and more, with a nouvelle sensibility. The inn still has guest rooms for

a romantic hideaway. (Lunch, daily noon–3:00 P.M.; dinner, Monday through Thursday 4:30–8:00 P.M., Friday and Saturday 4:30–9:00 P.M., Sunday 3:30–7:00 P.M.)

Continue your drive west on U.S. 40 to PA 519, taking a country short-cut north to meet I–79 at Canonsburg and then on home.

THERE'S MORE

Nemacolin Woodlands Resort and Spa. Pennsylvania's top-ranked resort (by *Zagat*) and golf course (Mystic Rock gets 4½ stars from *Golf Digest*) also features a unique sport-shooting academy in the English aristocratic tradition, a luxurious spa, an extensive public art collection, a classic car collection, and several restaurants, including creative spa cuisine at Seasons. It's found in Farmington (724–329–8555 or 800–422–2736; www.nemacolin.com).

Touchstone Center for Crafts. Serious crafts classes for adults in black-smithing, ceramics, and more, located in Farmington near the Summit Inn (724–329–1370 or 800–721–0177; www.touchstonecrafts.com).

Laurel Caverns Geological Park. The largest cave in Pennsylvania at 430 acres; take a guided tour of developed sections or a trip into the "wild" sections. Free if you're staying at the Summit Inn. Fees range from $9.00 for a basic tour to $25.00 for rappelling (release form required) to $5.00 for miniature cave golf (724–438–3003 or 800–515–4150; www.laurelcaverns.com).

Searights Toll House. Built 1835, this is one of two remaining tollhouses in Pennsylvania along the National Road. It's found 6 miles west of Union-town and open daily from Memorial Day to early fall (724–439–4422).

Washington Mill Run Park includes an eighteenth-century distillery, the only free standing fulling mill in United States, and the foundation of George Washington's gristmill, restored using the original stone. Plans are being made to replicate the mill. The park is on SR 4038 (Linden Hall Road) near Perryopolis (724–736–4073 or 724–736–4383).

Biking. Along the Youghiogheny River Trail, the 10 miles from Ohiopyle to Confluence is considered one of the most scenic bike rides in the world. The 204-mile Allegheny Trail Alliance rail-trail from Pittsburgh to Cumberland, Maryland, will eventually connect to the C&O Canal Towpath to Washington, D.C. The longest continuous completed stretch, more than 100 miles, runs from McKeesport to Meyersdale (www.atatrail.org).

SPECIAL EVENTS

March. Kites Over Kentuck. Go fly a kite and tour a Wright house (724–329–1901).

May. National Road Festival. Highlighting this four-day festival along U.S. 40 through Washington, Fayette, and Somerset Counties is a pair of wagon trains, one traveling east, the other west. Find 90 miles of street fairs, yard sales, church food sales, and other festivities (724–329–1560).

July. The Battle of Fort Necessity is commemorated every July 3. Later in the month is Queen Alliquippa Day, celebrating Native American and frontier cultures (724–329–5512).

OTHER RECOMMENDED RESTAURANTS AND LODGING

The Inn at Lenora's. Rich continental dishes with lots of tenderloins, crab, and sauces. Guest rooms are available. In Perryopolis (724–736–2509; www.theinnatlenoras.com).

River's Edge Cafe and B&B and Antiques. Casual but creative lunches and dinners are served indoors or overlooking the Youghiogheny in Confluence, just outside Ohiopyle State Park. Sweaty bicyclists and white-water rafters welcome (814–395–5059).

FOR MORE INFORMATION

Laurel Highlands Visitors Bureau, 120 East Main Street, Ligonier, PA 15658; 724–238–5661 or 800–925–7669; www.laurelhighlands.org.

Bedford County

GEORGE WASHINGTON
SLEPT HERE, TOO

---

1 NIGHT

---

*Frontier Life • Covered Bridges • Defying Gravity
Scenery • Winter Sports*

A quarter of a millennium ago, this area was Raystown, a bustling and most important frontier trading post. In 1758 came a sizable fort, named for the Duke of Bedford, protecting the traders and farmers from enemy French and Indians. General Forbes launched his successful march on Fort Duquesne from here, with his young aide George Washington at his side. An older Washington, by this time president of the new United States, personally led the army as far as Bedford to put down the Whiskey Rebellion. Since then, well, not a great deal has happened here. Sure, there are all the modern conveniences, but somehow the hustle and bustle of modern life whizzed right past Bedford County, first on the Lincoln Highway, now on the Pennsylvania Turnpike. What's left is mostly forest with the occasional farm, creating scenery that will just suck the film right out of your camera in pretty much every season. While historic attractions are most popular in warm weather, and fall foliage and harvest combine for autumnal popularity, the highest vertical drop in Pennsylvania means great skiing during a long, snowy winter.

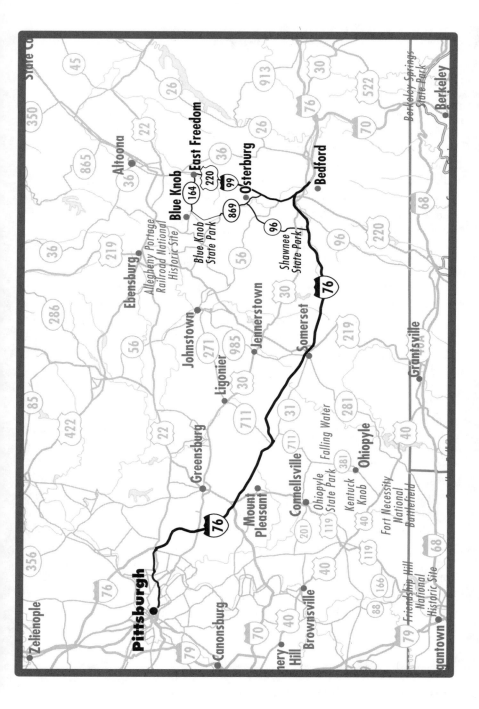

DAY 1

Morning

Head east on the Pennsylvania Turnpike to exit 11 (Bedford), about two and a half hours away. Turn south onto U.S. Business 220 for about a mile, then turn right at the sign for **Bedford Village** (814–623–1156), through your first covered bridge of the trip (there will be more, promise). One of our more successful Bicentennial projects, the seventy-two-acre village is a collection of about forty historic local structures, some original, some reconstructions using pieces of two or more buildings, and some reproductions designed to re-create eighteenth- and nineteenth-century life in Bedford. A popular photo op is the old-fashioned village stocks (no, they don't actually lock) on the path to the church and old houses with mini museums on such topics as African American life, Native American life, quilting, and the Whiskey Rebellion.

LUNCH: At the far end of the path is the **Pendergass Tavern,** which serves simple lunches in an eighteenth-century-style tavern: sandwiches, maybe stew, probably pickled eggs and beets. Go next door for ice cream and relax with your cone by the "opera house," the **Gardner Memorial Theater,** where somewhat more modern plays are staged on weekends June through December (814–623–1156), with both evening and matinee shows.

Afternoon

Continue your stroll through the village's "shops," where various artisans demonstrate and discuss colonial crafts. The chandler makes not only beeswax candles but also the rough lye soap used in the old days, and the cooper prides himself on "whiskey-tight" barrels, buckets and butter churns, all made of wood. You may also meet the village weaver, leather worker, blacksmith, and more, but the kids' favorite place is the old jail (for times when punishment in the stocks was not enough). The path leads to the crafts store, which includes handmade bonnets, lye soap, candles, and a few other things made on the premises. (Admission is $6.95. Open 9:00 A.M.–5:00 P.M. daily except Wednesday, Memorial Day through Labor Day; then Thursday through Saturday 10:00 A.M.–5:00 P.M., and Sunday 10:00 A.M.–4:00 P.M., till October 31. Classes are also available. Visit www.bedford.net/village.)

Return to U.S. 220 south and, in a few minutes, you'll reach U.S. 30—also Bedford's main drag, Pitt Street. You'll probably find free on-street parking, or you can use a public garage off Juliana Street (the top of the hill). Cross Juliana to visit **Founder's Crossing Market Place** (814–623–9120; www.geocities.com/founders99/), an old G. C. Murphy filled with three floors of country-crafty items—it's like visiting a small-town festival with 150 vendors. There's quite a variety: from handmade knickknacks to supplies for folks restoring old homes, with furniture on the lower level and pretty decent prices on dried-flower arrangements. (Open Monday through Saturday 9:30 A.M.–5:00 P.M., Sunday noon–4:00 P.M.)

There are only a few blocks of "downtown" Bedford, with a variety of shops, often with rather eccentric hours, but they're reliably open on Saturday afternoon. Stop by **Elaine's Wearable Art** (814–623–7216) for a nice array of handmade jewelry and accessories, and head down the hill for homemade brittle and fudge at **Bedford Candies** (814–623–1545). But the biggest attraction is the lineup of antiques shops in town and throughout the county. Just remember that this area has been a frontier outpost and country village: Figure more Grandma's attic than Grandma's parlor. There's a free booklet available at the visitors center on Juliana Street from the county Antique Dealers Association (800–765–3111).

You'll also find a nice combination of art and history at the **Bedford County Arts Council** (814–623–1538), which features changing exhibits in three rooms of the Anderson House, a historic Georgian mansion right at 137 East Pitt Street. (Free. Open Tuesday through Saturday 11:00 A.M.–5:00 P.M.)

DINNER: Just up the hill (not coincidentally) at 131 East Pitt Street is **Oralee's Golden Eagle Inn** (814–624–0800; www.bedford.net/oralee), the current incarnation of the Golden Eagle Tavern built by Dr. John Anderson of Anderson House fame. During the Whiskey Rebellion campaign, President George Washington and his troops ate here, and you can, too, from a colonial-inspired but modern seasonal menu that uses local produce when possible. Upstairs are sixteen guest rooms and suites furnished with antiques, and you can visit the National House Antique Gallery downstairs. (Open Tuesday through Saturday for lunch starting at 11:30 A.M., and dinner starting at 5:00 P.M. Last reservations are taken at 7:30 P.M. weekdays, 8:00 P.M. Saturday. Sunday brunch starts at 11:30 A.M.)

Evening

LODGING: Bedford House (814–623–7171), just slightly out of the hubbub on the edge of the Historic District at 203 West Pitt Street, is a 1798-vintage home with a range of comforts. All rooms have cable TV and private bathroom; the most sumptuous has a fireplace and a Jacuzzi.

DAY 2

Morning

BREAKFAST: Relax with home-baked goods and changing breakfast entrees at Bedford House, then stroll around town without the antiques-hunting crowds for a while. Take a self-guided tour with a free brochure available from your B&B or the visitors center, right across Juliana Street from the historic courthouse (in continual use since 1829, and the oldest in the state) and the *Man on the Monument,* an 1890 Civil War memorial. Farther down Juliana, at John Street, is a historic cemetery dating to 1772; while the tombstones are worn, you'll find Revolutionary War veterans as well as some of the earliest "western" settlers. Back on Pitt Street, make sure to take a look at the **Espy House,** President Washington's headquarters during the Whiskey Rebellion.

Turn back the clock even farther at the **Fort Bedford Museum** (814–623–8891 or 800–259–4284; www.bedfordcounty.net/attract/fort). The original fort has been gone for some 200 years—except for the original British colonial flag, which is on view—but the main building gives you some idea what it was like. There's a large replica of the five-sided fort, and the balcony around the central room mimics the walkway that would have been patrolled when the British were on watch for the French and Indians. The museum's three rooms feature exhibits of frontier life, including the story of "Indian Eve," who was kidnapped in 1777, sold to the British, and finally worked her way home. (Open 10:00 A.M.–5:00 P.M. daily, except Tuesday, in May, September, and October; and weekends only in April, November, and December. Closed January through March.)

Grab your camera for a drive up **Brumbaugh Mountain** north of town. From I–99, take the Osterburg exit and head east on PA 869. About 2.5 miles up you'll see a scenic overlook, which is absolutely spectacular in autumn. The light is best from late morning through early afternoon, when the fog has burned off. Enjoy another scenic tour by heading back through Osterburg and

Explore colonial life at Fort Bedford Museum.

continuing on PA 869 into **Blue Knob State Park** (814–276–3576), primarily 5,614 acres of wilderness area (watch for deer) and 12,000 acres of state game land named for Pennsylvania's second highest mountain (3,146 feet). This gives you both a spectacular view from Blue Knob Peak and a 1,050-foot vertical drop at **Blue Knob Four Seasons Resort** (814–239–5111 or 800–458–3403; www.blueknob.com).

For more great views, drive down SR 3003 and turn right onto PA 164 into East Freedom. Turn left onto U.S. Business 220. Just before the I–99 interchange, turn right onto an access road that makes a semicircular hook to pass the **Creekside Inn** (814–696–0377).

LUNCH: The blackened alligator at the Creekside will perk you up. Or you can go for traditional or creative sandwiches, stir-fries, and salads. (Open Sunday through Thursday 11:00 A.M.–11:30 P.M., till 12:30 A.M. Friday and Saturday.)

Afternoon

Get your camera back out for a whole lineup of covered bridges. Follow signs to U.S. 220/I–99, then head back to the Osterburg exit to PA 869. After you pass through Osterburg on PA 869, you'll see the **Bowser Bridge** on your left. Turn left onto Claycomb Road, right at the T onto Gordon Hall Road, and left again onto Chestnut Ridge Market Road past **Snooks Bridge.** Veer right and cross PA 56 onto Dunning Creek Road (SR 4013) to catch two more covered bridges (both burr truss bridges), then left onto PA 96 for one more before you reach New Paris.

It's time for the famous **Gravity Hill.** After New Paris, cross the metal-sided bridge and take the first right onto Bethel Hollow Road. Follow this road, which twists a couple of times (at mile 0.6, you'll bear left at the Y; after another 1.5 miles, bear right at the stop sign), until you come to the spray-painted GH on the road (and, most likely, other folks doing exactly the same thing you are). Stop your car between the two GH marks, put the car into neutral, and coast "uphill." Really. Or so it seems. Continue another 0.3 mile beyond the second spray-painted GH to the unmarked Gravity Hill (look for the pole marked 69 on your right). Try coasting again, and again it will seem like you're going uphill. The turnaround is about another 100 yards beyond. No, the "trick" doesn't work in the other direction, but you can try.

Back on PA 96, continue south to U.S. 30. Turn right, then take a quick left onto Mill Street (aka Skip Back Road) to **Colvin** (aka **Shiller**) **Bridge,** a multiple kingpost bridge. Turn left onto PA 31 and watch for the sign to turn left onto Faupel Road for **Turner's Bridge** and Turner Camp Road, which leads to **Shawnee State Park** (814–733–4218) for a nice view of the lake. There's also hiking (eight trails), boating, and, of course, fishing. Return to PA 31 and turn west onto Watson Road to **Herline Bridge,** the longest covered bridge (136 feet) in the county. From there, it's just a couple of miles north on Tulls Hill Road and a right onto U.S. 30 to reach a historic tavern.

DINNER: Jean Bonnet's Tavern (814–623–2250; www.bedfordcounty.net/bandb/jbt), dating to about 1760, was a major stopping point for western-bound travelers and troops (including General Forbes's). Upstairs are six rooms and one ghost, allegedly in residence for at least 200 years; downstairs, under native chestnut beams, is a tavern restaurant serving creative pizzas, pastas, steaks, and chicken. (Open for lunch and dinner daily, plus Sunday brunch; breakfast is for inn guests only.)

Return on U.S. 30 to Bedford, turn left onto U.S. Business 220, and head back to the turnpike and home.

THERE'S MORE

Teapot Cafe. Just west of Bedford's historic district on U.S. 30, on your right, is a whimsical, if run-down, building in the shape of an old-fashioned teakettle.

Bison Corral. Bring your cooler to stock up on bison meats, or watch 'em roam on the range. Off U.S. 30 west of Schellsburg (814–733–4908).

Fisher's Country Store. Lots of homemade noodles, jellies, and baked goods at this Mennonite store (so it's closed on Sunday). Just off U.S. Business 220 north of the turnpike (814–623–2667).

Warriors Path State Park. This small (334 acres) park in northeastern Bedford County is bound by the Raystown Branch of the Juniata River, good for canoeing and kayaking (814–658–3847).

SPECIAL EVENTS

June–October. A free guided tour of historic Bedford is offered every Friday at 3:30 P.M., from the visitors center (800–765–3331).

July. Pontiac's Uprising Reenactment and 18th Century Market Faire at Old Bedford Village (814–623–1156 or 800–238–4347).

August. The Bedford County Fair has agricultural exhibits, foods, and a midway (814–623–9011).

October. The Fall Foliage Festival features two weekends of events centered at the County Fairgrounds, but with related activities at pretty much every attraction and shop (814–623–1771 or 800–765–3331).

December. Old-Fashioned Christmas & Festival of Trees lights up Old Bedford Village.

OTHER RECOMMENDED RESTAURANTS AND LODGING

Landmark Restaurant. A popular spot for lunch next to the visitors center on Juliana Street (814–623–5488). There's a larger location out on U.S. Business 30 (814–623–6762).

Auberge de la Montagne. An upscale French restaurant at the Blue Knob Four Seasons Resort, open only on weekends in the ski season. Call ahead for reservations; it's often closed for private parties (814–239–5111).

Bedford's Covered Bridge Inn Bed & Breakfast. Found at 749 Mill Road, Schellsburg (814–733–4093; www.bedfordcounty.net/cbi.htm).

FOR MORE INFORMATION

Bedford County Visitors' Bureau, 114 South Juliana Street, Bedford, PA 15522; 814–623–1771 or 800–765–3331; www.bedfordcounty.net.

Gettysburg and Antietam

THE LAST FULL MEASURE

OF DEVOTION

3 NIGHTS

Historic Battlefields • Civilians in War • Antiques • Art

The very words Gettysburg and Antietam evoke high drama in American history: respectively the bloodiest battle ever on the North American continent, and the single bloodiest day in U.S. history. Civil War buffs already know this territory well, but this trip is geared toward the rest of us, who never really had much of a grasp of either battle's significance and are less wrapped up in the military maneuvers.

Both are major Civil War sites and, on today's highways, about an hour apart, but there are striking differences. An established, bustling commercial town when the famed battle took place, Gettysburg is still fighting a battle of sorts: against overcommercialization and the tackier aspects of being a tourist mecca. To a certain extent, it has succeeded. Much of the nineteenth-century town proper has been preserved—even many of the bullet-ridden walls are intact—and the controversial observation tower has been demolished. On the other hand, the site of the Antietam National Battlefield on September 17, 1862, was farmland outside the little town of Sharpsburg, Maryland. It's still largely farmland, and the town attracts few tourists, who are more likely to sleep and eat in nearby Hagerstown, the county seat and only 37 miles from Gettysburg.

A seasonal note: Unless you really want to relive some of the suffering of Union and Confederate soldiers, don't visit during summer, when you have

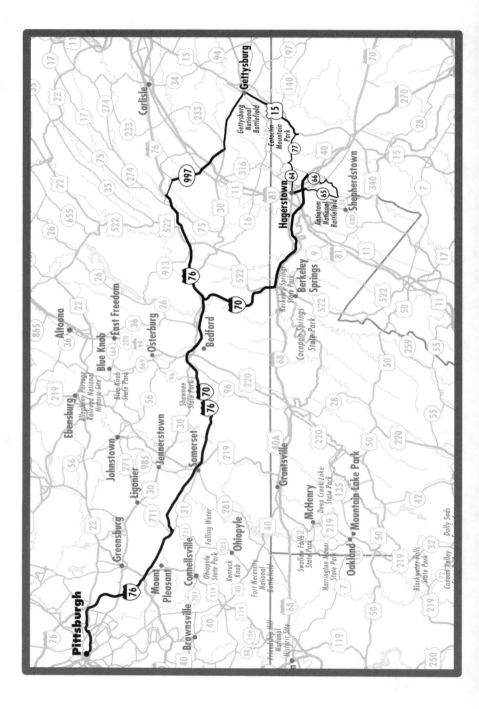

to battle crowds as well as heat. The battlefields are open practically every day of the year, and though other attractions and shops may curtail their hours, few shut down completely during the off season. And many prices are lower.

DAY 1

Afternoon

You could take U.S. 30 all the way to Gettysburg; it's scenic and direct. It's also very hilly, though, and at least half an hour longer than this three-and-a-half-hour route. Head east on the Pennsylvania Turnpike to exit 15 (Blue Mountain). Turn right and follow PA 997 south, through several small towns and over I–81, until it ends at a traffic light on U.S. 30. Turn left; in about twenty minutes you'll be in Lincoln Square, the heart of **Gettysburg.**

DINNER: Even if you arrive fairly late, you're likely to find sustenance at the **Pub & Restaurant** (21 Lincoln Square; 717–334–7100). Try a big salad, soup or chili in a bread bowl, creative pizzas, or entrees. On late evenings during the school year, you may be sharing space with partying undergrads from nearby Gettysburg College. (Open Monday through Thursday 11:00 A.M.–11:00 P.M., Friday and Saturday 11:00 A.M.–midnight, Sunday noon–10:00 P.M.)

Evening

LODGING: From Lincoln Square, take Baltimore Street (PA 34) south. Go through two traffic lights; just before the third light, turn left onto Locust Avenue then make a quick right to turn into the alley. Park in the second lot on the right. Follow the steps down to the **Brickhouse Inn** (452 Baltimore Street, 717–338–9337 or 800–864–3464; www.brickhouseinn.com), where rooms are named for states represented in the battle, and decorated with local Amish quilts.

DAY 2

Morning

BREAKFAST: Wake up to a selection of fruit and a hot breakfast entree. Innkeepers Craig and Marion Schmitz always have fresh shoofly pie on the table, too.

Your first stop is the **National Park Service Visitor Center** (97 Taney-town Road; 717–334–1124; www.nps.gov/gett), a short drive or comfortable walk up Steinwehr Avenue (U.S. Business 15, which veers right off Baltimore Street practically in front of the Brick House Inn); then turn left onto Taney-town Road. It's definitely worth the $3.00 to sit in on the **Electric Map** pro-gram (ext. 431, offered 8:00 A.M.–5:00 P.M. daily), which gives you the aerial overview of troop movements day by day, plus insights into why military lead-ers did what they did and how they messed up. Your battlefield visit later will make a lot more sense. Afterward, look through two floors of exhibits, which include not just the usual collection of uniforms and weapons but also arti-facts like playing cards to show how the soldiers passed their time. The most moving section, though, is the changing gallery of photos of actual battle par-ticipants, sent in by their descendants. (The visitors center is free. Open every day but Thanksgiving, Christmas, and New Year's Day, 8:00 A.M.–5:00 P.M.; summer hours, 8:00 A.M.–6:00 P.M.)

It's just a short stroll to the **Cyclorama** (717–334–1124, ext. 422), a National Historic Object; it's a painting measuring 356 feet by 26 feet depict-ing Pickett's Charge. Various exhibits and a film are included in the $3.00 admission. (Open 9:00 A.M.– 5:00 P.M. on the same days as the NPS Visitor Center.)

As you walk back down the hill, you'll see various clothing shops catering to the historical reenactor, specializing in everything from soldiers' regulation trousers (made from the same kind of flannel as in 1863) to ladies' crinolines and bonnets. The most seriously historically accurate stuff is more likely to be stashed in the back or available by special order only, but the casual shopper can usually find interesting accessories—costume jewelry, hats, lacy fans, and so on—at places like the **Centennial General Store** (717–334–9712 or 800–438–8971). The main store with men's gear, flags, and souvenirs is at 230 Steinwehr Avenue, with **A Lady's Boutique** in the rear, opening onto Taney-town Road. (Open 9:00 A.M.–6:00 P.M. daily except Wednesday till 9:00 P.M. Thursday through Saturday in summer.)

LUNCH: If you think Gettysburg is old, the **Dobbin House Tavern** (89 Stein-wehr Avenue; 717–334–2100; www.dobbinhouse.com) is even older—built 1776. Lunch in the more casual Springhouse Tavern features sandwiches, homemade soups, and "lite" entrees. The specialty at the more formal Alexan-der Dobbin Dining Rooms (actually six historic rooms) is Adams County duckling, or go for the "primal" rib. Stop in the house's Country Curiosity

Store for colonial-style crafts, dried flowers, and more. (The Springhouse Tavern is open 11:30 A.M.–9:00 P.M. daily, till 10:00 P.M. Saturday; the dining rooms open at 5:00 P.M., with the last seating at 9:00 P.M. The gift shop is open 11:00 A.M.– 9:00 P.M. daily, till 10:00 P.M. Saturday. There are also B&B accommodations.)

Afternoon

The Electric Map gave you a basic military overview, but now let's see what those three days in July meant to the townspeople. Head back up Baltimore Street (a few blocks south—uphill—from its intersection with Steinwehr) to the **Jennie Wade House Museum** (758 Baltimore Street; 717–334–4100), the preserved home of the only civilian casualty of the battle. The small house was actually a two-family home, and you'll walk through both sides because a Confederate cannonball created a passageway-sized hole in the common wall. That hole is still there, along with more than 200 bullet holes, including that of the bullet that instantly killed twenty-year-old Mary Virginia "Jenny" Wade as she baked bread for the Union soldiers. (Admission is $5.75, paid at the gift shop behind the museum. Open Memorial Day through Labor Day, 9:00 A.M.–9:00 P.M. daily; off season, 9:00 A.M.–7:00 P.M. daily.)

A few blocks north (downhill) is the recently preserved, somewhat more upscale home of Schriver's Saloon and Ten-Pin Alley, now the **Schriver House Museum** (309 Baltimore Street; 717–337–2800; www.schriverhouse.com). The house was commandeered by the Confederates, and their sharpshooting nest in the attic (uncovered during the 1996 preservation) is the high point, both literally and figuratively, of the four-floor house tour. (Admission is $5.50. From April through November, open Monday through Saturday 10:00 A.M.–5:00 P.M., Sunday noon–5:00 P.M.; December, February, and March, open Saturday and Sunday noon–5:00 P.M.)

Gettysburg Heritage Sites Walking Tour, a free brochure available from Main Street Gettysburg (717–337–3491; www.mainstreetgettysburg.org) and the Convention and Visitors Bureau (717–334–6274; www.gettysburg.com), suggests dozens of other sites in and around the center of town to take a look at. Many buildings sport historical plaques and/or illustrated markers telling the stories of Gettysburg. On your way up the street to dinner, you can read the one about the hausfrau who hid a Union general in her pigsty.

DINNER: Game pie with turkey, pheasant, and duck is the house specialty at the **Farnsworth House Inn** (401 Baltimore Street; 717–334–8838; www.

farnsworthhousedining.com), as much a mini museum as it is a restaurant and B&B, with more than one hundred bullet holes from the war. The dining room plays both sides of the Mason-Dixon Line with goober pea (peanut) soup, Yankee pot roast, Virginia ham, and Pennsylvania Dutch chicken potpie, which you can wash down with Civil War–era drinks like hot buttered rum. The casual-dining tavern behind the main restaurant has been dubbed the Killer Angel Tavern because it served as the "officers' club" during the 1992 filming of *Gettysburg,* based on the book *The Killer Angels.* You'll find Civil War–era memorabilia all over the complex—dinner guests can get a free look at the sharp shooters' post in the attic—but the things you see in the tavern are from the movie. (Open every day except major holidays. The tavern serves 11:30 A.M.–11:00 P.M. The dining room opens at 5:00 P.M.; the last seating is at 8:30 P.M. The Farnsworth also deals in military artifacts, books, and art.)

Evening

Haunted by the ghosts of Gettysburg? You could be. The Farnsworth Inn sponsors **ghost walks**, séances, and—you'll pardon the expression—live performances of ghost stories ($6.00 per person; daily in season, weekends only off season). **Ghosts of Gettysburg** (717–337–0445; www.ghostsofgettysburg.com) takes the spirit world more seriously with three tours based on the books of Mark Nesbitt, and one focusing on the Underground Railroad ($6.00–6.50; daily in season, weekends only off season). The tour headquarters at 271 Baltimore Street features exhibits of photos taken by members of the Pennsylvania Ghost Hunters Society.

DAY 3

Morning

BREAKFAST: Wake up to another hot breakfast at the Brickhouse Inn.

Now it's time to meet some real ghosts. There are many possibilities for touring the **Gettysburg Battlefield,** from a variety of bus tours with taped or live narration ($14.95–16.95) to biking tours (717–337–0700; $30.00). The most highly recommended are those led in your own car by **Park Service–licensed battlefield guides,** volunteers who have studied the battle and the 5,984-acre battlefield pretty thoroughly and can personalize a tour to your preference (maybe you want to know mostly about the action of the regiment your great-great-uncle Andrew served in). And they can answer most questions you may have about the battle or its more than 1,400 monuments, markers, and memorials. The guides are assigned from the NPS Visitor Center desk on a first-come, first-served basis beginning at 8:00 A.M. (Large groups and/or special-needs visitors may reserve in advance at 717–334–1124, ext. 439 or 717–334–4474 or 877–438–8929; www.gettysburgtourguides.org. Fees are $35 for one to five people; $45 for six to fifteen folks; $75 for sixteen or more of you.)

It's also pretty easy to tour on your own. The free map and guide from the NPS Visitor Center outlines a tour that's marked by signs along the streets and roads of Gettysburg and the battlefield, and there's no shortage of battlefield markers to help you along. You can get more details with the help of various guidebooks and audio tours on cassette or CD, widely available at most attractions and stores ($5.00–12.00 rental, $13.00–30.00 purchase. I went with the TravelBrains CD from the NPS Visitor Center's gift shop for $20.)

The Union forces of 93,000 suffered 23,000 casualties; the Confederate army lost as many as 28,000 of 70,000 men. The battlefield monuments are not great works of sculpture, but symbols of the passion still kindled here. While most of the monuments were built around the turn of the twentieth century, several memorials honoring Southern regiments date from the 1960s *(The Soldiers and Sailors of the Confederacy)* and 1970s (Mississippi, Louisiana, and more). The largest of the state memorials, not surprisingly, is Pennsylvania's, which includes the names of every one of the 34,500 Pennsylvania soldiers who fought here.

The tour ends at **Gettysburg National Cemetery** (open daily 8:00 A.M.–5:00 P.M.), across from the NPS Visitor Center. It was here at the dedication of a Soldiers' Cemetery on November 19, 1863, that President Lincoln gave the most famous speech in U.S. history. Head back to the center of town to see where he wrote it (and it wasn't on the back of an envelope). The **Lincoln Room Museum** (717–334–8188), on the southeast corner of Lincoln Square in the Historic David Wills House, includes the original furnishings in the bedroom where the president worked on the drafts of his Gettysburg Address. (Admission is $3.50. Open Memorial Day through Labor Day, 9:00 A.M.–7:00 P.M. daily; off season, Sunday through Thursday 10:00 A.M.–5:00 P.M., Friday and Saturday 10:00 A.M.–8:00 P.M.)

The square is the perfect place for shopping. The Wills House alone features more than eighty dealers in the **Antiques Center of Gettysburg** (717–337–3669; www.antiquecenter-getty.com; open Monday, Wednesday, Thursday, Saturday 10:00 A.M.–6:00 P.M., Friday 10:00 A.M.–8:00 P.M., Sunday

11:00 A.M.–6:00 P.M.; closed Tuesday). Just a block north at 103 Carlisle Street is another notable antiques destination, **Mel's Gettysburg Antiques and Collectibles Mall** (717–334–9387; open Friday through Sunday only, 9:00 A.M.–5:00 P.M.). Cruise the streets radiating from the square for dozens of gift shops, then head south again on Baltimore Street.

LUNCH: Not far from the NPS Visitor Center is **Gingerbread Man** (217 Steinwehr Avenue; 717–334–1100), but there's too tough a choice for me: its famous cream of crab soup or its hot crab dip in a bread bowl? (Open Monday through Saturday 11:00 A.M.– 11:00 P.M., Sunday 11:00 A.M.–10:00 P.M.)

Afternoon

Continue south on Steinwehr (U.S. Business 15) to U.S. 15; head south and soon you're in Maryland. Exit at Thurmont to head west on MD 77, up and around some impressive twists into and over **Catoctin Mountain Park** (301–663–9388; www.nps.gov/cato). Once inside the park, watch for the turnoff to the left for **Cunningham Falls,** an impressive 83-foot cascade. You won't see any sign of the park's only (yet famous) place to stay: Camp David, the presidential retreat on top of the mountain at 1,880 feet. (A visitors center, on Park Central Road—a right turn off MD 77 about 3.5 miles into the park—features nature exhibits and maps for the 25 miles of hiking trails and free rock-climbing permits for Wolf Rock; open daily 10:00 A.M.–4:30 P.M.)

Once outside the park, turn left onto Jefferson Boulevard (MD 64) and head west into **Hagerstown.** Turn left onto Cannon Avenue, right onto Franklin Street (U.S. 40), and left onto South Potomac Street (MD 65) to go through downtown. You'll see **Rose Hill Cemetery** (the final resting place for more than 2,000 Confederate soldiers) on your left; turn right onto Memorial Boulevard and continue for just a few blocks until you come to a traffic circle. Directly ahead is the **Hagerstown City Park,** with the **Washington County Museum of Fine Arts** (301–739–5727; www.washcomuseum.org) facing a small lake. Follow the circle to Key Street, bear left, then turn right into the parking lot. The museum was founded in 1929 by Mr. and Mrs. William Henry Singer Jr. of Sewickley after (so the story goes) none of the Pittsburgh museums expressed interest in Mr. Singer's postimpressionist paintings. So the museum opened in the hometown of his wife, Anna Brugh Singer. His works, and the many pieces the couple picked up in their travels, formed the original permanent collection, which has grown with the museum to include a good smattering of works from Old

Masters to Peale portraits to modern glass. The small but nicely designed museum includes a concert hall for regular recitals and performances—all free, as is admission to the museum. (Open Tuesday through Saturday 10:00 A.M.–5:00 P.M., Sunday 1:00–5:00 P.M.)

Return to South Potomac Avenue and head north, veering right at South Locust Street; be careful, because most streets become one-way downtown and often change names. Turn left onto Franklin Street then left again onto South Potomac; turn right into the parking lot of the Washington County Free Library. Cross the street to **Schmankerl Stube Bavarian Restaurant** (58 South Potomac Street; 301–797–3354; www.schmankerlstube.com), on the corner of South Potomac and Antietam.

DINNER: As you may guess, the food here has a definite German accent—not just the traditional wursts, schnitzels, and sauerbraten but also the shrimp, fish, and vegetarian dishes. If you can't decide, get a sampler platter for two. (Open Tuesday through Saturday for lunch 11:30 A.M.–2:00 P.M., for dinner till 10:00 P.M.; Sunday brunch is served on the last Sunday of the month, 11:30 A.M.–2:30 P.M.)

Evening

Watch those one-way streets: Turn left onto Baltimore Street, then left onto Locust Street. Head north for a while, then make a left turn onto Fairground Avenue, then a right onto Potomac. Cross the train tracks and turn left at the first traffic signal. Turn left onto Oak Hill Avenue, cross the train tracks again, and **Wingrove Manor** (635 Oak Hill; 301–797–7763; www.wingrovemanor.com) will be on your right.

LODGING: The terrace is long but not very steep, and there are parking spaces well off the street and just a few steps from the richly bricked stairs and porch of this lavishly decorated late-Victorian home.

DAY 4

Morning

BREAKFAST: Your continental breakfast of coffee, juice, home-baked breads, and cereal will get you going for another trip into the Civil War. A quick word about our destination: Many Civil War battles are known by more than one name. The North tended to name battles for landmarks (such as Antietam

Creek), especially in the unfamiliar territory of the South; Confederates named battles for the nearest town, in this case **Sharpsburg.**

Turn right onto Oak Hill Avenue, which merges with Potomac Street (MD 60) and, in downtown, with MD 65. Head south, crossing over I–70; about twenty minutes later, turn left for the **Antietam National Battlefield** (301–432–5124; www.nps.gov/anti). Start at the relatively small visitors center, which includes exhibits and a new theater featuring hourly showings of a short film about Lincoln's visit, but the hour-long documentary at noon provides a better background to the battle. Pick up a free NPS map and guide to take a self-guided tour. Note that much of the area is still active farmland, with cornfields and woods (and not so many monuments) standing where their predecessors did during the battle. The rural serenity and isolation could not be in starker contrast to Gettysburg, yet in a way this is an even more horrific killing field: Union casualties numbered 12,410, Confederate 10,700, in less than twelve hours of utterly futile battle. More than 1,800 bodies were never identified, and are among those buried in **Antietam National Cemetery** at the end of the 8.5-mile historic trail. (The visitors center is open every day June 1 through August 31, 8:30 A.M.–6:00 P.M.; September 1 through May 31, 8:30 A.M.–5:00 P.M. Admission is $2.00 per person, $4.00 per family, good for three days.)

From the cemetery, head northeast on Sharpsburg's Main Street (MD 34) and continue about 6 miles into Boonsboro, then turn left onto U.S. 40A to the **Old South Mountain Inn** (6132 Old National Pike; 301–432–6155).

BRUNCH: Built possibly as early as 1730, the inn was a stagecoach stop along the National Road and definitely a tavern during the Battle of South Mountain, a few days before the Battle of Antietam. (Open Tuesday through Friday 5:00–9:00 P.M., Saturday 11:30 A.M.–2:00 P.M. and 4:00–10:00 P.M., Sunday 10:30 A.M.– 8:00 P.M.)

Head north on MD 66 to I–70, then west to Breezewood and the Pennsylvania Turnpike; you'll be home in about three and a half hours.

THERE'S MORE

Eisenhower National Historic Site. This Gettysburg farm was the only place the thirty-fourth president and his wife called home. It's accessible only by shuttle bus from the National Park Service Visitor Center (717–338–9114; www.nps.gov/eise).

Cornfields still flourish at Antietam National Battlefield.

General Lee's Headquarters. Not a house museum, the original house commandeered by Lee is now a small, more personalized commemoration of some of the people involved. Near the battlefield (717–334–3141).

Gettysburg College. Chartered in 1832, just a few blocks north of what's now Lincoln Square, this small liberal arts college has a lovely and historic campus worth strolling. The current administration building (and oldest building on campus) was used as a hospital during the battle. The school sponsors many Civil War–related lectures and programs (717–337–6000 or 800–431–0803; www.gettysburg.edu).

Greystone's American History Store. Near the Brickhouse Inn; you'll find here a huge selection of Civil War– and Gettysburg-related books, including many for children, plus videos, miniature figures, and more. Not a souvenir-type shop (717–338–0631 or 888–581–8835; www. Ghistory.com).

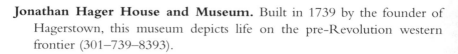
Jonathan Hager House and Museum. Built in 1739 by the founder of Hagerstown, this museum depicts life on the pre-Revolution western frontier (301–739–8393).

Crystal Grottoes Cavern. More geological formations per square foot than any other known cave. Open year-round, 6 miles from Antietam, just outside Boonsboro on MD 34 (301–432–6336).

Free Walking Tours of Historic Downtown Hagerstown (301–739–8577, ext. 116).

Golf. Black Rock Golf Course outside Hagerstown is ranked 4 stars by *Golf Digest* (301–791–3040).

SPECIAL EVENTS

April. History Meets the Arts. Dozens of historical artists, writers, and artisans congregate for three days in Gettysburg (717–334–8151).

June–July. Gettysburg Civil War Heritage Days commemorate the battle with encampments, concerts, lectures, battle reenactments, and more (717–334–6271; www.gettysburg.com).

September. Anniversary of the Battle of Antietam (Sharpsburg) (301–432–5124; www.nps.gov/anti). Sharpsburg Heritage Festival (800–228–STAY). Fire on the Mountain, Boonsboro: Reenactment of the Battle of South Mountain (301–241–4707; www.fireonthemountain. com). Boonsboro Days (301–432–5889). Eisenhower World War II Weekend—a living-history encampment with Allied soldiers and military vehicles at the Eisenhower National Historic Site, Gettysburg (717–338–9114; www.nps.gov/eise).

November. The anniversary of Lincoln's Gettysburg Address is observed with a memorial service in the Gettysburg National Cemetery. The day before, Remembrance Day, includes a parade (717–334–6271; www.gettysburg. com).

December. An Eisenhower Christmas features 1950s period decorations, storytelling, reduced admission prices, and free refreshments at the Eisenhower National Historic Site, Gettysburg (717–338–9114; www.nps.gov/ eise).

PREVIEWS OF COMING ATTRACTIONS

Antietam Campaign: Lee Invades Maryland. A 70-mile trail from White's Ferry in Montgomery County to Antietam National Battlefield in Sharpsburg should open by September 17, 2002, the 140th anniversary of the Battle of Antietam (www.mdisfun.org).

OTHER RECOMMENDED RESTAURANTS AND LODGING

Lincoln Diner. Desserts are homemade and breakfast is served 24/7. Off Lincoln Square in Gettysburg (717–334–3900).

Gettysbrew. This restaurant and brewpub in the historic Monfort Farm, one of the largest Confederate field hospitals, is about a mile outside town (717–337–1001; www.gettysbrew.com).

The Altland House Public Tavern. General Eisenhower's favorite restaurant features great turtle soup and offers guest rooms. East on U.S. 30 (717–259–9535).

Herr Tavern and Publick House. Food and guest rooms in an 1815 house that was involved in the battle (717–334–4332 or 800–362–9849; www.herrtavern.com/).

Cashtown Inn 1797. A stagecoach stop that became Confederate headquarters. The dining room is closed Monday. Guest rooms, breakfast, special theme weekends (717–334–9722 or 800–367–1797; www.cashtowninn.com).

Brafferton Inn. The oldest inn in the historic district (1786), close to Lincoln Square, this B&B has historic decor, antiques, and a bullet still in the mantel from the first day of the battle (717–337–3423).

Piper House B&B. Built in 1840 and practically right on Antietam Battlefield (301–797–1862).

Jacob Rohrbach Inn. Damage from the 1863 battle has been repaired in this B&B right in downtown Sharpsburg (877–839–4242 in the daytime; 301–432–5079 in the evening).

FOR MORE INFORMATION

Gettysburg Convention and Visitors Bureau, 89 Steinwehr Avenue, Gettysburg, PA 17325; 717–334–2100; www.gettysburg.com.

Washington County–Hagerstown Convention and Visitors Bureau, Elizabeth Hager Center, 16 Public Square, Hagerstown, MD 21740; 301–791–3246 or 888–257–2600; www.marylandmemories.org.

EASTERN

Carlisle, Harrisburg, Hershey

BEYOND THE MOUNTAINS

2 NIGHTS

History • Art • Science • Chocolate

Southeast Pennsylvania was the easy part: The flat, accessible reaches of south-eastern Pennsylvania were the first to be settled, and lent themselves readily to farming. Beyond the Susquehanna River lay the Appalachians, however—their long ridges, one after another, blocking the path west. It's no wonder that early pioneers nicknamed them the Endless Mountains.

In our travels to the other side of the mountains, we'll take a look at the days when plantations still existed in Pennsylvania, and how Pennsylvania's fertile farmland helped Milton Hershey convert chocolate from a luxury item to something kids could buy at the corner store (back when there were cor-ner stores). And, yes, there is our state government. We don't have to watch the sausage being made—just enjoy one of the most beautiful capitol buildings in the country.

DAY 1

Afternoon

Head east on the Pennsylvania Turnpike to exit 16 (Carlisle). Settled in 1751, **Carlisle** was a bivouac point for the British in the Revolution, a staging point for President Washington during the Whiskey Rebellion, and the starting point for settlers heading west (the Ohio Valley back then). And there's the Carlisle Barracks, the oldest U.S. Army post in the country and now home to the Army War College. Carlisle Cemetery contains a statue marking the grave

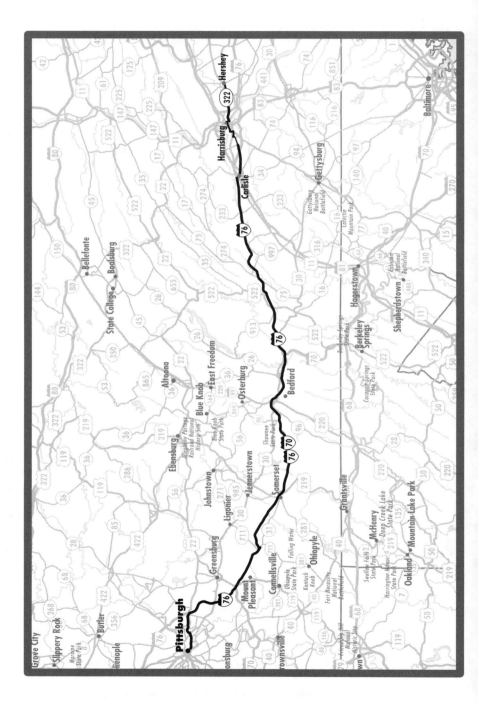

site of Mary Hayes, better known as Molly Pitcher, heroine of the Battle of Monmouth.

Start your tour of Carlisle at the square at the intersection of High and Hanover Streets. Downtown Carlisle is flat, laid out on a grid, and walkable. Though the Battle of Gettysburg is regarded as the high-water mark of the Confederacy, significant Civil War action took place even farther north here. Cumberland County's Old Courthouse, in the square at the intersection of High and Hanover Streets, still carries marks of Confederate shelling.

You can still see many of the town's nineteenth-century buildings, preserved in the 13-block downtown historic district bounded by Baltimore and East Penn Streets, and East and College Streets. View the results of preservation efforts in the restaurants and specialty stores lining West High Street between the square and Dickinson College, and the streets to the north and south running parallel to West High Street. You'll find a concentration of antiques stores on the blocks of North Hanover Street just north of the square.

DINNER: You're there. The chef-owned **Empire Restaurant & Bar** (149 North Hanover Street; 717–258–4888) is a regional favorite for its globally inspired approaches to seafood and game, infused with unusual seasonings like vanilla and sparked with fruits as well as vegetables. (Dinner is served Wednesday through Monday 5:00–10:00 P.M.; Sunday brunch 11:00 A.M.–3:00 P.M.)

LODGING: From downtown Carlisle, head east on PA 641. Turn left onto Hickorytown Road about 2 miles beyond the I–81 overpass. Watch on your left for the **Pheasant Field Bed and Breakfast** (150 Hickorytown Road; 717–258–0717; www.pheasantfield.com). The 200-year-old farmhouse features a tennis court, horse boarding, and ready access to trout streams and the Appalachian Trail. Ask about the homemade cookies.

Evening

Check the **Dickinson College** events calendar (www.dickinson.edu) for concerts, shows, and recitals.

DAY 2

Morning

BREAKFAST: Wake up and smell the coffee—and the muffins and the bread and the rest of the full country breakfast at the Pheasant Field Bed and Breakfast (on the back patio if the weather is obliging).

Follow U.S. 11 east to Camp Hill and the Susquehanna River. Where U.S. 11 turns left to follow the river, proceed straight ahead across the Taylor Bridge to downtown **Harrisburg.**

The **State Museum of Pennsylvania** (300 North Street; 717–787–4978; www.statemuseumpa.org) is just across North Street from the state capitol. Get the full history of Pennsylvania: geological, archaeological, and technological as well as political. Memorial Hall holds a photographic reproduction of the commonwealth's original charter, a painting of William Penn's *Treaty Under the Elm,* and William Penn himself as rendered in two tons of metal. Walk through the doorway to William Penn's left to view Brockerhoff House and its Federalist-Victorian decor comparison. Stroll down a colonial street in the Market, Shop and Home Exhibit. Other areas are devoted to Native American archaeology, Pennsylvania military history, and dioramas of Pennsylvania's plants and animals. The Industry and Technology exhibits feature technologies from the past and (maybe) the future; learn about the difficulties in predicting the course of technology and why dog power never caught on. Check the planetarium schedule for show times and a description of the current feature program. (Free; the planetarium is $2.00. Open Tuesday through Saturday 9:00 A.M.–5:00 P.M., Sunday noon–5:00 P.M.)

Market Street is 1 block south of the capitol grounds; Third Street forms the western border. Near their intersection, you'll find the **Whitaker Center for the Science and Arts** (222 Market Street; 717–221–8201; www.whitakercenter.org) and three floors of interactive science exhibits. Have fun with the sound effects and lighting stations at the Backstage Science exhibit, as well as the space-distorting False Perspective Room. Find out how you can see sound in the Galleries of Sound and Music. Walk through a giant kaleidoscope and create pictures from polarized light in the Galleries of Color and Light. Or enjoy nature's artistic efforts in the Gallery of Mathematics in Nature and Art. (Admission costs $6.75, or $9.75 with an Imax Theater show. Open Monday through Saturday 9:30 A.M.–5:00 P.M., Sunday 11:00 A.M.–5:00 P.M.)

LUNCH: Head north to the **Broad Street Market** (1233 North Third Street; 717–236–7923; www.broadstmarket.com) on Third Street between Sanford and Cumberland Streets. Third Street is a one-way street heading south; take Second Street and turn right onto Sanford. Restaurants in two buildings offer barbecue, sandwiches, Vietnamese soup, pasta, seafood, and Greek and Middle Eastern food. It's your choice; if you fancy curried goat for lunch, this is your

opportunity. (Stone Market is open Tuesday and Wednesday 9:00 A.M.–3:00
P.M., Thursday and Friday 7:00 A.M.–6:00 P.M., Saturday 7:00 A.M.–4:00 P.M.
Brick Market is open Thursday and Friday 7:00 A.M.–5:00 P.M., Saturday 7:00
A.M.–4:00 P.M.)

Afternoon

It's big (covering two acres) and it's grand (with a marble staircase modeled on
one in the Paris Opera House) and you've already contributed to the heating
and electric bills, so take advantage of the thirty-minute guided tours at the
state capitol (Third Street between Walnut and North Streets; 717–787–6810
or 800–868–7672; www.legis.state.PAus/WU01/VC/DOCS/visitor.htm).
You'll have the chance to see the aforementioned staircase, the dome (modeled after Michelangelo's dome of St. Peter's in Rome) and the ornate House
and Senate chambers. Architecturally significant and imposing though the
building is, the highlights of the tour are artistic: the murals, statuary, and
stained-glass windows. Note the five paintings by Pre-Raphaelite leading light
Edwin Austin Abbey behind the Speaker's platform in the hall of the House
of Representatives. (Free. The welcome center is open Monday through Friday 8:30 A.M.–4:30 P.M. Tours are offered Monday through Friday every half
hour 8:30 A.M.–4:00 P.M., Saturday and Sunday at 9:00 and 11:00 A.M., and
1:00 and 3:00 P.M.)

From downtown Harrisburg, travel north on Front Street, and continue on
North Front Street about 2 miles beyond the I–81 overpass.

First it was a frontier fort. Then it was a plantation. Then it was a dairy
farm, with strutting peacocks and grazing sheep. Now restored, **Fort Hunter
Mansion and Park** (5300 North Front Street; 717–599–5751; www.
forthunter.org) offers a view of sophisticated nineteenth-century country living. Tour the herb garden and the outbuildings, which complete what was
once a self-sufficient frontier village. After your tour, relax in the nearby park
and enjoy the view of the Susquehanna River and the forty-eight-arch
Rockville Bridge, a National Civil Engineering Landmark. The longest stone
masonry railroad bridge in the world is a heavily used rail link between Harrisburg and Pittsburgh. (Admission is $4.00. Open May through November,
Tuesday through Saturday 10:00 A.M.–4:30 P.M., Sunday noon–4:30 P.M.)

Return south on North Front Street, then take I–81 north to the U.S. 22
east exit (exit 23). When U.S. 22 splits off, continue south on PA 230. Turn
right onto PA 441, then make a sharp left.

DINNER: Choose between the salmon and duck—both highly recommended—at **Politesse** (540 Race Street; 717–236–2048), known as much for its service as for its wine list and its food. And make sure you end with the superb crème brûlée. (Lunch is served Tuesday through Friday 11:00 A.M.–4:00 P.M. Dinner, Tuesday through Thursday 5:00–9:00 P.M., Friday and Saturday 5:00–10:00 P.M.)

Head north on I–83. Continue east on U.S. 322 when I–83 splits off to the north. Exit onto PA 39 north, which becomes Hershey Park Drive in **Hershey.** Turn left on Sandbeach Road and follow the signs to the Hotel Hershey.

LODGING: On a rise, you'll see the distinctive Mediterranean-style rooftops of the **Hotel Hershey** (100 Hotel Road; 717–533–2171; www.hotelhershey.com). Amenities include seventy-two holes of golf, swimming pools, a fitness center, and a recently opened spa. Check to see if the shuttle to Hershey attractions is in operation for your next-day itinerary.

Evening

Take a carriage ride around the grounds, stroll through the Hotel Hershey gardens, or just lounge on the veranda and watch the sunset (or your fellow guests). And head upstairs to a balcony for a better look at the lobby and its central fountain.

DAY 3

Morning

BREAKFAST: Grab some juice or coffee (or cappuccino or espresso or latte) at the Hotel Hershey's **Cocoa Beanery** (717–534–8800; opens at 6:30 A.M. daily) to tide you over until brunch.

Head a short way down the hill, and plan on an early arrival to see **Hershey Gardens** (170 Hotel Road; 717–534–3492; www.hersheygardens.org) at their best. Stroll around the twenty-three-acre botanical display to see the dwarf and weeping conifer collections and the specimen trees. The award-winning rose gardens are among the world's best, with 7,000 plants of 275 different varieties—from ancient roses to the hybrid perpetuals of Mrs. Hershey's day to the most gorgeous modern roses. If the weather is cooperative and you arrive in season (mid-June through mid-September), you may get to see the residents of the Butterfly House unfurl themselves to flutter over to nearby blooms, forming striking color combinations. (Admission is $6.00. Open seven days a week, April through September, 9:00 A.M.–6:00 P.M.; October, 9:00 A.M.–5:00 P.M.; Memorial day through Labor Day, Friday through Sunday till 8:00 P.M.)

BRUNCH: There are three restaurants at the hotel, but the longtime favorite is the formal **Circular Dining Room** (717–534–8800), deriving its shape from Milton Hershey's exasperation with restaurants that placed low tippers in corners. Book first seating for the best brunch in the region. Enjoy the ice carvings and the view of the formal gardens and reflecting pool while you dine on the buffet of many seafood dishes, two soups, a carving station, eggs, and, of course, a plethora of chocolate desserts. Jackets are required for gentlemen; appropriate attire for ladies. Reservations are required. (Sunday brunch seatings are at 11:45 A.M. and 2:00 P.M. Lunch is served Monday through Saturday 11:30 A.M.–2:00 P.M., with seating every fifteen minutes. Dinner served every day, 5:30–9:00 P.M., seating every half hour.)

Afternoon

Head south on Sandbeach Road and turn right onto Hershey Park Drive. Watch for the left turn to **Hershey's Chocolate World** (800 Park Boulevard; 717–534–4900; www.HersheysChocolateWorld.com) for the chocolate-making tour ride simulating a trip through a chocolate plant. Follow chocolate bar creation from cocoa bean and cow to finished product, of which you'll receive a free sample at the conclusion. Want more? The gift shop has Earth's largest selection of Hershey's chocolates and candies, including five-pound bars and chocolate molds with personalized chocolate messages. The food court will satisfy your need for fudge, cocoa, and chocolate cookies as well as (non-chocolate) soup and sandwiches. You'll also have photo opportunities with costumed Hershey's product characters—maybe you've always wanted to shake hands with a giant milk chocolate bar. (Free. Hours vary from 11:00 A.M.–4:00 or 5:00 P.M. on winter Sundays to 9:00 A.M.–10:00 P.M. during summer prime time, with some summer dates 5:00–10:00 P.M. Closed only on Christmas.)

On a nearby rise overlooking the Hersheypark entrance is the **Hershey Museum** (170 West Hershey Park Drive; 717–534–3439; www.hersheymuseum. org), housing collections of Native American and Pennsylvania Dutch art as

Candy is big at Hershey's Chocolate World.

well as historical items from the town built on chocolate. But the showstopper is the 13-foot-tall Apostolic Clock dating to 1878, with a massive counterweight that drives an intricately choreographed procession of hand-carved wooden figures each hour. Arrive early for the explanatory talk, so you know where to watch for sudden surprise appearances of adversaries in the battle between good and evil. (Admission $6.00. Open seven days a week, Memorial Day through Labor Day, 10:00 A.M.–6:00 P.M.; off season, 10:00 A.M.–5:00 P.M. Closed Thanksgiving, Christmas, and New Year's Day.)

Take a look at those famous Hershey Kiss–shaped streetlights in town, then head back to Harrisburg on Hershey Park Drive, which leads to U.S. 322 west and I–83 south. Exit at 17th Street (exit 25) in Harrisburg; turn left onto 17th Street. Turn right onto Paxton Street (PA 441), then right onto Cameron Street (PA 230).

DINNER: Just a portobello sandwich or a quesadilla at the **Appalachian Brewing Company** (50 North Cameron Street; 717–221–1080; www. abcbrew.com) should hold you after that sumptuous brunch, or maybe you're ready for a Harrisburger. Go easy on the house brews, because it's about three hours home via the Pennsylvania Turnpike. (Open Sunday through Thursday 11:00 A.M.–10:00 P.M., Friday and Saturday 11:00 A.M.–11:00 P.M.)

THERE'S MORE

Cumberland County Historical Society Museum. Collections present the history of Cumberland County. In Carlisle (717–249–7610).

Hersheypark. Roller coasters. More roller coasters. Eight of them are found among fifty-five rides on 110 acres, as well as water rides, carousels, live bands, strolling entertainers, and specialty shopping. Your admission price includes ZooAmerica, North American Wildlife Park. In Hershey (717–534–3090 or 800–437–7439; www.hersheypark.com).

John Harris/Simon Cameron Mansion. Built by the city's founder. Located in Harrisburg, its exhibits focus on local history and art (717–233–3462).

SPECIAL EVENTS

June. Spring Antiques and Collectibles at Carlisle, at the Carlisle fairgrounds. The beginning of the outdoor East Coast antiques season (717–243–7855).

July. American Music Fest in Harrisburg's Riverfront Park and City Island celebrates the July 4 weekend with music and other activities, capped with fireworks (717–255–3020).

August–October. The Pennsylvania Renaissance Faire on weekends re-creates Elizabethan England at Mount Hope Estates with shows and jousting tournaments (717–665–7021; www.parenaissancefaire.com).

September. Fall Festival at Fort Hunter Mansion and Park. Free admission, crafts demonstrations, entertainment, and more (717–599–5751; www. forthunter.org).

OTHER RECOMMENDED RESTAURANTS AND LODGING

Firehouse Restaurant and Bar. Yes, it's a restored firehouse from 1871, serving New American cuisine. Seafood specials on Friday; "First Response" early-bird dinner specials 4:00–6:00 P.M. In Harrisburg (717–234–6064).

Market Cross Pub. Rock or blues music in the evening to go with your choice of more than 200 ales and lagers, in Carlisle (717–258–1234).

Piatto. Regional Italian cuisine in a Victorian–era home in Carlisle's historic district. Outdoor seating from May through September (717–249–9580).

Raspberries Restaurant. Power lunches and a popular Sunday brunch buffet in the Harrisburg Hilton, not far from the capitol (717–233–6000, ext. 419).

Ashcombe Mansion Bed and Breakfast. Enjoy the country view from your own little porch in this 1891 Queen Anne mansion on twenty-three acres outside Mechanicsburg (717–766–6820 or 888–580–8899).

Spinner's Inn. This motor inn near Hersheypark includes breakfast and homey touches (717–533–9157).

FOR MORE INFORMATION

Harrisburg–Hershey–Carlisle–Perry County Tourism and Convention Bureau, 25 North Front Street, Harrisburg, PA 17101; 717–231–7788 or 800–995–0969; www.visithhc.com.

Brandywine Valley

STOP AND SMELL THE ROSES

2 NIGHTS

A Revolting Day • Gardens • Art • Golf

That's just the war I'm talking about: a quick dip into George Washington and the Revolutionary War before settling into a weekend with the Du Pont legacy in magnificent mansions and even more magnificent gardens. The Du Ponts tended to have an excellent aesthetic sense, especially with gardens, sometimes to—shall we say?—eccentric extremes. Or let's call them visionary, creating plantings that are works of art.

This is horse country, and you'll see plenty of rolling fields and horse farms. It's also a hotbed of great golf and the nation's Mushroom Capital: one-fourth of the U.S. supply of fresh mushrooms comes from this little corner of Pennsylvania. There's a nice ecological balance here (not to mention an abundance of mushrooms in local cooking). The horses produce the, um, growing medium for all those mushrooms, which transform the stuff into the perfect fertilizer for keeping all those golf courses so perfectly green and all those gardens glowing with color. It's a bit pricey here, and more elegant than most weekend trips I've suggested. Figure a country-club look, and pack a jacket for dinner.

DAY 1

Morning

What was the hit of the 1939 World's Fair and an engineer's dream? The
Pennsylvania Turnpike (www.paturnpike.com) was the first limited-access

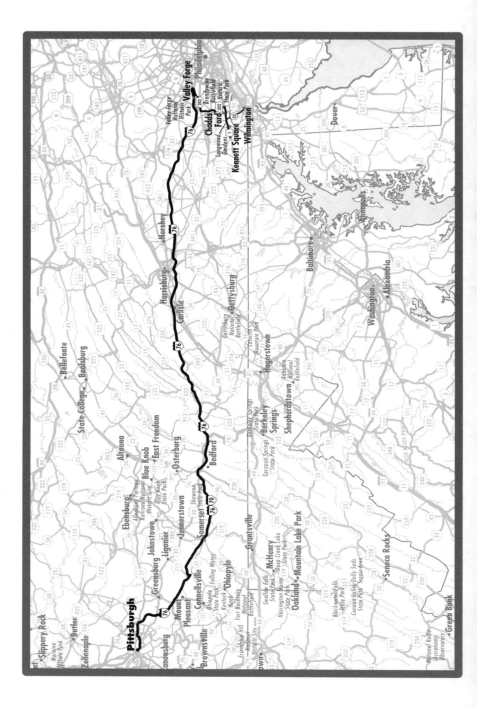

highway of its length (160 miles from Irwin to Carlisle to start) and type when it opened in 1940, after being designed by 1,100 engineers (who were virtually inventing highway engineering as they went along) and built in twenty months by 15,000 workers from eighteen states. (Think about that next time there's a slowdown because of construction.) You're driving on a piece of history as you head east to the **South Midway** (814–623–8011) service plaza, about 100 miles from Pittsburgh.

BREAKFAST: The South and North Midway plazas, the only matched set on the pike, are historic in their own right. Among the few of the original rest stops left on the nation's oldest expressway (you can read the historic plaque about its being the forerunner of the interstate highway system), the two were long connected by an underground tunnel. Now completely remodeled and, like all Turnpike service plazas, open twenty-four hours, Midway offers coffee and pastries at Cinnabon and somewhat more substantial breakfasts at Sbarro.

In about three more hours on the turnpike, you'll be ready to go even farther into America's past. Take exit 24 (Valley Forge), bearing right, and follow signs for Valley Forge: Head north on North Gulph Road for about 1.5 miles and, at the fifth traffic light, turn left at the entrance sign into **Valley Forge National Historical Park** (610–783–1077; www.nps.gov/vafo). Feel a chill? This is where General Washington and the Continental army battled the cold instead of the British in the winter of 1777–78. There is a tour bus, but you may prefer to stretch your legs for the walk to the typical eighteenth-century brick house that served as **Washington's Headquarters** ($2.00 admission). The 3,466-acre park includes a variety of programs explaining the significance of that cold-weather camp (such as how it led to an independent United States), including a free film, *Valley Forge: A Winter Encampment,* shown every half hour from 9:30 A.M. to 4:30 P.M. (Admission is free. The grounds are open daily, year-round, sunup to sundown. The visitors center and Washington's Headquarters are open 9:00 A.M.–5:00 P.M. every day but Christmas.)

From the visitors center, take Valley Forge Road (PA 23) to U.S. 422 and head south, going under the turnpike, to U.S. 202, and turn southwest. In about 15 miles U.S. 322 joins U.S. 202 (now the Wilmington Pike). Turn right onto U.S. 1 (Baltimore Pike), and head west for about 2.5 miles to PA 100 (South Creek Road) and **Chadds Ford.**

LUNCH: Stay in an eighteenth-century mood in one of the dining rooms of the **Chadds Ford Inn** (610–388–7361) for creative seasonal entrees and

salads. Save room for dessert. (Open Monday through Thursday 11:30
A.M.–10:00 P.M., Friday and Saturday 11:00 A.M.–10:30 P.M., Sunday brunch
11:00 A.M.–3:00 P.M., dinner till 9:00 P.M.)

Afternoon

Backtrack along U.S. 1 to **Brandywine Battlefield Park** (610–459–3342;
www.ushistory.org/brandywine) for a visit to what was the biggest battle on
U.S. soil until the Civil War. Strictly speaking, the park area is not where the
battle was waged (it was over a rather large area) on September 11, 1777, but
it does include the buildings that served as Washington's headquarters and
Lafayette's quarters (the nineteen-year-old marquis had a wound dressed here,
and got the French officially on our side). And strictly speaking, the Americans lost. But the good guys realized that it was because of faulty intelligence
reports, not because the colonials couldn't muster up a good fight against
British regulars, so at least it counts as a moral victory, and the first major battle of the American Revolution. (Admission to the park grounds and visitors
center is free; the historic buildings are open by tour only, $3.50. Open Tues-
day through Saturday 9:00 A.M.–5:00 P.M., Sunday noon–5:00 P.M.)

Just a few miles west on U.S. 1 is Pennsylvania's best wine maker, **Chaddsford Winery** (632 Baltimore Pike; 610–388–6221; www.chaddsford.com). I
prefer the Chambourcin and the Cabernet Sauvignon, but taste for yourself in
the restored seventeenth-century barn, or tour the wine-making process. Sample some of the popular spiced apple wine if you prefer, and check the bargain
bin for bottles marked as COOKING WINE for your next pot roast. Check out
the schedule for wine classes and special dinners. (Open daily noon–6:00 P.M.)

That was your aperitif. Continue west on U.S. 1, onto the bypass and the
Jennersville exit (PA 796). Turn left at the end of the ramp and go about a
quarter mile to a former colonial stagecoach stop.

DINNER: Beef Wellington is the specialty of the house at the **Red Rose Inn**
(100–107 South Jennersville Road; 610–869–3003), capped by a homemade
dessert in one of the period-decorated dining rooms. Rooms are also available. (Lunch is served Monday through Saturday 11:30 A.M.–4:00 P.M.; dinner,
Monday through Thursday 4:00–9:00 P.M., Friday and Saturday 4:00–10:00
P.M., Sunday 4:00–8:00 P.M.)

Return east on U.S. 1 and turn right onto PA 52, which becomes DE 52
(Kennett Pike), through the quaint shop-filled town of Centreville. Past the
Winterthur Museum, turn left at the second light to DE 82 (Kirk Road), and,

at the next light, turn right onto DE 100; then make a quick left into the parking lot.

LODGING: The **Inn at Montchanin** (Route 100 and Kirk Road; 302–888–2133 or 800–COW–BIRD; www.montchanin.com) is actually the entire village, with guest rooms and suites in its various cottages and a school-house. Though in the old days they were mainly home to laborers in the DuPont powder mills, the accommodations are now definitely luxurious.

Evening

Return to the Chaddsford Winery and pick out a spot to relax at an outdoor concert, usually jazz. Reservations are recommended; concerts are offered June through September (610–388–6221; www.chaddsford.com).

DAY 2

Morning

BREAKFAST: Head over to Montchanin's former blacksmith shop, now **Krazy Kat's** restaurant, for the complimentary breakfast. (Open for breakfast, week-days 7:00–9:00 A.M., Saturday and holidays, 8:00–11:00 A.M.; lunch, weekdays 11:00 A.M.–2:00 P.M.; dinner, Monday through Saturday 5:30–10:00 P.M., Sun-day 5:30–9:00 P.M.; Sunday brunch 8:00 A.M.–1:00 P.M.

Retrace your steps to DE 52 and the **Winterthur Gardens and Museum** (302–378–4069 or 800–448–3883; www.winterthur.org). Depend-ing upon how you feel about gardens, you could stay here all day, exploring some 1,000 acres of native and exotic plants in naturalistic rather than formal settings. Henry Francis du Pont "painted" with the color of his plants, partic-ularly azaleas, directing his crew of gardeners to replant again and again until his **Azalea Walk** was absolute perfection (generally at its height around Mother's Day; book your accommodations well in advance). The Winterthur (pronounced WIN-ter-ter) Museum, Henry's onetime home, now houses his huge collection of American decorative arts 1640–1860, displayed in three permanent and one changing exhibition in the Gallery, plus entire Period Rooms, which can be seen on the guided Highlights Tour only. Start with the garden, and move indoors as it gets warmer. (The $8.00 general admission includes the galleries and a thirty- to forty-five-minute tram ride of the gar-dens; $13.00 Highlights Tour adds the Period Rooms; the $13 Garden Walk adds a guided garden tour to general admission. More intensive one- and two-hour Decorative Arts tours are offered for $17 and $21; reservations required. The last tickets sold at 3:45 P.M., while the last Period Room tour starts at 4:00 P.M. Open Monday through Saturday 9:00 A.M.–5:00 P.M., Sunday noon–5:00 P.M.; in season, the gardens are open till dusk. Members may visit the gardens from dawn to dusk every day.)

LUNCH: Take a break in Winterthur's **Garden Restaurant** (302–888–4910) for a buffet luncheon of antipasti, smoked or poached fish, salads, fruit, and more (April through summer, Monday through Saturday 11:30 A.M.–2:00 P.M.; also afternoon tea, Thursday through Saturday 2:30–4:00 P.M., and champagne brunch on Sunday 10:00 A.M.–3:00 P.M.; reservations suggested.) Or just grab a quick salad and soup from the cafeteria–style **Pavilion.** (Open Monday through Saturday 11:00 A.M.–4:30 P.M., Sunday 11:00 A.M.–4:30 P.M.; hot food service stops at 3:00 P.M.)

Afternoon

Head south on DE 52 and turn left onto DE 141, then left onto Children's Drive, and left again onto Rockland Road; follow the signs to the parking lot on the right and get ready for eighteenth-century France at **Nemours Mansion and Gardens** (On the grounds of the Alfred I. du Pont Hospital for Children; 302–651–6912; www.nemours.org). Named for the Du Ponts' ancestral home, the Louis XVI–style chateau of Alfred I. du Pont includes 101 rooms filled with European antiques and art, and superb French-style gardens, including a maze garden, sunken garden, and grotto. The two-hour tour includes a lot of walking up and down steps in the house, but you get to sit down and take a bus tour of the gardens on this 300-acre estate, built 1909–10. (Admission costs $10. Reservations are recommended. Tours are conducted May 1 through November 30, Tuesday through Saturday 9:00 and 11:00 A.M., and 1:00 and 3:00 P.M.; Sunday 11:00 A.M., and 1:00 and 3:00 P.M.)

Nearby, also off DE 141 via Montchanin Road (DE 100) and Buck Road, is the **Hagley Museum** (298 Buck Road; 302–658–2400; www.hagley.org), which includes a look at Du Pont workers as well as the original Du Pont mills and home, Eleutherian Mills, built by company founder Eleuthere Irenee du Pont in 1803. The relatively modest Georgian home, lived in by five generations of the Du Pont family, includes a small garden that combines ornamentals with edibles. The 235-acre site also includes Blacksmith Hill, where interpreters in period dress show and talk about the company schools providing an education for children before there were public schools, and about daily life for the millworkers. Also visit the first office of the Du Pont Company, which started as a gunpowder maker. (Admission is $9.75. Open every day but Thanksgiving, Christmas, and New Year's Eve; mid-March through December 30, 9:30 A.M.–4:30 P.M.; January 1 through mid-March, weekdays, one guided tour only at 1:30 P.M., Saturday and Sunday 9:30 A.M.–4:30 P.M.)

Head back to Montchanin Road (DE 100) and turn left to go south to Kennett Pike (DE 52), continuing south as country turns to the outskirts of **Wilmington**. Bear right onto North Jackson Street and go southwest, up the ramp at the sign for I–95 to DELAWARE MEMORIAL BRIDGE/BALTIMORE, only to exit 6 (SR 9, Fourth Street, to Martin Luther King Boulevard and SR 4). Continue on North Jackson Street and turn left onto Lancaster Avenue, then right onto South Market Street.

DINNER: "Angry" mussels will make you happy at **Restaurant 821** (821 Market Street; 302–652–8821; www.restaurant821.com), which features exciting new wood-fired takes on traditional Mediterranean risottos and seafood, plus plenty of wines by the glass. For real extravagance, book the wine cellar for chef Tobias Laury's six-course tasting menu. (Open for lunch, Monday through Friday 11:30 A.M.–5:30 P.M.; dinner, Monday through Thursday 5:30–10:00 P.M., Friday till 10:30 P.M., and Saturday 5:00–11:00 P.M.)

DAY 3

Morning

BREAKFAST: Montchanin's Krazy Kat will keep you purring.

It's an easy trip back to DE/PA 52, a right turn onto U.S. 1, and a left into one of the largest and best-known gardens in the United States. **Longwood Gardens** (610–388–1000; www.longwoodgardens.org) includes forty gardens—half of them outdoors, half of them under glass—on 1,050 acres. Besides some 11,000 types of plants are such attractions as the world's largest residence aeolian organ, more fountains than any other garden (many have their own performance schedule), and special performances combining fountains, light shows, fireworks and a live orchestra. The theme in 2001 is Stravinsky 'Stravaganza (Tickets are $22; to order, call 610–388–1000, ext 100.)

And in May 2001, Longwood is set to reopen its newly refurbished **Chime Tower** with real bells. It was originally built by Longwood founder Pierre du Pont in 1929–30 with real chimes (which he could turn on from his home), then replaced with an electric carillon after his death in 1954; they

Longwood's fountains combine light shows with water and greenery.

haven't been played since 1989.

But for most of us, the real point of Longwood is flowers. Most outdoor gardens include free horticultural tips, and there's an entire garden (the Idea Garden) devoted to educating and inspiring the public. Self-guided tours are divided into East Garden, West Garden, and Conservatory, and could take about an hour and a half each if you want to see them all, which could lead to sensory overload. There's always something in bloom; check before your visit at www.longwoodgardens.org/Bloom/whatsinbloom.htm. And there's the **Peirce–du Pont House,** the oldest building at Longwood (built 1730) and the family homes of the Peirces till 1905, then the weekend residence of Pierre du Pont. (Admission is $12.00; $8.00 on Tuesday. Open January through March, daily 9:00 A.M.–5:00 P.M.; April and May, daily 9:00 A.M.–6:00 P.M.; Memorial Day through Labor Day weekend, Monday, Wednesday, Friday, Sunday 9:00 A.M.–6:00 P.M., till one hour after dusk on Tuesday, Thursday, and Saturday [Fountain Nights]; September and October, daily 9:00 A.M.–6:00 P.M.; November 1 through Thanksgiving, daily 9:00 A.M.–5:00 P.M.; Thanksgiving through January 7, daily 9:00 A.M.–9:00 P.M. The house museum is open every day 10:00 A.M.–5:00 P.M., till 6:00 P.M. in summer and till 9:00 P.M. during the Christmas display.)

BRUNCH: Longwood's **Terrace Restaurant** (610–388–6771) features a buffet brunch on most weekends, with roast beef, salmon, soups, omelettes, and more. (Brunch in March is served 11:00 A.M.–2:00 P.M.; March 31 through September 30, 11:30 A.M.–3:30 P.M.; till 4:00 P.M. for holiday brunches. Lunch is served generally 11:00 A.M.–3:00 P.M., till 4:00 P.M. weekends; dinner, generally in summer only, Tuesday, Thursday, Saturday 5:00–7:30 P.M. Reservations are recommended. Closed January 8 through March 25, except select weekends. Also, a cafeteria is available, generally open 10:00 A.M.–4:00 or 5:00 P.M.)

Afternoon

Continue north on U.S. 1 to the right turn into the lot for the **Brandywine River Museum** (610–388–2700; www.brandywinemuseum.org). Even around the parking lot there's something to see: the Wildflower Gardens, entirely designed with native plants. The museum, a nineteenth-century gristmill, specializes in American art—particularly of the Brandywine Valley, along with landscapes, still lifes, genre paintings, and illustrations—but is best known for its collection of works by three generations of the Wyeth family, especially N. C., Andrew, and James. The cafeteria-style museum restaurant serves local wine as well as hot entrees, vegetarian meals, and more. (Admission is $5.00. Open every day but Christmas, 9:30 A.M.–4:30 P.M. One-hour tours of the N. C. Wyeth House and Studio are available April 1 through mid-November, Wednesday through Sunday 10:15 A.M.–3:15 P.M. There's a charge of $3.00 over the regular admission.)

Let's just scoot south quickly on U.S. 1 before we leave town. The **Phillips Mushroom Place Museum** (610–388–6082 or 800–243–8644; www.phillipsmushroomplace.com) is more fun than you imagined a fungus could be. The tiny one-room museum (a token $1.00 admission includes a card that lets you come back) portrays mushroom lore and methodology, but the real attraction is the we're-everything-mushrooms gift shop. Stock up on several varieties of fresh mushrooms, not to mention dried mushroom powder, pickled mushrooms, dried exotic mushrooms, mushroom-motif aprons, and more. (Open every day except major holidays, 10:00 A.M.–6:00 P.M.)

Head north on U.S. 1 back to U.S. 202/322, and continue northwest for 3.3 miles, letting U.S. 322 go away to leave you on U.S. 202 (Old Wilmington Pike). Watch for the **Dillworthtown Inn** (1390 Old Wilmington Pike, West Chester; 610–399–1390; www.dilworthtown.com) on your left.

DINNER: The Inn, established 1758, managed to survive the Battle of Brandywine that destroyed many other buildings around here. Lucky us. Think of homemade pâté and the signature crabcakes with caramelized tomato and mango chutney. Think of the 900-bottle wine list. It's pricey, but heavenly. And heaven just got expanded into cooking classes in the new Innkeepers Kitchen. Remember jackets; ties are optional. (Open weekdays 5:30–9:00 P.M., Saturday 5:00–9:30 P.M., Sunday 3:00–8:30 P.M. Reservations recommended.)

If dinner is too good, you may want to stay booked at the Inn at Montchanin. Or you can begin the drive home on the Pennsylvania Turnpike.

THERE'S MORE

Golf. Given the relatively mild climate, not to mention the old-money culture, this is serious golf country nearly year-round. There's an amazing wealth of excellent golf courses, of which the following are only some highlights. Remember that in the height of the season, it's a good idea to schedule tee times well in advance; also, while all the courses listed here are open to the public, members do get preference. So do folks booking specific golf packages, available at about twenty (mostly chain) hotels on both sides of the Pennsylvania-Delaware line. (All ratings are from *Golf Digest*.)

Hartefeld National Golf Course. Rated 4½ stars; home of Bell Atlantic Classic. Avondale, Pennsylvania (610–268–8800 or 800–240–7373; www.hartefeld.com).

Wyncote Golf Club. Rated 4 stars; home of Exelon Invitational. Oxford, Pennsylvania (610–932–8900; www.wyncote.com).

Back Creek Golf Club. Rated 3½ stars; the sister course to Chantilly Manor. Middletown, Delaware (302–378–6499).

Chantilly Manor Country Club. Rated 3½ stars; the sister course to Back Creek. Rising Sun, Maryland (410–658–4343; www.chantillymanorgolf.com).

Three Little Bakers Country Club. Rated 3 stars. Pine Creek Valley outside Wilmington, Delaware (302–737–1377).

Rockwood Museum. A rural Gothic house museum with a garden, near Nemours and Hagley (302–761–4340; www.rockwood.org).

Historic Houses of Odessa. Winterthur Museum's off-site location of an eighteenth-century village relatively untouched by development. South of Wilmington (302–378–4069).

Barns-Brinton House and **John Chads House.** The former was built as a tavern in 1714; the latter dates to 1725. Historic demonstrations are offered. Both are on U.S. 1, Chadds Ford (610–388–7376).

Delaware Art Museum. A notable collection of Pre-Raphaelite English art, plus nineteenth- and twentieth-century American art. Wilmington (302–571–9590; www.delart.org).

Delaware Museum of Natural History. Notable collections of mollusks and birds, plus interactive exhibits. Practically across the road from Winterthur (302–658–9111; www.delmnh.org).

Delaware Toy & Miniature Museum. Dollhouses, dolls, toys from 1770, miniature vases from 600 B.C. are all found here off DE 141 in Wilmington (302–427–8697 or 302–658–0668).

Mykonos. An unusual shop with handcrafted jewelry, art clothing, and collector-quality kaleidoscopes at Glen Eagle Square in Chadds Ford (610–558–8000).

Centreville Merchants Association. A historic village of shops and restaurants off the Kennett Pike (DE 52; 302–655–1299).

Historic Kennett Square. Pennsylvania's oldest borough features antiques shops and guided tours. It's on U.S. 1, a mile south of Longwood Gardens (610–444–7181; www.kennett-square.pa.us).

Herr Foods Inc. Visitor Center. Free weekday tours of the chips and snacks maker in Nottingham (800–284–7488; www.herrs.com).

QVC Studio Tour. It's on all the time, and maybe you can even sit in on a show. Daily tours on the hour, 10:00 A.M.–4:00 P.M. In West Chester (800–600–9900; www.qvctours.com).

Covered bridges. A free brochure describing a driving tour of Chester County's fifteen covered bridges is available at the county's Tourist Information Center, a historic Quaker meetinghouse on U.S. 1 near the entrance to Longwood Gardens.

SPECIAL EVENTS

April–November. Brandywine Battlefield hosts special Second Sunday historic programs (610–459–3342; www.ushistory.org/brandywine).

May. Brandywine River Museum hosts the Wildflower, Native Plant and Seed Sale on Mother's Day weekend (610–388–2700; www.brandywinemuseum.org).

September. A reenactment of the Battle of Brandywine includes Quaker meeting, folk music, and crafts (610–459–3342; www.ushistory.org/brandywine). Mushroom Festival, Kennett Square: national cookoff, farm tours, arts, crafts (888–440–9920). Labor Day weekend jazz festival at Chaddsford Winery (610–388–6221; www.chaddsford.com).

November–January. Christmas at Longwood features special light displays, fountain shows, musical performances, dinner events, and extended hours till 9:00 P.M. (610–388–1000; www.longwoodgardens.org).

OTHER RECOMMENDED RESTAURANTS AND LODGING

Hank's Place. The shiitake omelette is famous. It's served 5:00 A.M.–7:00 P.M. at this casual eatery near Brandywine Museum (610–388–7061).

Harry's Savoy Grill. Casual upscale dining and a good wine list in Wilmington (302–475–3000).

Kennett Square Inn. This restaurant and tavern founded in 1835 also offers guest rooms (610–444–5688; www.kennettinn.com).

Flower Farm. A country B&B that features flower-themed Victorian rooms in Kennett Square (610–444–5659).

FOR MORE INFORMATION

Chester County Conference and Visitors Bureau, 601 Westtown Road, Suite 170, West Chester, PA 19380; 610–344–6365 or 800–228–9933; www.brandywinevalley.com.

Delaware Tourism Office, 99 Kings Highway, Dover, DE 19901; 302–739–4271 or 800–441–8846; www.visitdelaware.net.

SOUTHERN
ESCAPES

Parkersburg and Marietta

ROLLIN' ON THE RIVER

---

1 NIGHT

Glass • Dolls • Riverboats • Antiques

You can find your marbles—plenty of them—as well as unbelievably lifelike dolls, antiques, and a riverboat captain's dream just a short way downriver. Of course, you'll need to drive to these towns spanning the Ohio in West Virginia and Ohio, respectively. Both were prominent river towns in the nineteenth century and have retained much of their Victorian architecture and charm. And for those who favor West Virginia glass, there are still several notable small operations going on, as well as the biggest of them all: Fenton Glass, a major collectible (and it's so pretty). And speaking of collectibles, across the river is the nation's largest doll company, Lee Middleton. But there are many little gems as well: the nation's oldest five-and-dime, a treasure-trove hardware shop, a delectable pasta shop, and great antiques shops for browsing.

I originally discovered this area while exploring the North Bend Rail Trail, 72 miles roughly parallel to U.S. 50 along the old C&O Railroad right-of-way in West Virginia. There's plenty of fun there, too.

DAY 1

Morning

Head south for about two hours on I–79 to exit 119 and west on U.S. 50, part of West Virginia's limited-access Appalachian Corridor system. After a scenic 39 miles, exit at **Pennsboro;** turn right onto WV 74, continue north for 1 mile, and stop at the depot.

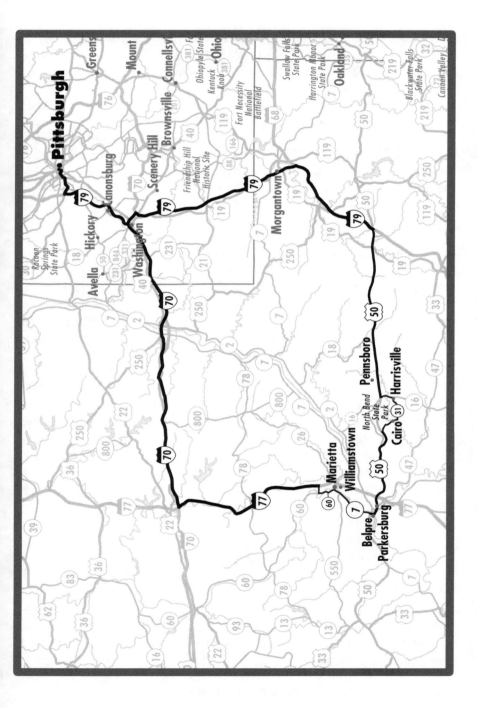

BREAKFAST: The **P&H Family Restaurant** (206 Kimball Avenue; 304–659–3241), right along the North Bend Trail, features basic home cooking in large portions. It's also a B&B. (Open Monday through Saturday 6:00 A.M.–8:00 P.M., Sunday 8:00 A.M.–3:00 P.M.)

Head south to Old Route 50, turn right, and continue west for about 3.5 miles; watch on your left for the **Mid–Atlantic Glass Company** (Old Route 50; 304–869–3351). Across the parking lot from the showroom, kilns protruding from a shed bring the glassmaking process out into the open. Go inside the showroom to see marbles, paperweights, and a selection of napkin rings in the shapes of flowers, as well as detailed hummingbirds in glass, hurricane glasses in a variety of colors, and brandy snifters in a wide range of sizes. (Open Monday through Friday 9:30 A.M.–noon and 12:30–5:00 P.M., Saturday 9:00 A.M.–2:00 P.M.)

Continue west to Ellenboro, and head south briefly on WV 16. Turn left just before the North Bend Rail Trail bridge to reach **West Virginia Glass Specialty Inc.** (107 Main Street; 304–869–3374) for glassware that has been colored, silk-screened, enameled, cut, and/or monogrammed by hand, including hand-painted marbles. Don't miss the eye-catching Z-stem martini glasses with an iridescent finish. (Open Monday through Friday 8:00 A.M.–3:30 P.M., Saturday 9:00 A.M.–4:00 P.M.)

Continue south 5 miles on WV 16, which becomes Main Street as it enters Harrisville. Turn right onto Court Street to head to **Berdines 5 & Dime** (106 North Court Street; 304–643–2217), the nation's oldest variety store, in operation since 1908. A glass-front case holds such treats as licorice strings and button candy. Along with notions, sewing supplies, and wooden clothespins, you'll also find toys of the child-powered, rather than battery-powered, variety. The shelves in the front of the store hold such a range of glassware produced by the area's glass factories that there's a chance you might find a piece from that pattern you've given up on as discontinued and lost. (Open Monday through Saturday 9:00 A.M.–5:00 P.M.)

Return to, and continue on, Main Street as it sheds its state route number and becomes County Road 5. Four miles of winding road, much of it guardrail-free, brings you to the entrance of **North Bend State Park** (304–643–2931; www.northbendsp.com). The four-season park includes cottages, a lodge, restaurant, swimming, tennis, and the 72-mile North Bend Rail Trail for biking, cross-country skiing, horseback riding, and more.

On leaving the park, take County Road 14 (Low Gap Run Road) for 3.4 miles and turn right onto WV 31 to Cairo. The imposing three-story brick building on your right, just past the center of town, is **R. C. Marshall Hardware Co.** (Main and McGregor Streets; 304–628–3321; www.rcmarshall.com), with supplies ranging from the eminently practical (nails in bins and cast-metal three-pound sausage stuffers) to the not entirely whimsical (hard hats with built-in lanterns for cyclists traversing the North Bend Rail Trail's many tunnels). Though you may not have any immediate need for oil-drilling supplies or galvanized washtubs available in full-sized or eight-ounce versions, note that the store produces a full line of preserves under its own label. (Open Wednesday through Sunday 10:00 A.M.–5:00 P.M., with extended summer hours.)

Continue on WV 31 and turn left onto U.S. 50 for 20 miles to downtown **Parkersburg.** As U.S. 50 turns left from Eighth Street onto Ann Street, move into the left lane to avoid being drawn across the Ohio River prematurely. Head south on Ann Street, and follow the WV 68 SOUTH signs up the ramp and across the Little Kanawha (pronounced ka-NOY) River. Less than a mile from the bridge, turn right at the Star Avenue exit, make a quick left onto Marrtown Road, and then make a right after 0.3 mile onto River Hill Road (County Road 30). On your right, 1.6 miles later, is **Point of View** restaurant (River Hill Road, Blennerhasset Heights; 304–863–3366).

LUNCH: Enjoy a spectacular view of the Ohio River and Blennerhasset Island along with chicken, pepper steak and a variety of sandwiches. (Open Monday through Saturday for lunch, 11:00 A.M.–2:00 P.M.; for dinner, Monday through Thursday, 5:00–9:00-ish, Friday and Saturday 5:00–10:00 P.M. There's a seafood buffet every Friday and Saturday. Reservations recommended for dinner.)

Afternoon

Retrace your route to downtown Parkersburg. At the downtown end of the Little Kanawha River Bridge, turn left and left again onto Ann Street, this time avoiding the bridge ramp. Turn left onto Second Street and right onto Juliana Street to the **Blennerhasset Museum** (Second and Juliana Streets; 304–420–4800; www.blennerhassett.org). The museum features a video telling the story of Harman and Margaret Blennerhasset, the aristocratic Irish couple who settled Blennerhasset Island and became entangled with Aaron Burr's mysterious expedition to the Southwest. It also offers three floors of archaeological and historical exhibits. (Admission is $2.00. Open December 1 through March 31, Saturday 11:00 A.M.–5:00 P.M., Sunday 1:00–5:00 P.M.; April 1 through May 1, Tuesday through Saturday 11:00 A.M.–5:00 P.M., Sunday 1:00–5:00 P.M.; May 2 through September 4, Tuesday through Saturday 9:30 A.M.–6:00 P.M., Sunday 11:00 A.M.–6:00 P.M.; September 5 through October 29, Tuesday through Saturday 9:30 A.M.–5:00 P.M., Sunday 11:00 A.M.–5:00 P.M.; October 30 through November 30, Tuesday through Saturday 1:00–5:00 P.M., Sunday noon–5:00 P.M.)

Head to **The Point,** a 2-block walk from the museum. Pass through the opening in Parkersburg's flood wall. When high water threatens, the openings are blocked with logs or aluminum bars stacked on top of each other to keep the floodwaters out. The Point is the boarding location for the stern-wheeler that travels to **Blennerhasset Island.** Blennerhasset Mansion, reconstructed on the foundations of the original, features authentic eighteenth-century furnishings that complement the many pieces once owned by Harman and Margaret Blennerhassett. During the 1760s the famous Delaware Indian Nemacolin made the island his home. Other famous visitors include King Charles X of France, Johnny Appleseed, Henry Clay, and Walt Whitman. Also on the island are a crafts village, refreshment and souvenir shops, picnic shelters and rental bicycles, and a narrated horse-drawn wagon ride. (Boat ride, $6.00; mansion tour, $3.00; wagon ride, $4.00. Open May 1 through September 6, Tuesday through Saturday 10:00 A.M.–4:00 P.M., Sunday noon–4:00 P.M.; September 7 through October 31, Thursday through Saturday 10:00 A.M.–4:30 P.M., Sunday noon–4:30 P.M.)

From the Blennerhasset Museum, head north on Juliana Street, staying in the left lane for the left turn to U.S. 50 and the Ohio River bridge to Belpre. Remain in the left lane on the bridge, and turn left at the end of it onto OH 618 (Washington Boulevard). On your left, 0.9 mile later, is the pastel facade of the nation's largest domestic doll factory, **Lee Middleton Original Dolls Inc.** (1301 Washington Boulevard; 740–423–1481 or 800–233–7479; www.leemiddleton.com). You don't "buy" these incredibly lifelike dolls; you "adopt" them. Painted, dressed, jointed, and weighted to feel like real infants, these collectibles have stood in for the real thing on TV shows like *ER,* as well as in plays, ads, and even living Nativity scenes. (The outlet store is open Monday through Saturday 9:00 A.M.–5:00 P.M.)

Return, via Washington Boulevard, to the Ohio end of the Ohio River bridge. Turn left and follow Main Street to the entrance ramp to OH 7 north and the 12-mile drive to **Marietta.** The scenic overlook south of town offers a panoramic view of the river valley as well as a view of Marietta itself. Follow OH 7 across the Muskingum River on Washington Street, turn right at the traffic light at the end of the bridge onto Second Street, turn right again onto Wooster Street, then turn left onto Front Street, which leads to the heart of downtown Marietta, lined with brick buildings with colorful gingerbread woodwork.

DINNER: Join the festivities at the **Marietta Brewing Company** (67 Front Street; 740–373–BREW; www.axces.com). Choose from the five brews made on site or the homemade root beer to wash down quesadillas, wraps, spicy pizzas, and sandwiches. The brewing equipment is enshrined in a multistory atrium in the front of the building; the brick walls are adorned with six-foot-high painted reproductions of period posters. High metal ceilings make the conviviality reverberate when local rock bands entertain on Friday and Saturday night. (Open Monday through Thursday 11:00 A.M.–11:00 P.M., Friday and Saturday 11:00–1:00 A.M., Sunday 4:00–9:00 P.M.)

Evening

LODGING: Built in 1918, the **Lafayette Hotel** (101 Front Street; 800–331–9336; www.historiclafayette.com) seems not so much to evoke the riverboat era as to be still part of it, with the 11-foot pilot's wheel in the lobby. Cap the night with the view of the Ohio and Muskingum Rivers from the Riverview Lounge.

DAY 2

Morning

BREAKFAST/BRUNCH: Line up for the Sunday brunch buffet in the Lafayette's **Gunroom Restaurant,** 8:30 A.M.–2:00 P.M. Check out the long-rifle collection (all from 1795 to 1880) in the dining room, decked out in a riverboat theme. (The restaurant is open for breakfast, Monday through Saturday 6:00–11:00 A.M.; lunch, daily 11:00 A.M.–2:00 P.M.; dinner, Sunday through Thursday, 5:00–9:00 P.M., Friday and Saturday 5:00–10:00 P.M., Sunday hours are 7:30 A.M.–9:00 P.M.)

Afternoon

Work off the carved ham and desserts by strolling along Ohio River Front Park or on Front Street, window-shopping at the town's antiques shops. One of the best, right across from the Lafayette, is **Riverview Antiques** (102 Front Street; 740–373–4068; www.riverviewantiques.com; open every day but Thanksgiving and Christmas, Monday through Saturday 9:30 A.M.–5:30 P.M., Sunday 10:30 A.M.–5:30 P.M.), with well-organized and extensive collections of Wedgwood, pewter, and glassware, plus an array of china, historic photographs of Marietta, Hummel plates, and bells. Continue up the street to **Antiques & Needful Things** (177 Front Street; 740–374–6206; www.marietta-ohio.com/antiquesandneedfulthings), which takes up two storefronts with both new and antique furniture and home accessories like clocks and quilts. A few steps away is the **Looking Glass** (187 Front Street; 740–376–0113 or 877–376–0113; www.thelookingglas.com—note that there's only one *s* in the URL) for local glass pieces, furniture, and more. (Most shops are open Monday through Saturday 10:00 A.M.–5:00 P.M., Sunday noon–5:00 P.M.)

Head north on Front Street to **The Ohio River Museum** (601 Front Street; 614–297–2332 or 800–860–0145; www.ohiohistory.org/places/ohriver) to dive into the history of the boats that linked the East to the frontier via the Ohio River. Displays include a model of a typical stern-wheel packet and ornate furnishings typical of the golden age of steamboat travel. A 30-minute video contains footage of old excursion boats and packets as well as views of present-day steamboats. Pittsburgh's *W. P. Snyder, Jr.,* moored in the Muskingum River adjacent to the museum buildings, is America's sole surviving steam-powered stern-wheel towboat. (Admission is $5.00. Open March through November, Wednesday through Saturday 9:30 A.M.–5:00 P.M., Sunday noon–5:00 P.M. Also open Monday and Tuesday 9:30 A.M.–5:00 P.M. from May through September. The riverboat is open for tours the same hours as the museum, mid-April through October.)

Head back down Front Street and turn left at the Lafayette onto Greene Street. They don't mind if you inhale when you visit **Rossi Pasta** (114 Greene Street; 740–376–2065 or 800–227–6774; www.rossipasta.com), and that's a good thing, because a good deep breath gives you a head start on your basil and garlic intake as you watch pasta being made. Variety No. 5 of the twenty-six distinct pasta flavors offered combines these two flavors. Not for the faint of heart is No. 28 in hot orange, combining cayenne pepper and paprika. Choose from eight red sauces to go with your pasta, and stock up on freeze-dried artichoke hearts if you're running low. (Open Monday through Saturday 9:00 A.M.–7:00 P.M., Sunday noon–5:00 P.M.)

Head upriver on Greene Street and turn right onto the Williamstown-Marietta Bridge into **Williamstown.** At the West Virginia end of the bridge, turn right onto WV 14 south. Turn left at the first traffic light 0.6 mile later, and right 0.3 mile later into the **Fenton Glass** (700 Elizabeth Street; 304–375–6122 or 800–319–7793; www.fenton-glass.com) parking lot. The nation's largest manufacturer of handmade colored glass features a variety of lamps, vases, and other giftware, including museum reproductions. An on-site museum is dedicated to preserving the heritage of Ohio Valley glassmaking. (Open Monday through Saturday 8:00 A.M.–5:00 P.M., Sunday 12:15–5:00 P.M. Hours are extended to 8:00 P.M. Monday through Friday from April through December. Tours are available Monday through Friday only.)

DINNER: Return to Marietta, turn left at the end of the bridge onto Greene Street, and turn right onto Second Street. **Oliver's Fine Food and Spirits** (203 Second Street; 740–374–8278) is a long, narrow room with a neighborhood feel. Try Oliver's cheese bread with your salad, or Chef Joe's beer chili. (Open Monday through Thursday 11:00 A.M.–10:00 P.M., Friday and Saturday 11:00 A.M.–11:00 P.M., Sunday 9:00 A.M.–9:00 P.M.)

Head north on Third Street to OH 60. Turn right onto OH 621. Take I–77 north to Cambridge, Ohio, and I–70 west to Washington, Pennsylvania. Return home via I–79.

THERE'S MORE

North Bend Rail Trail. This multipurpose recreational trail includes ten tunnels, plus three that can be seen from the trail. It runs 72 miles from WV 47 near Parkersburg to Wilsonburg, near Clarksburg. Easily accessible from I–77 and I–79, the trail nearly parallels U.S. 50 (304–643–2500 or 800–899–6278; www.wvrtc.org).

Oil & Gas Museum. Actual oil- and gas-drilling and -pumping equipment as well as models, along with Parkersburg historical displays disputing Pennsylvania's claim to be the birthplace of the oil industry (304–485–5446).

Historical Model Railroad Museum. A model railroad display, with more than eighteen trains operating simultaneously (740–374–9995; www.eekman.com/harmarstation/).

Campus Martius. This museum commemorates the founding of Marietta. A house that was part of the original fort is enclosed within a wing of the museum, which showcases period tools and furnishings (740–373–3750 or 800–860–0145; www.ohiohistory.org/places/campus).

Valley Gem. Stern-wheeler tours on the Ohio and Muskingum Rivers (740–373–7862 or mcnet.marietta.edu/~Vgem).

Schafer Leather Store. Operated by the fifth generation of the Schafer family this Marietta shop sells hats (which can be custom-shaped), clothing, boots, luggage, and more. Closed Sunday (740–373–5101).

Underground Railroad. Tours, a photo display, maps, books, and more are offered at the Levee House Cafe, 127 Ohio Street, Marietta (740–374–2233).

Oxbow Golf and Country Club. Designed by Jack Kidwell and rated 3 stars by *Golf Digest*. Golf packages are available at local hotels. County Road 85, Belpre (740–423–6771 or 800–423–0443).

Showboat *Becky Thatcher Theatre*. This National Historic Landmark in Marietta specializes in showboat-style plays and revues all summer, with an abbreviated season in fall and winter. It also serves lunch and dinner separate from the theater. Closed Sunday (740–373–6033 or 877–SHO–BOAT; www.marietta-ohio.com/beckythatcher/).

SPECIAL EVENTS

June. Mid-Ohio Valley Multi-Cultural Festival in Parkersburg City Park celebrates three days of food, music, arts, and culture of many nations (304–428–4405 or 304–428–1552).

June–July. The Annual Tent Sale at Fenton Glass runs from the last Friday of June to the second Monday in July (304–375–7772).

September. Ohio River Sternwheel Festival brings dozens of the big boats (and plenty of the smaller ones) for a weekend of music and food, capped by stern-wheeler races (740–373–5178).

October. Foliage tours are conducted up the Muskingum at 10:00 A.M. every Sunday on the *Valley Gem,* through America's last completely hand-operated lock system (740–373–7862; mcnet.marietta.edu/~Vgem).

OTHER RECOMMENDED RESTAURANTS AND LODGING

Third Street Deli. Soups, sandwiches, beer, and wine to take out or eat on the patio. In Parkersburg (304–422–0003).

The Becky Thatcher Theatre *is a real showboat.*

Levee House Cafe. Marietta's oldest riverfront building combines good food with history and romance, riverside or in the restored dining room. Closed Sunday (740–374–2233).

Historic Blennerhassett Clarion Hotel. Opened in 1889 in downtown Parkersburg; breakfast is included, and there's dining in Harman's Restaurant (304–422–3131 or 800–262–2536).

Avery-Savage House. A Queen Anne Victorian B&B in the Avery Historical District near downtown Parkersburg (304–422–9820 or 800–315–7121; www.averysavagehouse.com).

Claire E Sternwheeler. This floating B&B is listed on the National Register of Historic Maritime Vessels (740–374–2233 or 740–374–3876).

FOR MORE INFORMATION

Parkersburg/Wood County Convention and Visitors Bureau, 350 Seventh Street, Parkersburg, WV 26101; 304–428–1130 or 800–752–4982; www.parkersburgcvb.org.

Marietta/Washington County Convention and Visitors Bureau, 316 Third Street, Marietta, OH 45750; 740–373–5178 or 800–288–2577; www.mariettaohio.org.

SOUTHERN

Downstate West Virginia

A TASTE OF THE WILD

AND WONDERFUL

---

2 NIGHTS

Heights and Depths • Artistic Crafts
Antebellum Charm • Stargazing

Perhaps more than most trips in this book, this one serves up disparate destinations that could serve to inspire separate future trips. The heart of West Virginia in and around the Monongahela National Forest offers incredible beauty and charm of both the man-made and the natural sorts. Many already know this area as a superb place for white-water rafting, rock climbing, skiing, crafts, and food. And when people tell you to go jump off the bridge here, they really mean it—in a nice way.

West Virginia is not called the Mountain State for nothing. There are few stretches of straight, flat road, and some of the places you'll visit call for something highly maneuverable. But—let's dispel any misconceptions—the road system has benefited greatly from some serious highway construction in the last few years. And though West Virginia is definitely to the south, all those mountains mean it's actually likely to be a few degrees cooler year-round.

DAY 1

Morning

BREAKFAST: Take a break from I–79 by taking the Kirwin Heights exit and turning left onto PA 50 to **Gab & Eat** (1073 Washington Avenue, Scott Township;

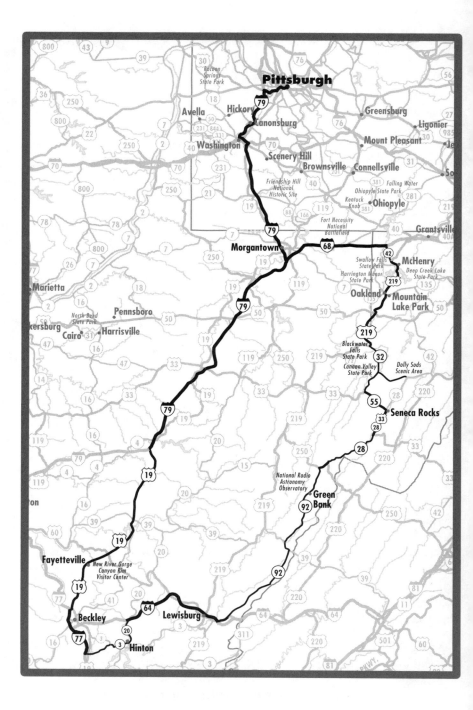

412–276–8808), famous for its large platters of mixed grill, eggs, and pancakes. (Serves Monday through Friday 7:00 A.M.–3:00 P.M., Saturday 6:00 A.M.–2:00 P.M., Sunday 7:00 A.M.–2:00 P.M.)

Continue south on I–79 for a couple of hours (past Washington, Pennsylvania, and Morgantown) to exit 57 and U.S. 19, which is limited access and very scenic for most of the 50 miles to **Beckley.** Watch for the turnoff to your left for the **New River Gorge National River's Canyon Rim Visitor Center** (304–465–0508; www.nps.gov/heri/), right before the bridge. While the center does include a tidy mini museum of local history, its main attraction is the view into the gorge, up to 1,300 feet deep. Some 53 miles of this river and its gorge—70,000 acres—are preserved as a free-flowing waterway. The misnamed river is actually one of the oldest in the world, older even than the Appalachian Mountains themselves, exposing rocks that date back about 330 million years (some of them superb for rock climbing). The bridge itself is something of an attraction. The longest single-arch steel-span bridge in the world is 3,030½ feet long and 876 feet high, and once a year hundreds of people come from around the world to—legally—rappel or jump to the bottom (see "There's More").

Your means of descent is a tad easier. Turn right out of the parking lot and right again onto WV 82. This is the route that local folks had to use before the bridge was opened in 1977. Take it slowly, because much of the road is one lane and steep with sharp turns, but also occasional turnoffs that allow you to stop and take pictures. While the ends of the road are two-way, the middle (including the Fayette Station Bridge crossing the river) is one-way; watch for cars, the occasional tour bus (I don't know how they manage it, either), and the intrepid souls who explore on foot. At the river, you may catch sight of rafters. With a 750-foot drop in 50 miles, the New River offers excellent white-water rafting. At the top, turn right onto U.S. 19, then make a quick right onto WV 16 into **Fayetteville,** on what used to be the Giles, Fayette and Kanawha Turnpike, now simply Court Street.

LUNCH: Yes, the **Cathedral Cafe** (134 South Court Street; 304–574–0202) really is a former church. Select from creative sandwiches like chorizo with pizza sauce or smoked turkey with bacon and avocado, and don't overlook the homemade soup. Save room for carrot cake, check out the books at the in-store bookstore, then head upstairs to **Trillium Crafts** for West Virginia–made pottery, jewelry, salsas, jams and more. (Open for breakfast, Monday through Saturday 7:30–11:30 A.M., Sunday 7:00 A.M.–noon. Lunch, Monday through

Saturday 11:30 A.M.–4:00 P.M., Sunday noon–4:00 P.M. Dinner, during white-water season, April through October, Wednesday, Thursday, Sunday 5:00–9:00 P.M., Friday and Saturday 5:00–10:00 P.M.; off season, Friday and Saturday only, 5:00–9:00 P.M.)

Afternoon

Head south on U.S. 19 to the West Virginia Turnpike, I–77/64, and go southeast on I–77/64 for 1 mile to exit 44. Take WV 3 (Harper Road) east, following the signs for EXHIBITION COAL MINE, then turn left onto Ewart Avenue to go down the hill to New River Park. The **Beckley Exhibition Coal Mine** (304–256–1747; wvweb.com/www/exhibition_coal_mine) used to be the real thing. Forget the "good" old days. Just off the parking lot are a few buildings from a coal camp: a spacious one for the superintendent, and tiny cramped shacks for the miners. Even more of an eye-opener is the thirty-five-minute tour on a sort of tram called a man-trip car. An affable former miner recounts the history of coal-mining methods and of coal miners themselves as he takes you 186 feet underground and more than one hundred years into the past in damp and cool tunnels (bring a jacket and a hat; you will get dripped on). This National Historic Site is open April 1 through November 1; tours leave every half hour, 10:00 A.M.–5:30 P.M.; museum and gift shop are open 10:00 A.M.–6:00 P.M. (Admission is $7.00 or, for the coal camp only, $2.00.)

Right next door (you don't need to move your car) is the **Youth Museum of Southern West Virginia & Mountain Homestead** (304–252–3730)—just look for the boxcars. The museum features interactive science stations, changing exhibits, and the outdoor Mountain Homestead of reconstructed log houses that re-creates a West Virginia frontier settlement, complete with one-room schoolhouse and blacksmith shop. (Admission is $2.00 each for the main gallery and Homestead, $3.50 for both. Open Memorial Day through Labor Day, Monday through Saturday 10:00 A.M.–6:00 P.M., Sunday 1:00–6:00 P.M.; the rest of the year, Monday through Saturday 10:00 A.M.–5:00 P.M.)

Return up Ewart Avenue and turn west onto WV 3, past the Country Inn and Suites Hotel in a few minutes, to the first fork in the road. Bear right onto Dry Hill Road, then take the first right onto Tamarack Park Drive, and you'll see the distinctive building (based on a traditional quilt pattern) on your left.

Tamarack (304–256–6843 or 88–TAMARACK; www.tamarackwv.com) is the nation's first and still its only statewide arts and crafts collection. Boasting "the best of West Virginia," Tamarack is a destination unto itself with more than 1,800 juried artists, artisans, and craftspeople represented. Its 59,000 square feet includes half a dozen studio spaces where resident and visiting artists can demonstrate their specific media (classes available). There's also a theater/concert hall (free performances every **Sunday@Two**), two fine art galleries, and an outdoor sculpture garden, but perhaps the biggest attraction is the range of products—more than 30,000 of them—handmade jewelry, glassware, pottery, toys, musical instruments, furniture, baskets, clothing, and foods, especially various fruit spreads, mustards, sauces and salsas. (Admission and parking are free. Open every day but Christmas, January through March, 8:00 A.M.–7:00 P.M.; April through December, 8:00 A.M.–8:00 P.M.)

DINNER: Can you ask for more than Greenbrier cuisine? **A Taste of West Virginia** food court in Tamarack is managed by the world-famous resort and spa. Various stations feature soups, salads, deli sandwiches, grilled entrees (with luck, local trout), and baked goods, all top of the line but economically priced. (Open for breakfast, lunch, and dinner, the same hours as Tamarack.)

Take I–77 south (I–64 will split off) to exit 28 (Ghent). Turn left and, in 0.2 mile, turn right onto U.S. 19. Continue south for 2.2 miles. You'll pass **Winterplace Ski Resort** (304–787–3221 or 800–607–7669; www.winterplace. com). Turn left onto Ellison Ridge Road, check your odometer, and go 9 miles to Boland Road. This is fairly secluded, but the road isn't difficult. Watch for deer. In about a quarter mile, turn right at the FOXWOOD sign and follow the driveway for more than a mile to a mountain aerie.

LODGING: Foxwood B&B (304–466–5514; foxwoodwv@aol.com) is a hideaway on 250 acres in Jumping Branch. It's great for bird-watchers, or just casual strollers in the garden and around the pond. Spacious rooms and suites include free video.

Evening

Watch the sun go down and listen to the birds, then stargaze with no light pollution to interfere with the Milky Way.

DAY 2

Morning

BREAKFAST: Enjoy eggs, baked goods, and coffee on the covered veranda, and watch hummingbirds have their breakfast.

Return to Boland Road, turn left, then turn right onto Ellison Ridge Road. This is a very winding but beautiful road through the mountains, ending in the small town of Minitz. Turn right onto WV 3 and head down the mountain to WV 20. Turn left and follow the road through **Hinton**, a lovely little historic town and the other end of the New River Gorge National River. The road heads uphill. Watch on the left for the scenic overlook to **Sandstone Falls,** and get your camera. Shortly after the falls comes the town of Sandstone and I–64. Head east on I–64 to exit 169 (Lewisburg), then drive south on U.S. 219 to U.S. 60: Washington Street, the main street of historic **Lewisburg.**

Listed in *America's Most Charming Towns and Villages, The 100 Best Small Arts Towns in America,* and the National Register of Historic Places, Lewisburg is also manageable and affordable. Turn right onto Washington Street, go 2 blocks, and make a left onto Church Street, site of the visitors center (304–645–1000) in **Carnegie Hall** (304–645–7917). This arts and education center hosts free art exhibits, touring and local performing groups, and a film series.

Pick up a booklet outlining a walking tour of the historic district. Right across the street is **Old Stone Presbyterian Church,** built in 1796 and the oldest church in continual use west of the Alleghenies, but more famous for its role in the Battle of Lewisburg on May 23, 1863 (spot the bullet holes). Return to Washington Street and turn left to visit the **John A. North House Museum** (304–645–3398; www.greenbrierhistorical.org) for more than 200 years of local history, especially Civil War artifacts. (Admission is $3.00. Open Monday through Saturday 10:00 A.M.–4:00 P.M.)

There's a 235-acre historic district of sixty eighteenth- and nineteenth-century buildings to explore, and a main street lined with dozens of interesting shops. Tough decision. Contemplate it over a roast beef sandwich and a beer in the open-air plaza across the street.

LUNCH: The Market (304–645–4084) at 215 West Washington Street does a brisk take-out business. (Open Monday through Saturday 8:00 A.M.–8:00 P.M., Sunday noon–6:00 P.M.)

Afternoon

Combine history, art-grazing, and shopping with a stroll down Washington Street. Shops and galleries are generally open Monday through Saturday 10:00 A.M. to 5:00 or 5:30 P.M. A few places are also open Sunday. Find New Age tapes, videos, aromatherapy, and such at **O'Shea's** (304–645–3500), 201 West

Washington, and funky clothes as **Linda Blue's Unique Boutique** (304–645–5464) at 123 West Washington. Next to the entrance to the Greenbrier Valley Theatre is **Glass Roots** (304–647–5996), 113 East Washington. Check out **J. Fenton Gallery/Quilts Unlimited** (304–647–4208) at 117 East Washington for handcrafted jewelry, kaleidoscopes, and clothing; and, in the same building, **Honnahlee** (304–645–6123) for toys. A must-stop for antiques lovers is the new **Robert's Antiques** (304–647–3402), featuring early American items, primitives, furniture, and glassware (and it's open Sunday). Keep your historical guide handy; you could walk west on Washington (the hill is gentle) as far up as Edgar Drive to see the **Stuart Grant House** (now a private home; the original log cabin dates to 1870), one of the oldest land grants in the country (1830).

Work your way back down Washington on the other side. Explore fine art photography, painting, sculpture, and other media at the **Cooper Gallery** (304–645–6439 or 888–868–5129; www.coopergallery.com) at 122 East Washington; next door is the original **Robert's Antiques** (304–647–3404). Among the stops on the 100 block of West Washington are the **Tuckwiller Gallery** (304–645–2070) for works by local artist Robert E. Tuckwiller; **Wolf Creek Gallery** (304–645–5270) for wind-dancer-style clothing and jewelry; the **Old Hardware Gallery** (304–645–2236) for folk art; the **Stonehouse General Store** (304–647–5300), featuring West Virginia gourmet food (including its signature salsa), crafts, and more; and **Gallery 1897** (304–645–1656) for old prints and new art. And you're almost back where you started.

DINNER: Cross Washington to **Food & Friends** (213 West Washington Street; 304–645–4548; www.foodandfriends.com), a popular hangout with an extensive menu of salads, sandwiches, entrees, pastas, and more. Steaks are the specialty, creatively finished with bourbon and other touches, but don't overlook the crab-scallop cakes and grilled sweet bourbon salmon fillet. (Reservations are recommended, by phone or online. Open Monday through Saturday 11:00 A.M.–9:00 P.M.) Head east again on Washington until you see the stagecoach on your right.

LODGING: The **General Lewis Inn** (304–645–2600 or 800–628–4454; www.generallewisinn.com), owned and operated by the same family since 1928, actually dates to 1834. This country inn, named for the town's founder, is furnished with antiques, including a history-filled Memory Hall exhibit. And, yes, there is purportedly a ghost (or two), as reported by various guests.

Evening

The **Greenbrier Valley Theatre** (304–645–3838; www.gvtheatre.org) presents a summer season at the **Barn Theatre** near the Greenbrier Valley Airport, and year-round at its new, versatile black-box theater downtown. Or check to see if there's a performance at **Carnegie Hall** (304–645–7917). Or just lounge in the General Lewis livingroom and play with the games and puzzles available.

DAY 3

Morning

BREAKFAST: Stroll down to the General Lewis dining room (301 East Washington Street) and order from the menu. Start the day with a plate of fried potatoes with mushrooms, scallions, tomatoes, banana peppers, and cheese served with salsa and sour cream. Don't pass up French toast with spiced apples, or try southern biscuits and sausage gravy. (Open Monday through Saturday, for breakfast 7:00–11:00 A.M., lunch 11:30 A.M.–2:00 P.M., dinner 6:00–9:00 P.M.; Sunday, breakfast 7:30–11:00 A.M., dinner noon–9:00 P.M.)

Head east on U.S. 60, admiring the historic old homes. In less than half an hour, you'll be going through White Sulphur Springs, home of one of the nation's oldest and most famous resort spas, The Greenbrier (see "There's More"). Outside town, turn left onto WV 92 and continue for about an hour through the countryside until you see what looks like a giant satellite dish, bigger than a football field. It's actually the world's largest fully steerable telescope, operated by the **National Radio Astronomy Observatory** at its Green Bank site (public programs, 304–456–2164; www.gb.nrao.edu). Free tours of the NRAO facility are offered on the hour, 9:00 A.M.–4:00 P.M., Memorial Day weekend through Labor Day. Cameras are welcome. You can also take a tour of the solar system on your own with the help of the scale model near the parking lot, or sign up for one of the occasional educational programs or star parties (generally $3.00 to $5.00).

Back on the road, WV 92/28, stick with WV 28 when it splits from WV 92, and head north to Judy Gap; then take U.S. 33 west through serious mountains in and out of the Monongahela National Forest. You can even take a slight detour to head to the very top of Allegheny Mountain, at 3,950 feet. The road is good, the scenery even better. Continue on U.S. 33 and soon you'll see the distinctive treeless face of **Seneca Rocks** and the turnoff to the new

Seneca Rocks is one of the most popular spots for rock climbing in the East.

visitors center (304–567–2827). The Spruce Knob–Seneca Rocks National Recreation Area offers 100,000 acres of trails, wildlife, and one of the best-known sites for rock climbing in the eastern U.S. From the center you get a spectacular view, access to easy walking trails, and, on request, admission to the Sites Homestead, an 1830 farmhouse. (The center is open April 1 through October 31 every day 9:00 A.M.–5:30 P.M.; November 1 through March 31, weekends only, 9:00 A.M.–4:30 P.M.)

Stay on U.S. 33/WV 55 north to Harman, then veer right onto WV 32 and head up and up to the Canaan (pronounced kuh-NANE) Valley: At 3,200 feet, this is the highest valley in the East. Not surprisingly, it's also a superb ski area, akin to the best New England skiing. Even though the road is pretty straight, be careful. You will see deer. They're protected and thus rather bold here in the national wildlife refuge, home to more than 200 species of birds,

600 of wildflowers. Turn left at the sign for the **Canaan Valley Resort State Park** (304–866–4121 or 800–622–4121; www.canaanresort.com).

LUNCH: Enjoy the view in the resort's glass-walled **Aspen Dining Room,** along with basic sandwiches and salads. You can see the championship golf course and, in the distance, the slopes that attract skiers and snowboarders with a vertical drop of 850 feet; the longest run of the thirty-four slopes is 6,000 feet. The 6,000-acre resort and park also features a 250-room lodge plus twenty-three secluded cabins. (The dining room serves breakfast, daily 7:00–11:00 A.M.; lunch, daily 11:00 A.M.–2:00 P.M.; dinner, Sunday through Thursday 5:00–9:00 P.M., Friday and Saturday 5:00–10:00 P.M.)

Afternoon

Backtrack about a mile on WV 32 to WV 45, turn left and follow the signs to **Dolly Sods Wilderness Area** (no visitors center, no phone; vault toilets only in campground and picnic site) of the Monongahela National Forest. Ranging from 2,600 to more than 4,000 feet high, this part of the Allegheny Plateau seems much more like northern Canada given the fierce ecoclimate and unusual vegetation: sphagnum bogs, heath barrens, stunted red spruce. And it is true wilderness. You can drive through the 2,000-acre Dolly Sods Scenic Area on Forest Road 75, but it's not plowed in winter. Try a short walk along the 0.3-mile Northland Loop for berry picking and wildflower hunting, but real hiking should be attempted only by the very experienced and prepared. You'll need to backtrack along FR 75 to FR 19 toward Laneville, then follow WV 45 back to WV 32.

Head through the county seat, Davis, the highest town in West Virginia, and turn left at the sign for BLACKWATER FALLS STATE PARK (304–259–5216 or 800–CALL–WVA; www.blackwaterfalls.com). There are many trails for walking, hiking and cross-country skiing, but the must-see attractions are, of course, the falls, not just the 63-foot cascade that gives the park its name but also several smaller waterfalls. Pick up a free trail guide. The park also includes horseback riding, boating, fishing, a lodge with fifty-four guest rooms and a restaurant, and twenty-five modern cabins.

Return to WV 32 north to Thomas, where you meet U.S. 219 and head north. Shortly before you cross the state line into Maryland, you'll go through Silver Lake, home of **Our Lady of the Pines,** which claims to be the smallest church in the U.S. The mailing office there (ZIP 26716) also claims to be the nation's smallest. Photo op time. Continue north through Deep Creek Lake (see Southern Escape 3), then take MD 42 north to I–68, and turn west to drive into Morgantown. Switch to I–79 north and exit 155 (Star City). Turn right onto Monongahela Boulevard, past the West Virginia University Coliseum; the road turns into Beechurst Avenue. Continue about a quarter mile to the new warehouse district and your pick of restaurants lining the Caperton Trail and the Monongahela River.

DINNER: Dip into guacamole and salsa on the deck with a river view (you didn't know the Mon could look this good) at **La Casa Mexican Grill** (156 Clay Street; 304–292–6701) in a historic warehouse. (Open Sunday through Thursday 11:30 A.M.–9:00 P.M., Friday and Saturday 11:30 A.M.–10:00 P.M.)

Return home via I–79.

THERE'S MORE

White-water rafting. Besides what's available on the New River, the nearby Gauley River can exceed Class V with spring rains and the scheduled water releases from Summersville Dam in fall. Summer rafting tends to be easier and more family oriented. More than twenty local outfitters offer classes, excursions (day and overnight), rental gear, and meals. Most also offer fishing, rock climbing, hiking, mountain biking, and other outdoor sports excursions. Reservations are recommended several months in advance for fall rafting.

Class VI River Runners Inc. Trips end at the new Smokey's on the Gorge, a restaurant in the woods with a New River view (800–252–7784; www.800classvi.com, which includes links to check water levels).

Ace Adventure Center. A 1,400-acre resort (888–223–7238; www.acecraft.com).

Extreme Expeditions. Camping, cabins, hotel packages (304–574–2827 or 888–463–9873; www.go-extreme.com).

Fayetteville. The antebellum county seat, site of the Battle of Fayetteville, includes art galleries such as **Court Street Gallery** (304–574–9010), **Historic Fayette Theatre** (304–574–4655), the **Fayette County Museum**

in the former county jail, and a historic district (a free map is available from the Historic Visitors Bureau, 304–574–1500 or 888–574–1500).

Hawks Nest State Park. Get another view of New River Gorge from the Canyon Tramway (Memorial Day through October) in this 276-acre park, one of seven state parks near the New River Gorge National River. A lodge is also available (800–CALL–WVA).

Skiing. Pipestem Resort State Park (304–466–1800 or 800–CALL–WVA; www.pipestemresort.com) is a popular ski area in Bluestone Canyon, near Foxwood B&B. Timberline Four Seasons Resort (800–766–9464; www.timberlineresort.com) is in the Canaan Valley. Check for specials combining Canaan and Timberline at www.skithevalley.com.

The Greenbrier. The nation's first organized golf club was here in White Sulphur Springs. The historic landmark is home to three courses, including The Greenbrier Course, one of the best in the world (304–536–1110 or 800–624–6070), and the Greenbrier Sam Snead Golf Academy (800–793–3254). The 6,500-acre resort is almost as famous for its cooking classes, including a series conducted by celebrity chefs, plus of course the mineral waters, first mentioned in 1784 by Thomas Jefferson (www.greenbrier.com).

SPECIAL EVENTS

February–March. Dinner theater at Tamarack.

June. Captain Thurmond's Challenge Team Relay, Thurmond to Fayetteville: Bike 11 miles, kayak on Class IV or V rapids for 8 miles, and run more than 5 miles, starting at the bottom of New River Gorge (304–465–5617; www.captainthurmonds.com).

September. The Leaf Peepers Festival celebrates frogs and fun in Canaan Valley (304–259–5315 or 800–782–2775).

October. On Bridge Day, the third Sunday, arts and crafts booths line the entire span of the New River Gorge Bridge, which is open only to pedestrians, parachutists and climbers. This is the official end of rafting season (304–465–5617 or 800–927–0263; www.newrivercvb.com).

OTHER RECOMMENDED RESTAURANTS AND LODGING

Washington Street Inn. Fine dining in a 200-year-old home in downtown Lewisburg. Reservations recommended (304–645–1744).

Julian's Restaurant & Coffee Bar. Famed Lewisburg classical cuisine (304–645–4145).

White Horse B&B. Right in downtown Fayetteville (304–574–1400 or 877–574–1400; www.1historicwhitehorsebb.com).

Swift Level. Equestrian trips are available at this country-mansion-turned-B&B 3 miles west of Lewisburg (304–645–1155).

Bright Morning Inn. Hope for wild blueberry pancakes for breakfast at this B&B in Davis, near Canaan Valley (304–259–5119).

FOR MORE INFORMATION

West Virginia Division of Tourism, State Capitol Complex, Charleston, WV 25305; 800–CALL–WVA; www.callwva.com.

New River Convention and Visitors Bureau, 310 Oyler Avenue, Oak Hill, WV 25901; 304–465–5617 or 800–927–0263; www.newrivercvb.com.

Southern West Virginia Convention and Visitors Bureau, 511 Ewart Avenue, Beckley, WV 25802–1799; 304–252–2244 or 800–847–4898; www.visitwv.org.

Lewisburg Visitors and Convention Bureau, Carnegie Hall, 105 Church Street, Lewisburg, WV 24901; 304–645–1000 or 800–833–2068; www.greenbrierwv.com.

Tucker County Convention and Visitors Bureau, P.O. Box 565, Davis, WV 26260; 304–259–5315 or 800–782–2775; www.canaanvalley.org.

Garrett County, Maryland
ALONG THE CONTINENTAL DIVIDE

1 NIGHT

Crafts • Nature • Amish • History

The Deep Creek Lake area has been a popular tourist spot since buddies War-ren G. Harding, Thomas Edison, Henry Ford, and Harvey Firestone went camping at the foot of Muddy Creek Falls in 1919 in what's now Swallow Falls State Park. The area still offers major outdoor attractions with its seven state parks, the highest peak in Maryland, and, of course, various lakes and streams. But there are some surprises south of the border: thriving "Pennsyl-vania Dutch" communities, high-end glassware, and a subarctic relict.

It's a popular summer colony—many folks maintain cottages or condos for the season—but a new interest in skiing, snowboarding, and other winter sports (plus an annual average of 17 more inches of snow than Fairbanks, Alaska) has made this a popular four-season destination. Please note, however, that while the outdoors is always open, many indoor attractions, especially Amish areas, are closed on Sunday.

DAY 1

Morning

Head south on I–79 past Washington, Pennsylvania, to Morgantown, West Vir-ginia, then drive east on I–68 to exit 19, Grantsville, about two hours.

BREAKFAST: Penn Alps Restaurant & Craft Shop (U.S. 40, half a mile east of Grantsville; 301–895–5985) has grown since the days when three of its din-ing rooms (there are now six) comprised an original National Road stage-

coach stop in 1818. Order from the breakfast menu or belly up to the weekend brunch buffet (Saturday 7:00 A.M.–2:00 P.M., Sunday 7:00 A.M.–3:00 P.M.); make sure you try the homemade apple butter and the smoked sausage from nearby Yoder's. Explore the attached shop, which features works by 400 Appalachian artisans, including quilts, wooden toys, ironwork, and rockers, plus gifts like carved chess sets from overseas areas served by Mennonite missions. (The restaurant is open Monday through Saturday 7:00 A.M.–8:00 P.M., Sunday 7:00 A.M.–3:00 P.M. The shop's hours are Monday through Thursday 9:00 A.M.–7:00 P.M., Friday and Saturday till 8:00 P.M., Sunday till 3:00 P.M.; www.pennalps.com.)

There's no need to move your car to continue your exploration of the **Spruce Forest Artisan Village** (301–895–3332). Check the sign at the entrance to see which artists are in residence that day in twelve historic structures, two of which date to colonial times, and watch them make pottery, carve wood into birds, weave baskets, and more. Visit a one-room schoolhouse, then stroll on over to the **Casselman River Bridge,** the largest single-span stone arch bridge in the world when it was built back in 1813, now a National Historic Landmark. (The village is open Monday through Saturday 10:00 A.M.–5:00 P.M.)

Take a quick detour to the other side of Grantsville, to **Yoder Country Market** (north on MD 669; 301–895–5148 or 800–321–5148), a Mennonite "supermarket" of homemade fruit butters and preserves, canned meats, bulk foods, recipes, and more, plus a selection of Amish furniture across the road. When you're parking, make sure you don't block access to the hitching post for Amish buggies. (Open Monday through Saturday 8:00 A.M.–6:00 P.M.)

Head west on U.S. 40 to U.S. 219 and turn south. The view becomes spectacular at 2,800 feet, and there's a scenic pulloff so you can enjoy The Cove, a panoramic natural "amphitheater" of farmland surrounded by woods.

LUNCH: As you approach Deep Creek Lake in McHenry, Deep Creek Drive pulls away and parallels U.S. 219 to cruise along the shore to the **Point View Inn** (301–387–5555; rooms are also available). You get a lakeside view whether eating indoors or out; try the local take on a Pittsburgh salad, or the crabcake sandwich. (Open seven days, 7:00 A.M.–10:00 P.M.)

Afternoon

Continue south, leaving the lake area for the moment to visit Oakland, the county seat. The eighteenth-century "frontier town" became a vital link on the

B&O line, which inspired several Confederate raids during the Civil War. You'll find plenty of war memorabilia in the cozy little **Garrett County Historical Society Museum** (107 South Second Street; 301–334–3226), plus Native American artifacts from local archaeological digs, period clothing and toys, and lots of information on the B&O Railroad. The historic Queen Anne–style 1884 B&O station, just around the corner from the museum, is undergoing a massive restoration and should be ready for visitors in 2001. Across Liberty Street is **Saint Matthew's Episcopal Church,** where vacationers like Presidents Grant, Harrison, and Cleveland (and Chester A. Arthur before he became president) have worshiped since 1868; it's still open to visitors. (The museum is open Monday through Saturday 11:00 A.M.–4:00 P.M.; it's free.)

Head farther south on U.S. 219, and within minutes you'll find yourself in open farmland and Amish country. Turn left at Paul Friend Road and watch for hand-painted signs declaring quilts, furniture, pies, and more for sale as you explore the side roads. For example, the Yoder farm on Pleasant Valley Road (at the end of Paul Friend) sells hydroponically grown (and respectably tasty) tomatoes starting in March.

Double back through Loch Lynn to MD 135, then head east to Mountain Lake Park and the **Simon Pearce** art glass factory (265 Glass Drive; 301–334–5277; www.simonpearce.com). Even on Saturday you'll be able to watch artisans mouth-blow or hand-mold glass in the modern factory behind the showroom, where the handmade glass and pottery are for sale. The serving pieces, vases, and glassware are stunningly flawless (even the "seconds" look great)—and pricey. (Open daily 9:00 A.M.–5:00 P.M.)

DINNER: Return to Oakland and U.S. 219, and turn right on Memorial Drive to **Cornish Manor** (301–334–6499), a flamboyantly country French restaurant and bakery. It's casual but romantic (cozy up to the fireplace if it's cold), and reservations are a good idea, as is the homemade pâté. (Open Tuesday through Saturday 11:00 A.M.–2:00 P.M. and 5:00 P.M.–whenever.)

Return to U.S. 219 and return north to the Deep Creek area; turn right onto Glendale Road; in about a mile you'll cross a bridge and bear right, continuing about a mile to Carmel Cove. Turn left, then bear left for the B&B (the sign can be tricky to see).

LODGING: Carmel Cove (301–387–0067; www.carmelcoveinn.com), a former monastery retreat house for the Discalced Carmelite Fathers, is simple but not spartan, with a hot tub for evening relaxation, billiards, games, wine, and other amusements.

DAY 2

Morning

BREAKFAST: Work up an appetite with a swim off Carmel Cove's dock, just a walk down the hill from the B&B, or fish, or borrow one of the B&B's bikes or canoes for a morning ride. The sumptuous breakfast changes daily, and likely includes local Amish sausage, maple syrup, and fruit plus homemade baked goods.

Retrace your drive on Glendale Road, this time turning right at the bridge instead of crossing it, to enter the **Deep Creek Park Interpretation Center** (301–387–5563). Casually explore both the fauna and the history of the area in the center's exhibits, and get acquainted with the 1,818-acre park and its 6-square-mile man-made lake. It's an easy walk down to the "beach"; there are plenty of hiking opportunities (6 miles of snowmobile trails in winter), plus every water sport, from sailing to scuba diving.

After a stroll, take in more of the scenery on a hayride ($5.00). **Broken Bar Riding Stables** (301–334–3114) generally has a wagon in the parking lot (horseback riding and camping are also available; Open Monday through Saturday 10:00 A.M.–6:00 P.M., Sunday 1:00–6:00 P.M.).

LUNCH: Just 4 or 5 miles back north on U.S. 219, next to the visitors center, is the **Deep Creek Brewing Co.** (301–387–2182), a brewpub in a lodge setting providing a vista of the valley as well as chili or stew served in a bread bowl, plus basic bar sandwiches and munchies. (Monday through Thursday 11:30 A.M.–11:00 P.M., Friday and Saturday 11:30 A.M.–midnight, Sunday 11:30 A.M.–9:00 P.M.)

Afternoon

From the pub, turn left onto Sang Run Road (the area is named for the plentiful ginseng there). You'll pass the renovated **Friend's Store,** an 1890s general store (it's more a photo op than a must-stop), and climb the mountain (Ginseng Hill). Don't rush; enjoy the scenery, and even a little nick of West Virginia as you follow the twists and turns of Sang Run Road to Lake Ford Road. Watch for signs to the **Cranesville Swamp Nature Preserve:** 0.2 mile along Lake Ford, bear right at the fork, and head down a dirt road another 0.2 mile to the entrance to an ecological oddity.

The Cranesville Swamp (no phone, no amenities, no admission fee), one of the first designated National Natural Landmarks, is a subarctic relict from

Deep Creek offers placid waters for boaters.

the last ice age, about 15,000 years ago. This 850-acre peatland bog is home to hundreds of plants (including small carnivorous ones) and a few small animals (like shrews) normally found far to the north; it's a great place for bird-watching. There are three trails to explore, but make sure you stay on the boardwalk so you don't damage rare and delicate bog plants. (Owned and maintained by The Nature Conservancy, www.tnc.org.)

Get an eyeful of more recent forms of nature at Maryland's state parks (there are seven in the county, overlapping with three state forests). You can easily visit two of them now. Back on Lake Ford Road, turn right onto Cranesville Road and drive about 4 miles to **Swallow Falls State Park** (301–334–9180). There's usually a nominal (about $2.00 per car) entrance fee, and an easy walk to the spectacular scenery of Youghiogheny River gorges and Muddy Creek Falls, 63 feet tall. There are also hiking and skiing trails, one of which leads to nearby **Herrington Manor State Park** (301–334–9180). If you're really into nature, there are comfy log cabins right in the park for rental,

a tidy fifty-three-acre lake with a sandy beach for swimming, a variety of boats for rent (open to nonmotorized craft only).

Return to Oakland via Herrington Manor Road. From Oakland, head east on MD 135 for about 5 miles. Turn right onto Deer Park Hotel Road. In another quarter mile, you'll see the Deer Park Inn on your left.

DINNER: The **Deer Park Inn** (65 Hotel Road, Deer Park; 301–334–2308; www.deerparkinn.com) is housed in an officially historic Victorian mansion. Dine inside or out on exquisite country French food (the duck is great), enjoying good wines by the glass and a variety of antiques. As the name implies, overnight guest accommodations are also available. (Dinner only; hours vary.)

Head back home via U.S. 219 to MD 42, picking up I–68 at Friendsville; then take I–79 home, about two hours.

THERE'S MORE

State parks. The county is also home to Big Run, New Germany, and Casselman State Parks, all near Grantsville (301–895–5453 or 301–746–8359), and the Youghiogheny Scenic and Wild River, west of Deep Creek Lake (301–387–5563). Fishing, hunting, lake boating, and more. All except the river have campgrounds (www.dnr.state.md.us/publiclands).

Hoye Crest on Backbone Mountain, the highest point (3,360 feet) in Maryland and the Eastern Continental Divide, is most easily reached from a mile-long hiking trail, 5 miles south of U.S. 219 and U.S. 50 in Red House.

White-water fun. If white-water rafting is your idea of a good time, try the Upper Yough in Friendsville (800–477–3723; www.precisionrafting.com).

Wisp Ski & Golf Resort. Considered one of the 500 best courses in the U.S., the *Golf Digest*–ranked 4-star Golf Club at Wisp is twin to a hundred-acre slope with twenty-three trails, from beginner to black-diamond runs (301–387–4911; www.gcnet/wisp).

SPECIAL EVENTS

January. The Kick & Glide Cross-Country Ski Race in Herrington State Park is among several snow-sport events in the area (301–334–9180).

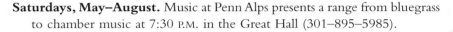
Saturdays, May–August. Music at Penn Alps presents a range from bluegrass to chamber music at 7:30 P.M. in the Great Hall (301–895–5985).

July. Summerfest and Quilt Show features about one hundred juried artisans, musicians, and storytellers in Spruce Forest (301–895–3332).

August. The Garrett County Agricultural Fair offers livestock displays, demolition derbies, country music, and more down-home fun (301–334–4715, ext. 2321).

October. The Springs Folk Festival links the tiny Pennsylvania town of Springs with Grantsville for Pennsylvania Dutch crafts, music, and food (814–662–4158).

The four-day Autumn Glory Festival celebrates the peak of fall foliage with statewide banjo and fiddle competitions, tall tales, and much more (301–387–4386).

For the Autumn Glory Train, the Western Maryland Scenic Railroad gets very scenic in a 110-mile round trip from Cumberland to Oakland (301–759–4400 or 800–TRAIN–50; www.wmsr.com).

OTHER RECOMMENDED RESTAURANTS AND LODGING

McClive's Restaurant & Courtyard Lounge. This longtime popular spot features seafood strudel, lake views, and evening entertainment. (Dinner seven days a week; lunch in summer only; 301–387–6172.)

Canoe on the Run. For a lighter touch in healthful soups, salads, and sandwiches. (Open every day for breakfast, lunch, and dinner; 301–387–5933.)

Black Bear Restaurant (301–387–9400) and **Tavern** (301–387–6800). Start with breakfast and end the day with dancing and bar games. Closed Sunday.

Savage River Inn. Stay right in Savage River State Forest in an updated 1934 farmhouse, with amenities that range from a shooting range to toboggan runs to massage (301–245–4440; www.savageriverinn.com).

Elliott House. All rooms are equipped with CD players, binoculars, and real Amish quilts, adjacent to Penn Alps and Spruce Forest Artisan Village (800–272–4090; www.elliotthouse.com).

FOR MORE INFORMATION

Garrett County Chamber of Commerce, 15 Visitors Center Drive, McHenry, MD 21541; 301–387–4FUN (4386); www.garrettchamber.com.

Berkeley Springs

IT RUBS ME THE RIGHT WAY

---
2 NIGHTS

Spas • Art • Antiques • George Washington's Bathtub

Folks who love this little piece of West Virginia often call it a remnant of the 1960s, or at least the 1960s as we'd like to be able to remember them. Casual. Artsy. Laid-back, with time and leisure to ponder great philosophical issues. Tolerance of any and all eccentricities. No fast-food restaurants. Cheap movies. And all with great food like from Alice's Restaurant—Alice is really named Tari, but you can still get anything you want. And everything's afford-able and manageable (heck, the entire town has only one telephone exchange number). Mix that in with a spa tradition that's eighteenth-century Bath mixed with twentieth-century New Age, one of the nation's leading artists' colonies, and, yes, you'll probably see Sasha the dog, too.

You could spend your entire weekend floating from spa to spa, or simply from "treatment" to "treatment" within one spa (many folks do; note that appointments are generally necessary), but I'll include some arts happenings, too. Everything is casual here—nothing more formal than clean socks. Oh, and pack some water jugs, too.

DAY 1

Afternoon

Head east on the Pennsylvania Turnpike to exit 12 (Breezewood), and con-tinue east on I–70 to Hancock, Maryland. Then take the left exit to go south for about 6 miles on U.S. 522. About three hours after leaving Pittsburgh,

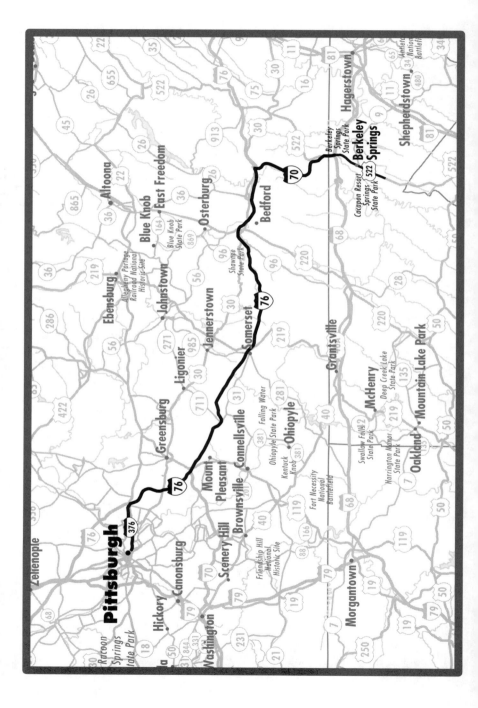

you'll pull into the tiny town (population 800) of **Berkeley Springs.** There's often street parking even on the main street, Washington (U.S. 522).

DINNER: Get an instant overview of the local arts scene at **Tari's Premier Cafe** (123 North Washington Street; 304–258–1196; www.tariscafe.com). The front windows are filled with locally made glass pieces, the walls are adorned with a changing array of local paintings and prints, and even the flower holders decorating the table are handmade and for sale. Settle down for another artistic endeavor. Tari Hampe-Deneen chars, grills, sautés, marinates, rubs, and sauces some of the most creative meats, fish, and pastas, using produce from her father's garden in season. And she sells her own brand of WV Wild Woman salsas and other products. (Dining seven days a week, 11:30 A.M.–9:00 P.M., with later snacks in lounge. Sidewalk tables are available at lunch. There's also a B&B upstairs.)

Evening

Head next door to the **Star Theater** (North Washington Street at Congress Street; 304–258–1404) to see a current popular movie in the type of neighborhood moviehouse you remember from your childhood. One screen, and a real popcorn maker (a 1947 Manley), with real butter on the popcorn, just $1.00. Jeanne Mozier runs the show literally here; she's unofficially the town's leading outspoken spokeswoman, and officially the author of *Way Out in West Virginia* and a member of the West Virginia Commission on the Arts. You want to know anything about Berkeley Springs or local art? Ask Jeanne. (Flicks change weekly, running Friday through Sunday at 8:00 P.M., plus Thursday in summer, and admission is only $3.00. Couch seating 50 cents extra.)

LODGING: Just a few blocks south of Tari's is the **Country Inn** (304–258–2210 or 800–822–6630; www.countryinnwv.com), built in 1932 to fit the colonial ambience of the town founded by George Washington's family. A recent remodeling added more modern rooms behind the inn on 207 South Washington Street.

DAY 2

Morning

BREAKFAST: Stroll through Berkeley Springs State Park to the **Fairfax Coffee House & Eatery** (116–120 Fairfax Street; 304–258–8019). If you're not

up for coffee, go for one of the fruit or veggie smoothies with a fresh-baked muffin. Recross the street to enjoy them in the park. (The coffee bar is open every day at 8:00 A.M., the eatery Wednesday through Friday 9:00 A.M.–5:00 P.M., Saturday and Sunday 9:00 A.M.–5:00 P.M., plus Sunday brunch 9:00 A.M.–3:00 P.M.)

The center of town is at the corner of Fairfax and Washington, two key names in this town. Back in 1748, Thomas Lord Fairfax owned pretty much this whole area, including the warm (always 74.3 degrees Fahrenheit) mineral springs whose purported healing powers had been attracting Native Americans from as far as the Saint Lawrence Seaway. White settlers got the word, too, and the Washington family (George was a kid) were among those who "took the waters," and even dreamed of setting up a spa town like the then-ultrafashionable Bath, England (read your Jane Austen). Thus **Berkeley Springs State Park** (304–258–2711; www.wvparks.com/berkeleysprings) adds justifiable fame to its claim as America's oldest spa. The Washingtons called the town Bath (still its official name), and all of them, including George, came fairly regularly—on the western side of the park, near the springs, you can see the bathtub that George used, the oldest outdoor tub used by any U.S. president.

Today's amenities are all indoors, and pretty inexpensive if on the very traditional side, at two facilities in the park. You can soak in one of nine restored 750-gallon individual sunken pool in the **Roman Bath House,** constructed in 1815 on the site of the town's first bathhouse, built in 1784. More familiar tubs are available as well in the "newer" (1930s era) bathhouse on the south end of the four-acre park (springwater is heated to 102 degrees). Before or after your soaking (bathing suits optional), you can also try such physiotherapies as infrared heat, steam cabinets, and various Swedish-style massages from the professional staff—male masseurs on the men's side of the building, female masseuses on the women's. Or you can just drink the water. It's free, by order of Lord Fairfax, when he conveyed the land to Virginia in 1776. And that's why you'll see folks lined up with boxes of gallon jugs under the historic Gentlemen's Spring House. There are two spigots. Just remember that they get pretty heavy once they're filled.

Climb the steps to the second floor of the Roman Bath House (there's a less strenuous entry on the Fairfax Street side) to the **Museum of the Berkeley Springs** (free; open May through October, Monday and Tuesday 10:00 A.M.–1:00 P.M., Thursday and Friday 4:00–6:00 P.M., Saturday 10:00 A.M.–4:00 P.M., Sunday noon–4:00 P.M.). Or proceed directly to the shops of North Washington Street. The crown jewel is right at the corner of Washington and

Fairfax: **Mountain Laurel** (101 North Washington Street; 304–258–1919 or 888–809–2041; www.mtn-laurel.com) offers two floors of handcrafted pottery, glass, clothing, prints, home accessories, Judaica, and more, primarily by Berkeley Springs-area artists, but also by artists from around the nation. (Open Monday through Saturday 10:00 A.M.–5:00 P.M., Sunday noon–5:00 P.M.)

The **Heritage Trail Antiques Mall** (304–258–5811) at 109 Washington Street is home to silver, glass, china, toys, and clothes from sixteen dealers (open Wednesday through Monday 10:30 A.M.–5:00 P.M.). **Tari's Wild Women Fine Art** (304–258–1196) at 123 North Washington Street features women's work, as you can guess, including jewelry, sculpture, and clothing, sponsored by the lady from the famous cafe (open seven days a week, about 10:30 A.M.–5:00 P.M.). Cross Congress Street to **Rhonda's Closet** (304–258–1560) at 205A North Washington for great costume jewelry, wedding dresses, and prom gowns among the used-clothing selection (also open every day).

LUNCH: Continue along North Washington Street and cross at Union Street to the classic old house that's now a B&B and **Inspirations Bakery & Cafe** (312 North Washington Street; 304–258–2292; www.inspirationscafenbnb. com). Place your order at the counter for funky but massive sandwiches, serve yourself soup from the antique sideboard in the dining room, and sit down at comfortable but mismatched tables and chairs. Your server will deliver your order. Cap it off with a piece of homemade pie; if it's pawpaw season (mid-September), check for specialties made from that elusive southern fruit. (Open February through December, Thursday through Monday, breakfast 7:30–10:30 A.M., lunch 11:30 A.M.–3:00 P.M. on Thursday, Sunday, and Monday till 3:30 P.M. Friday and Saturday.)

Afternoon

Continue your stroll north on Washington, then turn left at Depot Street and climb the stairs to visit **Heath Studio Gallery** (304–258–2482 or 304–258–9840; www.jheath.com), home of Jan and Jonathan Heath. She produces dreamy and dream-filled limited-edition woodcuts, linocuts, and monoprints. He produces limited-edition prints of wry watercolors of people and animals drenched in wit. One or the other is usually there to chat. (Open Saturday and Sunday 11:00 A.M.–5:00 P.M., and by appointment.)

Start heading south on Washington, but turn left at Independence Street, and left again at Mercer Street to the **Ice House** (corner of Independence and Mercer Streets; 304–258–2300; www.macicehouse.org). Yes, it was an ice-

house. Now it's an arts center under development, but the large gallery space is open, showing paintings, handmade furniture, jewelry, pottery, and more by local artists. There's also a theater space being developed by the Morgan Arts Council, which owns and operates the center. (Open Saturday and Sunday 11:00 A.M.–5:00 P.M.; closed January until Presidents' Day.)

Oh, dear, a crick in your neck from looking at all that art? How many hours since your last spa treatment? On your walk south on Washington, turn right onto Congress Street for **Atasia Spa** (206 Congress Street; 304–258–7888 or 877–258–7888; www.atasiaspa.com), staffed by licensed massage therapists and cosmetologists. Choose from Thai, Swedish, hot-stone, or specialized massage; a quick fifteen-minute whirlpool soak; a full body polish or herbal wrap; or—what with all that walking—reflexology, a pressure-point foot massage with aromatherapy oils; or even a fabulous spa pedicure with massage, whirlpool, exfoliation, and more. (A variety of pampering packages is available, some taking up so much of the day that lunch is included. Open every day but Thanksgiving, Christmas, and Easter, 9:00 A.M.–6:00 P.M.)

You may want to pick up the car and drive the few blocks south of town to the left turn onto WV 9 (Martinsburg Road), followed by an immediate left onto Mercer Street and an immediate right onto Warren Street.

DINNER: The art of Jan and Jonathan Heath transmutes into a different medium in **Lot 12 Public House** (302 Warren Street; 304–258–6264; www.lot12publichouse.com). Their son, Damian Heath, produces a spectacular and constantly changing Italian-influenced haute cuisine menu (great venison sausage) in one of the oldest homes in Berkeley Springs. Oh, and there's more artwork to enjoy as well. (Reservations are highly recommended. Open Wednesday and Thursday 5:00–10:00 P.M., Friday and Saturday 5:00–10:30 P.M., Sunday brunch 10:30 A.M.–3:00 P.M., dinner 3:30–8:00 P.M.)

Evening

There are free concerts on many summer Saturday evenings in Berkeley Springs State Park, and often Branson-type shows at the Country Inn starring Tom Netherton of *The Lawrence Welk Show* (304–258–2210 or 800–822–6630). Or just sit on the porch and enjoy the air.

DAY 3

Morning

BREAKFAST/BRUNCH: If you haven't explored the antiques-filled lobby area of the Country Inn, take a look at the hallways and sitting rooms (most antiques are for sale) before heading into the English-inspired **Garden** (304–258–1120), which looks like a perpetual garden party. Dig into the house specialty, smoked trout and eggs (available in season; after dinner the night before, one order was plenty for two of us to share, with a side of fruit). And you're far enough east and south to also choose scrapple, grits, or chipped beef on a biscuit. (Open every day; breakfast 7:00–11:00 A.M., lunch 11:30 A.M.–2:00 P.M., dinner 5:00–9:00 P.M., till 10:00 P.M. Saturday.)

Afternoon

Take the elevator behind the inn to the **Renaissance Spa,** perched above Berkeley Springs for a view with your pampering (services must be booked before checking into the hotel: 304–258–2210 or 800–822–6630). Perhaps a honey-almond body polish or a peppermint and seaweed wrap? What sort of facial: C-sea, thermoplastic, algo mask, hydralifting? There are also massages, a whirlpool, manicures, pedicures, and salon stylings. Choose various combinations in packages that include hotel rooms and some meals (the best bargains are weekdays from November through April).

Stroll across the park again, this time for the shops along Fairfax. The **Berkeley Springs Antiques Mall** (304–258–5676) hosts thirty dealers at 100 Fairfax with lots of furniture and, most interesting, **J&A Political Collectibles** (304–258–9286) in case you were looking for I LIKE IKE campaign buttons and other fun effluvia from presidential campaigns (open Thursday through Tuesday 10:00 A.M.–5:00 P.M.). Interested in homeopathy? **Homeopathy Works** (124 Fairfax Street; 304–258–2541 or 877–286–0601; www.homeopathyworks.com) is not just a shop but also a manufacturer and museum of homeopathic remedies. (Open every day 10:00 A.M.–5:00 P.M.). Zip next door to the **Book Keeper** (130 Fairfax Street; 304–258–6100) for new and used books, including works on alternative medicines (also open seven days a week, 10:00 A.M.–5:00 P.M.). And your nose leads you to the **Bath House** (114 Fairfax Street; 304–258–9071 or 800–431–4698; www.bathhouse.com) with its huge variety of locally made soaps in herbal varieties and other bath supplies, plus books about herbal healing and, oh my, spa services. Need a ther-

apeutic rub? With or without heat, aromatherapy and/or a hot tub? (No salon services. Open Monday and Tuesday 10:00 A.M.–3:00 P.M., Wednesday, Thursday, and Sunday 10:00 A.M.–5:00 P.M., Friday and Saturday 10:00 A.M.–7:00 P.M.)

Before leaving town for good (or at least for now), take a scenic drive south along U.S. 522 south (don't look at the chain stores along the highway) and make a right turn into Cacapon (pronounced kuh-KAY-pon) Resort State Park (see "There's More"). Follow the signs to the 2,300-foot summit of **Cacapon Mountain.** Enjoy the view of farms, woodlands, and small towns. For the strenuous minded, there's a trail along the crest of the mountain.

Return north on U.S. 522 through town, turning left up the hill onto Union Street (WV 9). Shortly after the turn you'll pass **Berkeley Castle** (the future of the English Norman building was still in flux when I was there); continue for about 3 miles to a scenic overlook on your right. Pull in and park, and be careful while crossing the road.

DINNER: Enjoy an early dinner along with the spectacular view of the Potomac and Great Cacapon River Valleys at **Jackie's Panorama Steak House** (WV 9; 304–258–9370 or 304–258–9847) atop Prospect Peak. Make sure you get plenty of hot bread to soak up the butter-wine sauce of seafood Norfolk, or tackle a meaty portion of the house specialty prime rib. (Open Wednesday through Friday 4:00–10:00 P.M., Saturday and Sunday 3:00–10:00 P.M.)

Return home via U.S. 522, I–70, and the turnpike.

THERE'S MORE

Cacapon Resort State Park. The narrow 6,000-acre park features more than 20 miles of hiking and bridle trails, tennis and volleyball courts, lake swimming, fishing, and more, but the crown jewel is the 4-star golf course designed by Robert Trent Jones, just steps from the lodge entrance (304–258–1022 or 800–CALL–WVA; www.cacaponresort.com).

Coolfont Resort, Conference, Spa and Wellness Center. Stay in the manor house, lodge, cabins, or chalets. Spend your day in various spa treatments, tennis, hiking, snow tubing, and such. A variety of ecotourism and arts programs is offered. Coolfont Treetop House Restaurant with view of lake and an emphasis on "healthy" cooking (1777 Cold Run Valley Road, off WV 9, above Berkeley Springs; 800–888–8768; www.coolfont.com).

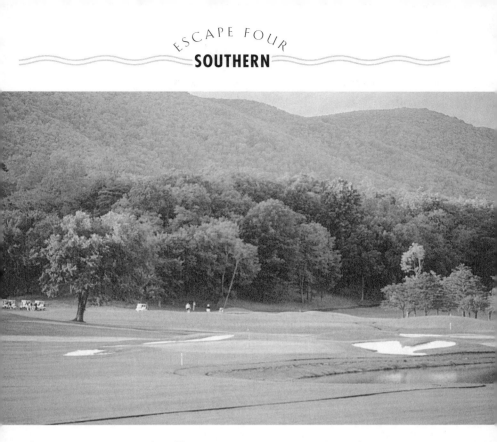

The greens are greener at the golf course in Cacapon Resort State Park.

Hsu Studios. Carol and Jean-Pierre Hsu (pronounced SHOO) fashion anodized aluminum into wall hangings, mobiles, and chic (but not expensive) jewelry. Work from their Berkeley Springs studio is available in local shops and many arts festivals around the country; also by appointment (304–258–1911; www.hsustudios.com).

The Parks House. This old home south of Berkeley Springs State Park (look for the buggy in the front yard) offers country-cute candles, bears, linens, et cetera, but it's notable as an outlet for high-quality and locally made Tom Seely Furniture (304–258–6871; www.theparkshouse.com).

The Old Factory Antiques Mall. This old factory between Williams and Union Streets, not far from the Ice House, offers antiques and collectibles, new furniture, and arts and crafts (304–258–1788).

SPECIAL EVENTS

January–March. Winter Festival of the Waters features events and special travel packages capped monthly by the **Spa Feast** (January), **International Water Tasting** (February; municipal and bottled waters from around the United States and several other countries compete), and **George Washington's Bathtub Celebration** (March) (304–258–3738 or 800–447–8797; www.berkeleysprings.com).

April. Uniquely West Virginia highlights state products throughout town, with a wine and food festival in the Ice House (304–258–3738 or 800–447–8797; www.berkeleysprings.com).

August. The Annual Studio Tour showcases most of the fifty-plus artists who live and work in the area (304–258–2300; www.macicehouse.org).

October. The Apple Butter Festival includes hundreds of booths with locally made crafts, art, food, and produce (304–258–3738 or 800–447–8797; www.berkeleysprings.com).

OTHER RECOMMENDED RESTAURANTS AND LODGING

Cacapon Eatery. A casual family restaurant with ribs and cheesesteaks across from the entrance to Cacapon State Park (304–258–1442).

Maria's Garden & Inn. This popular Italian restaurant (closed Sunday) and B&B includes a shrine to the Blessed Virgin Mary (304–258–2021).

River House Bed and Breakfast. Enjoy a country stay overlooking the Cacapon River, outside the village of Great Cacapon (304–258–4042).

FOR MORE INFORMATION

Berkeley Springs–Morgan County Chamber of Commerce, 304 Fairfax Street, Berkeley Springs, WV 25411; 304–258–3738 or 800–447–8797; www.berkeleysprings.com.

Alexandria and Baltimore

VINTAGE PORT(S)

---

2 NIGHTS

Art and Antiques • Nightlife • Arts and Crafts
George • Nontraditional Art

Although Alexandria celebrates its great antiquity, Baltimore is officially a tad older. They're both eighteenth-century towns (founded in 1749 and 1729, respectively), well established as important ports when Pittsburgh was still a handful of traders outside Fort Pitt. And though a couple of centuries later they're a bit in the megalopolis shadow of their johnny-come-lately neighbor, Washington D.C., both have found new life for the twenty-first century by rejuvenating their waterfronts. Alexandria's Old Town along the Potomac River pulses with shopping and history-hopping all day, bars and clubs at night, while Baltimore's Inner Harbor jumps with museums, Oriole Park at Camden Yards, PSINet Stadium (home of the Ravens), and, of course, shopping. Both towns feature lots of great restaurants, with no shortage of seafood. And there's a George Washington connection for both.

This is probably the funkiest trip in the book—any itinerary with Baltimore is likely to include a few curveballs—with some rather unusual, perhaps even unique stops. And while it's actually possible to sample both towns on a single weekend, it's not difficult to stretch either leg of this trip into a full-blown vacation.

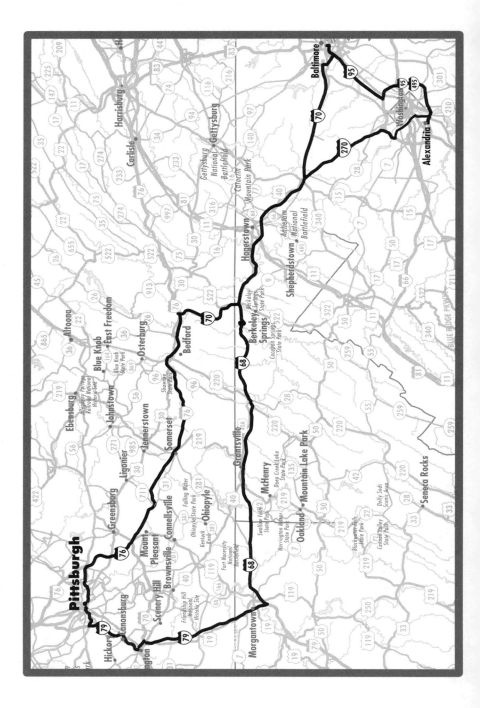

SOUTHERN

DAY 1

Morning

Head south on I–79 to exit 12 (Kirwin Heights/Heidelberg), and turn right onto PA 50.

BREAKFAST: The twenty-four-hour **Eat'n Park** (1197 Washington Pike; 412–221–8771; www.eatnpark.com) features a la carte breakfast specials like the "Breakfast Smile" of eggs, bacon, or sausage, and potatoes; or just head up to the breakfast buffet. (Breakfast buffet is served Monday through Friday 7:30–10:30 A.M., Saturday 7:30–11:00 A.M., Sunday brunch buffet 11:00 A.M.–2:00 P.M.)

Return to I–79, heading south into Morgantown. Then go west on I–68 to exit 62 (15-Mile Creek Road). Turn left and, at the top of the mountain, bear left at the Y in the road. A bit over a mile later, there's another Y; bear right. Watch on the left for the Amoco sign out front and the **Road Kill Cafe** (Artemas, Pennsylvania; 814–784–3257). You've driven a bit more than three hours from Pittsburgh.

LUNCH: The name is a joke, but the barbecued ribs are for real and the helpings are huge. Souvenir menus promise "Awesome Possum" and other roadside treats, but they're just part of the decor, along with photos of celebrities who've been drawn by the name and the food. (Open Monday through Saturday 8:00 A.M.–8:00 P.M., Sunday 1:00–3:00 P.M.)

Afternoon

Return to I–68 and continue about 20 miles to the **Sideling Hill Exhibit Center** (301–842–2155) right on the interstate (it's also a rest stop and picnic area). Park and take the pedestrian bridge over I–68, pausing to look at the layers of the mountain exposed in the highway cut. The geologic cross section is a 350-million-year-old rock formed by a massive compression of the earth's crust when the Appalachian Mountains arose some 245 million years ago. Even if you're not into geology, the curved, colored layers are pretty. Inside the mini museum is a four-story-high timeline of geologic development and evolution (Sideling Hill is 100 million years older than the dinosaurs), as well as exhibits on mountain building, local history and geology, and the progression of technology in building various versions of the National Road (U.S. 40).

(Free admission. The exhibit area is open 9:00 A.M.–5:00 P.M. every day but major holidays. The rest area is open 24/7.)

From here it's about two hours to **Old Town Alexandria.** I–68 ends in just a few miles near Hancock, Maryland, and joins with I–70. Continue east to Hagerstown and I–270 south to the Capital Beltway. Take the outer loop of the Beltway (I–495) west. Just after crossing the Potomac River into Virginia, exit onto the George Washington Parkway south and follow it directly into Alexandria.

On the narrow, eighteenth-century cobblestone streets of Old Town Alexandria, walking will get you around faster than driving. There are eighteen public garages, but street parking is tricky, with lots of permit-parking-only areas. Your B&B host or hostess can give you a temporary permit—and I do mean temporary. They're designed to fade in twenty-four hours (in hot weather, yours might fade faster) after activating, so you'll need to get a new permit every day. You can also get a free twenty-four-hour "parking proclamation" at the **Ramsay House Visitors Center** (221 King Street; 703–838–4200). The passes are valid at two-hour metered spaces only. While at the center, a modest 1724 home, pick up brochures on local attractions, especially the listing of art galleries and antiques stores. Read them in the house's tiny sheltered garden, or people-watch across the street next to the fountain in Market Square. (Open every day 9:00 A.M.–5:00 P.M.)

Perhaps, after all that driving, you need afternoon tea. The recently relocated and enlarged **Pineapple Inc.** (106 North Lee Street; 703–836–6112 or 800–847–4942) has added a **tearoom** (703–836–8180) to its offerings of museum reproductions, early American brass, imported linens, and more on two floors. Take a break with finger sandwiches, scones and, of course, a nice hot cuppa tea. (The shop is open Monday through Wednesday 10:00 A.M.–6:00 P.M., Thursday through Saturday 10:00 A.M.–9:00 P.M., till 6:00 P.M. in winter, Sunday noon–5:00 P.M. The tea room is open Tuesday through Sunday noon–4:00 P.M.)

A mercantile center for more than a quarter of a millennium, Old Town has more than forty antiques shops. The highest-quality ones are west of Washington Street, several blocks from the touristy waterfront—which is fun but not the place to look for seventeenth-century Old Masters. That's the sort of thing you can find at **Castle Swan** (1007 King Street; 703–519–6900; open noon–6:00 P.M. seven days a week). Look across the street for Provençal linens, pottery, and more at **French Country Antiques** (1000 King Street;

703–548–8563; open Monday through Saturday 10:30 A.M.–6:00 P.M., Sunday noon–5:00 P.M., closed Tuesday). Continuing west, you can get even more serious with French selections at **Micheline's Antiques** (1600 King Street; 703–836–1893; open Tuesday through Saturday noon–5:00 P.M., Sunday noon–4:00 P.M.)

DINNER: You could pick just about any place along King Street and not go wrong. If you're used to eating early (say, 6:00 P.M. or earlier), you may not even need reservations. Things tend to heat up at 8:00 P.M., and late suppers aren't unusual. Stay in a country French mood at **Le Gaulois Cafe Restaurant** (1106 King Street; 703–739–9494), starting with an assortment of homemade pâtés, pike dumplings with lobster sauce, a succulent cassoulet of duck, lamb, and sausage, and finishing with a raspberry and passion fruit cake. Ooh la la. (Open Monday through Thursday 11:30 A.M.–10:30 P.M., Friday and Saturday 11:30 A.M.–11:00 P.M.)

LODGING: Old Town B&Bs generally don't have signs, accept no walk-ins, and can be booked only through the **Alexandria & Arlington B&B Network** (512 South 25th Street, Arlington, Virginia 22202; 703–549–3415 or 888–549–3415; fax 703–549–3411; aabbn@juno.com; www.aabbn.com), which also handles guest houses and furnished houses. Since these are often in eighteenth-century homes, amenities can be somewhat modest, but make no mistake: These are in very high demand. Not only do you need to book well in advance with a credit card, but there are also pretty stiff penalties for cancellations. Still, there's something to be said for sleeping in a house that's even older than the nation. The high ceilings, local antiques (not to mention local restaurant advice and local gossip—which can include some high movers and shakers), and proximity to the heart of Old Town make the possible lack of luxury inconsequential.

Evening

Get a nighttime view of Alexandria, Georgetown, and our nation's capital on a ninety-minute **Washington by Water** tour aboard the *Matthew Hayes* of the **Potomac Riverboat Company** (City Marina, at the foot of King Street; 703–548–9000). When the nation's monuments are lit up, D.C. never looked so good. You can even get off in Georgetown to shop, then return on the next boat. (Tours are available April through October and cost $16. They depart Tuesday through Friday at 11:30 A.M. and 1:30, 3:30, 7:30, and 9:30 P.M.;

Tour boats provide transit to and unusual views of Washington, D.C., Georgetown, and Mount Vernon.

Saturday 11:30 A.M. and 1:30, 3:30, 5:30, 7:30, and 9:30 P.M.; Sunday 11:30 A.M. and 1:30, 3:30, and 5:30 P.M. The schedule may expand to include hourly trips in the peak season.)

DAY 2

Morning

BREAKFAST: At your B&B, it's likely to be a continental selection, enough to get you started for a short stroll toward the waterfront.

I like to think of the **Torpedo Factory Art Center** (105 North Union Street; 703–838–4565; www.torpedofactory.org) as a shopping mall for the soul. More than 160 juried artists, artisans, and craftspeople work in studio spaces created in this onetime U.S. Navy torpedo factory, built 1918–19. At any given time you're likely to find the artist in residence—part of the deal for the choice studio space is a commitment to interact with visitors, so you'll be able to discuss their works or commission one. Many artists are there a lot anyway, especially the jewelers who do custom work (this is wedding-ring nirvana). Or browse through watercolors, acrylics, dolls, art clothing, musical instruments, collage, photography, glass, ceramic, enamel, and more. You could take classes, too. (Open every day except major holidays, 10:00 A.M.–5:00 P.M.)

Stroll up Cameron Street to the side entrance of **Carlyle House and Historic Park** (121 North Fairfax Street; 703–549–2997), a key site in leading up to U.S. independence. On April 14, 1755, General Edward Braddock, before his ill-fated march west (see Eastern Escape 1), met here with five royal governors of His Majesty's colonies about paying for the war. They recommended what would be the first colonial tax, which, without representation, was hardly well accepted. Things started coming to a head on July 18, 1774, when Virginia leaders like George Washington and George Mason met here and called for an end to trade with England. The rest, as they say. . . . You can stroll around the garden, then take a house tour, offered every half hour. (Admission is $4.00. Open Tuesday through Saturday 10:00 A.M.–5:00 P.M., Sunday noon–5:00 P.M.)

Continue up Cameron to the oldest church in town, indeed one of the oldest in the nation. **Christ Church** (118 North Washington Street; 703–549–1450), a modest country church built 1767–73, includes the pew of George Washington. Robert E. Lee (another local boy) also attended. (Contributions accepted. Open Monday through Saturday 9:00 A.M.–4:00 P.M., Sunday 2:00–4:30 P.M.)

LUNCH: Stroll back down Cameron a bit to the popular **Gadsby's Tavern** (138 North Royal Street; 703–548–1288). It's a bit on the touristy side, but the period food, clothing, and atmosphere give you the full historic Old Town experience. The original tavern (now the adjoining museum, 703–838–4242) was built in 1770, while the "new" building dates to 1792. (Open Monday through Saturday, for lunch 11:30 A.M.–3:00 P.M., dinner 5:30–10:00 P.M., Sunday brunch 11:00 A.M.–3:00 P.M. Reservations are recommended.)

Afternoon

Ready to visit George Washington at home? **Mount Vernon Estate & Gardens** (703–780–2000; www.mountvernon.org), the nation's second most visited home (after the White House—which, by the way, George never lived in), is just an 8-mile drive away, but first take a quick detour up King Street to see the **George Washington Masonic National Memorial** (Mount Vernon; 703–683–2007) at Callahan Drive. Head to U.S. 1 and go south to the Mount Vernon Highway—there are plenty of signs. The *Miss Christin* also sails regularly from the Alexandria waterfront (703–684–0580; $22 includes Mount Vernon admission).

Various other trips in this book look at George Washington the surveyor, the soldier, the land speculator, the war hero, and the president, but here you'll meet George Washington the farmer, the livestock breeder, the athlete, the husband, the stepfather, and, yes, the slave owner. The 500-acre site includes continuous tours of the mansion he built up, plus the new George Washington Museum, four gardens, four acres of farmland, an archaeology area, a gift shop (new in 2001), and more than a dozen outbuildings, including a reconstructed "necessary". Generally, you can roam the grounds as you please (note that there are some steep hills), but there are also several walking tours offered April through October on the gardens, on slave life, and on the funeral processions. Both President and Mrs. Washington are buried here; there's a wreath-laying ceremony every day (in season) at 10:00 A.M. (Admission is $9.00. Open April through August, 8:00 A.M.–5:00 P.M.; March, September, and October, 9:00 A.M.–5:00 P.M.; November through February, 9:00 A.M.–4:00 P.M.)

Relax back in Old Town in **Waterfront Park** at the foot of Prince Street, a pleasant place to sit and watch the Potomac. You can also take a look at the area's newest historical addition, the **Shipbuilder Monument** (installed spring 2001), celebrating the two centuries of shipyards here, from 1752 to 1954. Thus inspired, let's head back to the heart of town for seafood.

DINNER: There are more touristy places offering seafood, but the best is at the relatively modest **Landini Brothers Restaurant** (115 King Street; 703–836–8404), known for great Italian food in a cozy room with old stone walls and a small bar near the window. The carpaccio and osso buco are also noteworthy. (Open Monday through Saturday 11:00 A.M.–11:30 P.M., Sunday 4:00–10:30 P.M.)

Evening

Follow the crowds or your own whims for jazz at the **King Street Blues Bar** (112 North Saint Asaph Street; 703–836–8800), dancing at **Bullfeathers** (112 King Street; 703–836–8088), Irish music at **Murphy's Irish Pub** (713 King

Street; 703–548–1717), piano bar at the **Morrison House** (116 South Alfred Street; 703–838–8000), a modern range of music in a 1700s building at the **George Washington Tavern** (6 King Street; 703–549–2341), and lots more.

DAY 3

Morning

BREAKFAST: Another simple repast at your B&B.

On a Sunday morning the Beltway should be less insane than the last time you saw it, and it's less than an hour to **Baltimore.** Head south from Alexandria and take the Beltway east (outer loop) across the Potomac. At Greenbelt, leave the Beltway for the Baltimore-Washington Parkway. Near Baltimore, head north on I–95 to exit 55 (Key Highway). At the bottom of the ramp, turn left onto Key Highway, and continue about 1.5 miles to the corner of Key Highway and Covington Street. Turn left onto Covington and into the parking lot ($3.00 per day), then cross the street—you'll see the giant whirligig—to one of the most unusual art museums you'll ever encounter.

The **American Visionary Museum of Art** (800 Key Highway; 410–244–1900; www.avam.org) is devoted to the work of self-taught artists—"outsider artists" considered fanatic geniuses by some, gifted folk artists by others, and complete wackos by more than a few (think Howard Finster, but more so). There's not much in the way of subtlety, whether in color or in subject, and the technique—depending upon your point of view—is crude or breathtaking in its power. Perhaps both. Opened in 1995, the museum has grown from its main building to include several more indoor and outdoor art spaces. The central facility, a three-story elliptical former industrial building, builds single-theme art exhibits in its six galleries. *Treasures of the Soul: Who Is Rich?* continues through September 2, 2001. Outside are the Sculpture Plaza, home to that famous whirligig; the Tall Sculpture Barn, whose 45-foot ceilings accommodate some of the more heroic efforts by visionary artists; and the Wildflower Garden, the setting for the meditation chapel and wedding altar. (Admission is $6.00. Open Tuesday through Sunday 10:00 A.M.–6:00 P.M.)

BRUNCH: Take the elevator in the main building to the top floor for **Joy America Cafe** (410–244–6500) for a fabulous brunch that vies with the museum in creativity and daring, using variations on American cuisine, from southwestern U.S. to Latin and South America. (Open Tuesday through Saturday 11:00 A.M.–10:00 P.M., Sunday brunch 11:00 A.M.–4:00 P.M.)

Afternoon

You're on the southern edge of the **Inner Harbor.** You can walk around the large C to the various attractions, or take the **Baltimore Water Taxi** (410–563–3901 or 800–658–8947; www.thewatertaxi.com), shuttle boats that scoot around to the dozens of attractions in the Inner and Outer Harbors from more than a dozen landings. A $5.00 fare lets you ride all day and includes (in season) a trolley to **Fort McHenry** (see "There's More"). May through September the "taxis" run about every fifteen to eighteen minutes from most landings (Monday through Thursday 10:00 A.M.–11:00 P.M., Friday and Saturday 10:00 A.M.–midnight, Sunday 10:00 A.M.–9:00 P.M.). Service out of season tends to be more sporadic, as much as a forty-minute wait, and runs only until 8:00 P.M. weekdays in April and October, till 6:00 P.M. all days November through March. There are different routes, so you need to tell the pilot where you're going when you board. Taxis don't run during storms.

Or take a stroll past Inner Harbor attractions like **Harborplace** (410–332–4191 or 800–HARBOR–1; www.harborplace.com), a shopping-dining complex of more than 200 shops in three buildings: The Gallery (across Pratt), Pratt Street Pavilion, and Light Street Pavilion. They're all connected by sky-walks. (Open Monday through Saturday 10:00 A.M.–9:00 P.M., Sunday 11:00 A.M.–7:00 P.M.)

As you wind your way along Pratt Street (the top of the C), it's hard not to notice the ships ahead. One of them might be the topsail schooner **Pride of Baltimore II** (410–539–1151), a replica of the 1812-era Baltimore Clippers and now Maryland's "goodwill ambassador," spending much of its time traveling the world. Of slightly more recent vintage is the USS **Constellation** (Pier 1, 301 East Pratt Street; 410–539–1797; www.constellation.org), a 1,400-ton, 179-foot sloop (built 1854) and the only surviving Civil War–era naval vessel and all-sail warship built by the Navy. (Admission is $6.50. Open May 1 through October 14, 10:00 A.M.–6:00 P.M., with extended hours June through August; October 15 through April 30, open 9:00 A.M.–4:00 P.M.)

There are three more ships as part of the **Baltimore Maritime Museum** (Pier 3, East Pratt Street; 410–396–3854 or 410–396–3853; www.baltomaritimemuseum.org). The USS *Torsk* submarine, a National Historic Landmark, sank the last two Japanese warships lost in World War II. The USCG cutter *Taney* is the last survivor of Pearl Harbor. The lightship *Chesapeake* was a "floating lighthouse" at the mouth of the Chesapeake Bay. (Admission $5.00. Open spring through fall, Sunday through Thursday 10:00 A.M.–5:30 P.M., Friday and Saturday 10:00 A.M.–6:30 P.M. In winter open Friday through Sunday 10:30 A.M.–5:00 P.M. The ticket booth closes half an hour before the ships do.)

The Maritime Museum's ticket booth is right in front of the **National Aquarium in Baltimore** (Pier 3 at 501 East Pratt Street; 410–576–3800; www.aqua.org), home to more than 10,000 water critters: more than 600 species of fish, mammals, birds, reptiles, and amphibians. You'll walk up a gently sloping spiral up, then down five levels (elevators also available) for most exhibits, from stingrays to puffins, but the seals have their own home near the entrance, and you can check out the dolphin show in a separate building. And visit the newest addition: an Amazon River forest. (Admission $15. Open March through June and September through October, 9:00 A.M.–5:00 P.M. every day, till 8:00 P.M. on Friday; July and August, every day 9:00 A.M.–8:00 P.M.; November through February, 10:00 A.M.–5:00 P.M. every day, till 8:00 P.M. Friday. Visitors can continue touring for two hours after closing.)

As you leave the aquarium and walk over the pedestrian bridge, you'll probably notice the crowds to your right heading into the **Power Plant** (601 East Pratt Street; 410–752–5444). The large remodeled industrial building is now an entertainment complex with a **Hard Rock Cafe** (410–347–7625) and the first **ESPN Zone** (410–685–3776) among others. (Bars tend to stay open till 2 A.M.)

Pick up your car and return to I–95, driving south to I–70 and west to exit 49 to U.S. 40A; turn left, toward Braddock Heights, and in Boonsboro turn left onto MD 34 toward **Shepherdstown,** the oldest town in West Virginia (settled 1730). About an hour and a half after leaving Baltimore, the first right after crossing the Potomac River Bridge brings you to the **Bavarian Inn and Lodge** (off WV 480; 304–876–2551; www.bavarianinnwv.com).

DINNER: The Greystone mansion, part of the Bavarian's twelve-acre country hideaway, includes several tastefully decorated dining rooms that serve a sort of German-fusion cuisine, with several traditional dishes and a wide variety of Continent-influenced game and steak dishes. The curried crab soup is heavenly. The wine choices are vast, with several superb selections for those who just want a glass. (Reservations are recommended. Breakfast is served every day 7:00–10:00 A.M. Lunch, Monday through Saturday 11:30 A.M.–2:00 P.M. Dinner, Monday through Friday 5:00–9:00 P.M., Saturday 4:00–9:00 P.M., Sunday noon–8:00 P.M.)

You may just decide to stay in the lodge for an extra day of play, or take the three–hour drive home: Head into downtown Shepardstown on WV 480, then turn right onto WV 45. In Martinsburg turn right onto WV 9 west. Head north on I–81 to I–70 west and home via the Pennsylvania Turnpike.

THERE'S MORE

Del Ray/Potomac West. A little more than 2 miles north west of Old Town is the back-in-fashion neighborhood of Del Ray, aka Potomac West, with about thirty unusual shops and restaurants, mainly along the 2000 block of Mount Vernon Avenue (703–838–4200 or 800–388–9119; www.funside. com).

Civil War. Alexandria was the longest-occupied territory during the war— almost the entire duration—but its heart was in the Confederacy. Notable sites include the boyhood home of Robert E. Lee (703–548–8454) near the Ramsay House, the Ford Ward Museum and Historic Site (703–838–4848) of changing Civil War exhibits, and the statue *Appomattox* at Prince and South Washington, where the 700 members of the 17th Virginia Volunteer Infantry left to fight for the Confederacy on May 24, 1861, when Union troops occupied the area. A new brochure for a self-guided Civil War–themed tour is available (888–CIVIL–WAR).

Alexandria Seaport Foundation's Seaport Center. A floating museum between the Torpedo Factory and Founders Park includes boats to rent (703–684–0569).

Lexington Market. A few blocks north of Baltimore's Inner Harbor is the nation's oldest public market (founded in 1782), featuring hundreds of independent food vendors selling seafood, meat, prepared foods, and more on a 2-city-block complex. Look for the big bull's head. Closed Sunday (410–685–6169; www.lexingtonmarket.com).

Fort McHenry National Monument. O, say can you see—the original of this restored star-shaped Baltimore fort was the site of the War of 1812 battle where the star-spangled banner inspired Francis Scott Key to write his famous poem (410–962–4299).

Maryland Science Center. Three floors of interactive family-oriented exhibits, plus planetarium laser shows and an Imax theater on the Inner Harbor (410–685–5225; www.mdsci.org).

Top of the World. Get the eagle's-eye view of Baltimore from the twenty-seventh floor of the World Trade Center in Inner Harbor (410–837–4515).

Oriole Park at Camden Yards. Inspired in part by Forbes Field. Tours depart regularly from the Baseball Store in the former B&B Warehouse on Eutaw Street. Game tickets can be hard to come by (410–685–9800; www.theorioles.com).

PSINet Stadium. Tours every Saturday 10:00 A.M.–2:00 P.M., except when there's an event. Single-game tickets are available, but Raven-Steeler games sell out very very quickly (410–261–RAVE [7283]; www.ravenszone.net).

The Dr. Samuel D. Harris National Museum of Dentistry. A short walk from Camden Yards is the world's only dental museum, the final resting place of George Washington's false teeth (no, they're not wood), antique dental instruments, and wisdom to help you understand and keep your own pearly whites (410–706–0600; www.dentalmuseum.umaryland.edu).

SPECIAL EVENTS

April. A highlight of the Baltimore Riverfront Festival is the American Visionary Art Museum's Kinetic Sculpture Race, in which "Kinetinauts" vie for the Mediocre Award, the Next to the Last Award, and prizes for art and engineering (410–244–1900; www.avam.org).

May. Memorial Day Jazz Festival in Old Town's Jones Point Park (888–738–2764; www.funside.com).

June–October. First Thursdays in Alexandria's Potomac West area, many shops and restaurants stay open 6:00–9:00 P.M. with special food and wine tastings, music, events, and more (703–838–4200 or 800–388–9119; www.funside.com).

September. Tour of Alexandria Historic Homes. Get a full view of local architecture and lifestyles (888–738–2764; www.funside.com).

Thanksgiving weekend–mid-December. Mount Vernon by Candlelight tours include the rarely seen third floor, plus a bonfire, caroling, historic characters, and hot cider and cookies (703–780–2000; www.mountvernon.org).

OTHER RECOMMENDED RESTAURANTS AND LODGING

Alexandria

Virginia Beverage Company. Happy hour (Monday through Friday 5:00–7:00 P.M.) features not just lower prices on house ales and beers but also 10 percent off all entrees, which tend toward the spicy Cajun (702–684–5397).

Bilbo Baggins. Good eclectic cuisine, a romantic setting, and an extensive wine list including wines by the glass (703–683–0300).

Chart House. Great view, a nice wine sampler. The menu is limited but good, with great coconut shrimp (703–684–5080).

Il Porto Ristorante. Close to Landini Brothers, with a smaller menu but almost as good (703–836–8833).

La Bergerie. Alexandria's best-known (and pricey) traditional French restaurant (703–683–1007; www.labergerie.com).

Geranio Ristorante. This small eclectic family-run Italian restaurant has a nicely lit, intimate atmosphere and some imaginative dishes (703–548–0088).

Warehouse Bar & Grill. Fantastic she-crab soup, creative menu. Pricey for dinner (703–683–6868).

The Mount Vernon Inn. Lunch and dinner just outside the gates of George Washington's home (703–780–0011).

Morrison House. An intimate European-style hotel right in Old Town (703–838–8000 or 800–367–0800; www.morrisonhouse.com).

Hilton Alexandria Old Town. A new luxury hotel—opened February 2000—near Metro stop (703–837–0440).

Holiday Inn Select Old Town. This is the only sizable hotel right in Old Town (703–549–6080 or 800–368–5047).

Baltimore

Little Havana. A casual Cuban bar and restaurant with lots of chorizo, plantains, spices, and vegetarian specialties like spicy black bean cakes, plus a breezy waterfront setting (410–837–9903).

Ban Thai. North of Inner Harbor, enjoy great chicken satay and just-hot-enough chicken Panang with red curry and crushed peanuts, in understated decor (410–727–7971).

Corks. New American food, but the place is best known for wine: all American and sensibly priced at $11.00 over wholesale (410–752–3810).

Victor's Cafe. Near the new Marriott by Pier 6. The food is imaginative, and it seems even better when you're out on the water with a good view of the harbor (410–244–1722).

Paolo's. Combines northern Italian with California sensibility for fresh salmon and wood-fired pizza (410–539–7060).

Burke's Cafe. An old-fashioned watering hole with steak, seafood, and late hours (410–752–4189).

McCormick & Schmick's. This popular seafood restaurant is in the same complex as the Pier 5 Hotel (410–234–1300; www.mccormickandschmicks.com).

Pier 5 Hotel. A waterfront boutique hotel with sixty-five rooms and the Dish Cafe for breakfast (410–539–2000 or 877–207–9047; www.harbormagic.com).

Brookshire Suites. A European-style Inner Harbor hotel with complimentary American-style hot breakfast in the rooftop Cloud Club. Ninety-seven rooms, including seventy suites (410–625–1300 or 877–207–9046; www.harbormagic.com).

FOR MORE INFORMATION

Alexandria Convention and Visitors Association, 221 King Street, Alexandria, VA 22314; 703–838–4200 or 800–388–9119; www.funside.com.

Baltimore Area Convention and Visitors Association, 100 Light Street, 12th Floor, Baltimore, MD 21202; 410–659–7300 or 800–343–3468; www.baltimore.org.

INTO THE
HEARTLAND

ESCAPES

Westmoreland and Somerset Counties

HISTORIC HIGHWAYS

---

1 NIGHT

History • Art • Parks • Glass

Why make war when you can make a road? What became part of U.S. 30 is the real reason why the British were eventually victorious at Pittsburgh's Point and, at least in part, why we don't speak French. The redcoats never "captured" Fort Duquesne; the French abandoned and burned it after General Forbes started building his supply road from Bedford (see Eastern Escape 2). Realizing that the road would enable the British to easily resupply and reinforce their troops, the French gave up their idea of an empire in the West. The Forbes Trail, as it became known, was the major route west, eventually becoming part of the Philadelphia–Pittsburgh Turnpike, then the Lincoln Highway, U.S. 30, the nation's first coast-to-coast road. But back in pioneer days, many settlers heading west actually preferred Glades Pike, a modest but still very useful road today as PA 31. You'll find other historic roads in this very scenic part of the country.

This is another adventure in your own backyard, with just about every site doable as a day trip, and many gems that you might not be aware of: beautiful regional museums, reconstructed pioneer sites, theater, and, of course, glorious scenery.

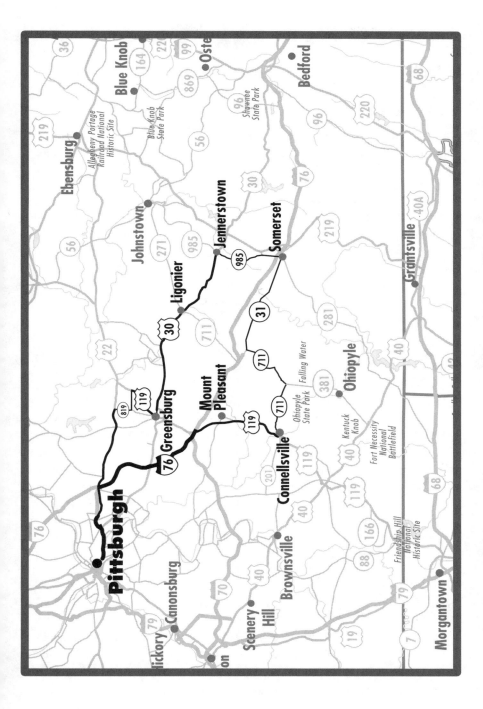

DAY 1

Morning

A quick trip east on U.S. 22 brings you to Monroeville and the **Park Classic Diner** (3893 William Penn Highway, Monroeville; 412–373–6395).

BREAKFAST: Stoke up on eggs, pancakes, and pastries baked in house at this recreation of an old-time diner. (Open 6:00 A.M.–11:00 P.M. seven days a week.)

Continue east on U.S. 22 into Murrysville to Five Points, turn right onto PA 819 and drive south for 4 miles, turn left onto SR 1032 leading into **Hanna's Town** (724–836–1800; www.wchspa.com), then left at the crossroads, and finally a quick left into the parking lot. The eighteenth-century town, the first county seat west of the Allegheny Mountains and the original seat of Westmoreland County (which back then included most of today's Allegheny County), was destroyed on July 13, 1782, as one of the last acts of the American Revolution. The reconstructed town is now open for tours by volunteers in period dress. You can visit the Courthouse-Tavern, jail, log palisade fort, and a log cabin with period furniture, as well as archaeological excavations of the original site and demonstrations of colonial crafts. (Admission is $3.00. Open Memorial day through Labor Day, Tuesday through Saturday 10:00 A.M.–4:00 P.M., Sunday 1:00–4:00 P.M.; weekends only in May, September, and October.)

Turn right out of the parking lot onto SR 1055; at the next crossroads, turn right onto U.S. 119 to head into Greensburg. Turn right up the hill on Main Street to the **Westmoreland Museum of American Art** (221 North Main Street; 724–837–1500; www.wmuseumaa.org). The recently remodeled two-story museum groups artworks by theme, with the nineteenth-century landscapes providing an interesting "before" to the industrial scenes' "after." You'll also see portraits, furniture, and examples of such famous local glass companies as Jeannette and Westmoreland. (Admission is $3.00. Open Wednesday through Sunday 11:00 A.M.–5:00 P.M., till 9:00 P.M. Thursday. Closed Monday, Tuesday, and most holidays.)

Go back down the hill on Main Street to Pittsburgh Street (PA 130), follow the signs to U.S. 30, and head east out of town, past Latrobe—home of Saint Vincent College (summer camp for the Pittsburgh Steelers) and Latrobe Brewing Company (sorry, no tours of the home of Rolling Rock Beer, though you can see the visitors center; see "There's More"), and birthplace of Arnold Palmer, Fred Rogers, and the banana split. Loyalhanna Creek splits

Find some familiar faces at the Westmoreland Museum of American Art.

U.S. 30 for perhaps its most scenic stretch in the country, a valley through Chestnut Ridge. Soon after you pass Idlewild Park, home of *Mister Rogers' Neighborhood of Make-Believe,* you enter **Ligonier,** a French and Indian War fort town now known for its upscale shopping in one of the last bastions of true preppiedom. Where U.S. 30 meets PA 711, turn left onto South Market Street and drive 3 little blocks to the center of town, aka the Diamond.

LUNCH: Lupe and Lucina Barragan were enticed to come to western Pennsylvania in 1999, and then to their current location in Ligonier because of the authenticity and quality of their Mexican food; check it out at **Casa Chapala** (724–238–7399). Climb the steps at 122 North Market Street for an eclectic collection of architectural artifacts, *pollo ala crema,* and a very spicy *mole ranchero.* (Open Tuesday through Thursday 11:00 A.M.–8:30 P.M., Friday and Saturday 11:00 A.M.–10:00 P.M., Sunday noon–8:30 P.M.)

Afternoon

There are dozens of shops clustered around the Diamond, selling clothing (including great resale shops for women, children and, no kidding, equestrians; check out **Harmony's Attic** (724–238–3230), 110 North Fairfield Street, for antiques and a surprising selection of needlework supplies with four shops. A must-stop is **G Squared Gallery** (724–238–4106) at 212 East Main Street, featuring top-of-the-line crafts and contemporary art. My favorite place is the **Toy Box** (724–238–6233; www.toyboxligonier.com), with six rooms of fun in a narrow three floors in a Civil War–era building—and one of the few shops open on Sunday. Most are open Monday through Saturday only, 10:00 or 11:00 A.M.–5:00 P.M.

It's a short stroll down Market Street to **Fort Ligonier** (216 South Market Street; 724–238–9701; www.fortligonier.org), a full-scale reconstructed fort. The original was damaged in 1758 when the French, fearing the imminent attack of General Forbes, decided to go on the offensive, but lost—subsequently abandoning Fort Duquesne. A second fort, built to withstand attacks from Native Americans in 1777, later fell into disrepair. Get into the period at the museum, featuring eighteenth-century paintings and a video about the fort's strategic importance and history, before visiting the fort itself. (Admission is $6.00. Open May 1 through October 31, Monday through Saturday 10:00 A.M.–4:30 P.M., Sunday noon–4:30 P.M.)

It's walkable but tricky to cross U.S. 30, so you may want to drive the quarter mile to the **Southern Alleghenies Museum of Art at Ligonier** (1 Boucher Lane; 724–238–6015; http://sama-sfc.org). This tiny museum in a replica farmhouse features many of the same traveling exhibits as the other museum branches (see Heartland Escape 2), but is the permanent home of the Walter Carlyle Shaw Paperweight Collection: 169 paperweights spanning 150 years of craftsmanship. (Donations accepted. Open Tuesday through Friday 10:00 A.M.–5:00 P.M., Saturday and Sunday 1:00–5:00 P.M. Closed Monday.)

Continue east on U.S. 30, up and over Laurel Mountain, and at Jennerstown turn right onto PA 985, which runs into PA 601 (the Old Somerset Pike from the 1840s), then heads south as it turns into Center Avenue in downtown **Somerset,** the seat of the state's highest county, known as the Rooftop Garden of Pennsylvania.

DINNER: Chef-owner Scott Schumucker at the **Pine Grill** (800 North Center Avenue; 814–445–2102) had worked around the nation, but he wanted to come back to his home town and cook up creative entrees using local produce. (Open Monday through Saturday 10:30 A.M.–10:00 P.M., Sunday 11:00 A.M.–9:00 P.M.)

LODGING: Practically across the street is the **Bayberry Inn** (611 North Center Avenue, Bayberry; 814–445–8471), where owners Marilyn and Bob Lohr can fill you in on the best places to pick up the 70-mile **Laurel Highlands Hiking Trail** and on the attractions of nearby state parks **Laurel Hill** (814–445–7725), **Laurel Ridge** (724–455–3744), **Laurel Mountain** (724–238–9860), **Linn Run** (724–238–6623), and **Kooser** (814–445–8673).

Evening

Feeling musical, or comical, or thrillable? Backtrack to **Jennerstown** and head to the **Mountain Playhouse** (814–629–9201; www.mountainplayhouse. com) for an evening of professional theater June through October, just a courtyard away from the **Green Gables Restaurant** (814–629–9201), filled with works of art as well as lamb chops, trout, pork loin, and steaks. (Saturday 8:00 P.M. theater tickets cost $17–26.) Still peckish on the way back? Stop in the classic **Summit Diner** (791–795 North Center Avenue; 814–445–7154) for its Midnight Special: two eggs, sausage or bacon, potatoes, and toast for $2.99, served 11:00 P.M.–11:00 A.M.

DAY 2

Morning

BREAKFAST: You'll need just a light breakfast of juice, coffee or tea, and homemade muffins at the Bayberry Inn.

The next stop is to take a look at the region's newest ski area. Sorta. Long after they closed, the Wildcat trails clandestinely attracted serious skiers to the slopes of General Richard King Mellon's once-private resort, which he opened in the 1930s. That makes the **Laurel Mountain Ski Resort** (724–238–9860 or 877–SKI–LAUR; www.skilaurelmountain.com) the area's oldest, but with new management sprucing up the place and reopening in December 1999, it's also the newest. And it's the highest in this part of the state, with a 900-foot vertical drop. The killer double-black Lower Wildcat is one of the steepest slopes you'll find anywhere. To get there, head back to U.S. 30 and west to the top of Laurel Mountain; watch for the turnoff to your left, then head up the 2-plus-mile Summit Road through the woods to enjoy the view from the lodge in this "upside-down" four-seasons resort (you ski, mountain board, whatever, down the hill, then ride one of the lifts back up to the lodge) on 493 acres in Laurel Mountain State Park. The lodge includes the Whiteout Cafe and the Wildcat Lounge, which features local bands most Saturday nights and some Friday nights.

Return to PA 985 and, 4 miles before you get to town, watch on your right for the **Somerset Historical Center** (10649 Somerset Pike; 814–445–6077; www.somersetcounty.com/historicalcenter). The complex of indoor exhibits, antique farm machinery, and both original and reconstructed historic buildings traces the change from hand farming on the eighteenth-century frontier to commercial agriculture in the industrialized twentieth century. (Admission is $3.50. Open Wednesday through Saturday 9:00 A.M.–5:00 P.M., Sunday noon–5:00 P.M. Closed Monday, Tuesday, and holidays except Memorial Day, July 4, and Labor Day.)

Resume your westward course into Somerset, and take a moment to admire the **Somerset County Court House,** built in 1906 of Indiana limestone with a distinctive copper-sheathed dome that you can see for miles (guided tours available weekdays, 814–443–1434). Turn right onto Main Street (PA 31 or Glades Pike) and wind your way out of town and into the countryside for about 6 miles.

LUNCH: One of the most popular big feeds for travelers in these parts is the **Oakhurst Tea Room** (2409 Glades Pike; 814–443–2897), an expansive but inexpensive buffet from the pre-salad-bar days of country cooking. If you're lucky, there will be a tub of maple butter to slather onto homemade rolls. (Open Tuesday through Saturday, lunch buffet 11:00 A.M.–3:00 P.M., dinner 4:00–9:00 P.M.; Sunday brunch 11:00 A.M.–2:00 P.M., dinner till 8:00 P.M.)

Afternoon

As you drive along Glades Pike, you'll pass the entrances of two of the most popular ski resorts in this end of the state, **Seven Springs** and **Hidden Valley** (see "There's More"), as well as entrances to Kooser State Park and other natural areas. When you approach Donegal, PA 31 joins with PA 711 (historically the Scenic Byway). Stay with PA 711 as it climbs up and through Forbes State Forest (why do you think they call it scenic?), and brings you into **Connellsville,** then turns into Crawford Avenue. Turn right at what looks like (and is) an old railroad station, now the home of **Youghiogheny Station Glass and Gallery** (900 West Crawford Avenue; 724–628–0332) and an official National Historic Place. There's a stunning collection of Tiffany-style glass, not just finished pieces like vases, lamps, and even windows but also the basic materials for artists or those who want to be artists. (Open Monday through Saturday 10:00 A.M.–5:00 P.M., till 7:00 P.M. Thursday; and Sunday noon–4:00 P.M.)

Watch for the right turn onto U.S. 119 and head north just a few miles to the Scottdale exit and PA 819. Turn left at the end of the ramp and follow PA 819 to the right turn for **West Overton Village** (724–887–7910), the only pre–Civil War village still intact in Pennsylvania, and the birthplace of steel and coke magnate Henry Clay Frick. Still being developed, the forty-five-acre site includes nineteen buildings, only a few of which are presentable for now. Tours start in the Overholt Museum, the onetime distillery where Frick's grandfather made Old Overholt Whiskey and his fortune. You can watch a short video on the coal and coke process, and on the Frick and Overholt families, then go on to visit the largest brick barn in Pennsylvania, a springhouse, a garden, and the Overholt Homestead, where scenes from the TV movie of August Wilson's *The Piano Lesson* were shot. (Admission is $3.00. Open May 1 through October 15, Tuesday through Saturday 10:00 A.M.–4:00 P.M., Sunday 1:00–5:00 P.M.)

Return east on PA 819, but cross over U.S. 119 and continue into **Mount Pleasant.** At the Dough Boy statue in the middle of town, turn right; you're again on PA 31. Go down the hill and up, watch for the sign to turn right at Factory Street, then drive a short block to the **L. E. Smith Glass Company** (900 Liberty Street, Mount Pleasant; 724–547–3544 or 800–752–4846 or 800–537–6484; www.lesmithglass.com). You've seen those covered "turkey" bowls that Martha Stewart is so fond of, or the "chicken" egg plate that was an Easter hit in Williams-Sonoma? This is where they come from, along with hundreds of other pressed-glass servingware and gift items made the same way since 1907. Make sure you go downstairs to the "preferred seconds" room; you may score some terrific bargains. (Tours are available weekdays. Open Monday through Saturday 9:00 A.M.–5:00 P.M., Sunday noon–5:00 P.M. Closed weekends from January through March 31 and major holidays.)

Return to PA 31, and in little more than half a mile you'll easily see the **Lenox** factory (724–547–9555 or 800–423–8946; www.lenox.com) to your right. As you head up the driveway, you'll see to your left the Lenox China Store, which features pretty much the full range of Lenox dinnerware and many gift pieces, all first quality. And to your right, you'll see a much larger parking lot and signs indicating the entrance to the factory outlet store and clearance center, which features Dansk and Gorham as well as Lenox seconds.

True bargains aren't so plentiful, but they can be found. (Open Monday through Saturday 9:00 A.M.–6:00 P.M., Sunday 10:00 A.M.–6:00 P.M.)

DINNER: Head back to PA 31, continue east for about 2 miles, and turn left onto PA 982; on your right is the **Barn** (Laurelville; 724–547–4500; www.thebarnrestaurant.com). It really is an old barn, but done up with piz-zazz—and crystal chandeliers, paintings, tapestries, and a modern-classic approach to such dishes as pork loin and plum duckling. If you're homesick for Ben Gross onion rings or mushrooms, enjoy them as appetizers. (Open Tuesday through Thursday 11:30 A.M.–8-ish, Friday through Sunday 11:30 A.M.–10-ish, Sunday brunch 11:30 A.M.–2:00 P.M. Reservations can be made online.)

Evening

The Barn features live music Sunday evening from 5:30 to 9:00, so sit back and enjoy your dessert and coffee, because you're only about an hour from home via the Pennsylvania Turnpike. (Go west on PA 31 to U.S. 119, then head north to the New Stanton interchange.)

THERE'S MORE

Desert Storm 14th Quartermaster Detachment Memorial. No Allied unit suffered greater casualties during Operation Desert Storm than this Greensburg-based corps, which lost thirteen soldiers and forty-three wounded—81 percent of its sixty-nine soldiers—to a Scud missile attack. The monument includes a life-sized bronze of one male and one female soldier, on Armory Road; follow signs to Greensburg Central Catholic from U.S. 119. In Hempfield Township.

Hidden Valley Four Seasons Resort. The 2,000-acre resort includes downhill and cross-country skiing, mountain biking, indoor and outdoor swimming, and the 3½-star Golf Club (814-443–8444), plus various types of lodgings, not a hotel as such (814–443–8000 or 800–458–0175; www. hiddenvalleyresort.com).

Seven Springs Mountain Resort. Self-billed as Pennsylvania's largest year-round resort, it features snow tubing as well as downhill skiing, snow-boarding, sleigh rides, and such indoor fun as bowling, racquetball, and skating, plus a 3½-star golf course (814–352–7777, ext. 7142). It's also the home of the noted restaurant Helen's (ext. 7827) and various other eateries and shops, plus live entertainment (814–352–7777 or 800–452–2223; www.7springs.com).

Bushy Run Battlefield. Colonel Henry Bouquet's victory over several Native American nations in Pontiac's Rebellion of 1763 opened up the area for white settlers. The visitors center sponsors nature and history programs. It's found on PA 993, near Harrison City (724–527–5584).

Latrobe Brewing Company Rolling Rock Gift Shop & Visitor's Center. You can buy Rolling Rock caps and tchotchkes, but not the beer. In Latrobe (724–539–3394).

Saint Vincent Summer Theatre. Saint Vincent College students and Pittsburgh actors present light comedies June through August. A cabaret follows each performance (724–537–8900).

SPECIAL EVENTS

January. Icefest in Ligonier features two days of fun and ice carving (724–238–4200; www.ligonier.com).

July. Steelers' training camp opens at Saint Vincent College. Fans can watch morning and afternoon practice sessions Monday through Saturday for free during the first two weeks to collect autographs and practice clichés for the season (www.steelers.com).

May–September. Hannastown Antiques & Collectibles Sale every second Sunday of the month features more than 300 dealers and parking for 2,000 cars. Food booths (724–836–1800).

September. The Masters Wildlife Art Show features top wildlife artists from around the nation. Ligonier Valley YMCA (724–238–7560).

Mountain Craft Days at the Somerset Historical Center features more than 125 craftspeople demonstrating traditional crafts (814–445–6077; www.somersetcounty.com/historicalcenter).

October. Fort Ligonier Days include a re-creation of the 1758 battle in a three-day festival (724–238–9701; www.fortligonier.org).

November–January. The Annual Holiday Toy and Train Exhibition at the Westmoreland Museum of American Art showcases antique and modern toys and miniature trains both from the museum's collection and on loan from private collections (724–837–1500; www.wmuseumaa.org).

OTHER RECOMMENDED RESTAURANTS AND LODGING

DiSalvo's Station Restaurant. Italian specialties and wine by the glass in a restored railroad station in Latrobe (724–539–0500; www.westernpa. com/disalvos).

Ligonier Tavern. Dine on game, seafood, or a trout hoagie in a historic 1895 home (724–238–4831; www.ligonier.com/tavern).

Brass Duck Restaurant & Lounge. A longtime local favorite of folks from the old-school crowd, found between Ligonier and Donegal. Closed Tuesday (724–593–7413 or 724–593–7440).

Glade Pikes Inn Bed and Breakfast. An 1842 stagecoach stop that's now part of a dairy farm, which includes a winery. In Somerset (814–443–4978 or 800–762–5942).

The Inn at Georgian Place. This mansion built in 1915 by local coal and cattle baron crowns an outlet mall that includes more than fifty stores (814–443–1043).

FOR MORE INFORMATION

Laurel Highlands Visitors Bureau, 120 East Main Street, Ligonier, PA 15658; 724–238–5661 or 800–925–7669; www.laurelhighlands.org.

INTO THE HEARTLAND

The Southern Alleghenies: Altoona and Johnstown

A MOVING EXPERIENCE

1 NIGHT

Trains • Tragedy • Triumph

The beauty of the southern Allegheny Mountains has been attracting vacationers since the nation was young, but their size blocked the path of westward expansion. On this escape you can enjoy their beauty while exploring the two engineering marvels of the nineteenth century that ultimately made westward travel possible. The famous Horseshoe Curve still stands after nearly 150 years. What it replaced, the Allegheny Portage Railroad—though now nearly forgotten—was perhaps even more of a marvel.

It's often boasted that the railroads built this country. And Altoona built the railroads, or at least the biggest and the best of them: the Pennsylvania Railroad, on exhibit in all its glory (and warts) at a new museum.

The mountains offered respite and peace; the valleys, hard work and rapid growth. Johnstown enjoyed both, but it wasn't its might as the nation's largest steel producer in 1873 that led to its place in history, but the fact that this serendipitous combination worked to create America's worst man-made peacetime disaster: the Johnstown Flood. You can try to get your mind around the enormity of this foreseeable tragedy at several key historic sites.

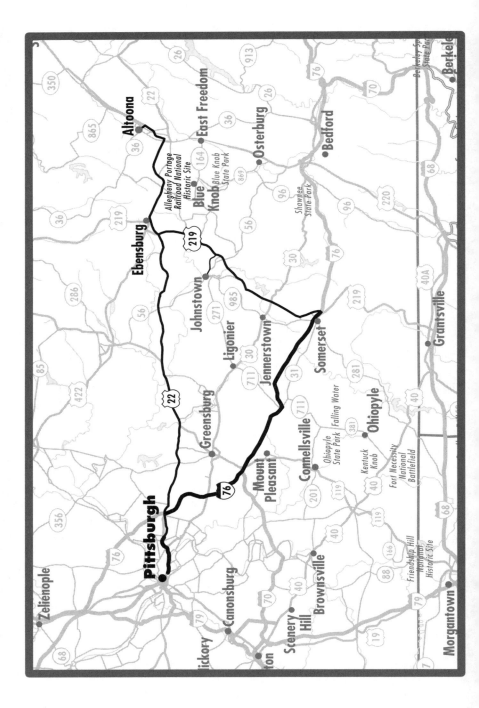

DAY 1

Morning

Head east on U.S. 22, past the suburban sprawl into increasingly rural country. In about an hour and a half, you'll pass the turnoff for the Chestnut Ridge
Golf Club, one of the area's best golf courses. Soon you'll reach the interchange for I–99, which you'll take north; in a few more minutes, exit at 17th
Street. Turn right onto Pleasant Valley Boulevard at the light and watch for the
green sign at **Granny's** (814–942–0491) on the right-hand side of the road at
613 Valley View Boulevard.

BREAKFAST: The weekday breakfast buffet (6:00–11:00 A.M.) features about
ten changing specials, and grows to a brunch array on weekends till 1:00 P.M.,
but you can order breakfast off the menu (including chocolate-chip pancakes)
anytime.

Backtrack to 17th Street (because of one-way streets, you'll need to take a
cross street west to catch Valley View Boulevard heading south), turn right up
the hill, and follow the signs to the **Railroaders Memorial Museum**
(814–946–0834; www.railroadcity.com) at 1300 Ninth Avenue, in the former
railroad station. Three floors of interactive exhibits give you an insider's view
of working on the railroad—warts and all. It was dirty, dangerous work, and
you'll have the chance (in all safety) to see if your skills are up to the test. Learn
how the railroads changed the country in big and little ways (did you know
Standard Time was developed because of the railroads?); if any of your rela-
tives ever worked for the railroad, log on to the "Call Board" database. Railroad buffs aren't the only ones who enjoy the gift shop selection of train-related
videos, books, and toys, or the combo price of $10 for adult admission to both
the museum and the Horseshoe Curve. The museum alone is $8.50. (Open
9:00 A.M.–5:00 P.M. every day.)

Before you turn left onto 17th Street from Ninth Avenue, you'll notice the
Boyer Candy Co. (814–944–9401) on your right. Stop at the outlet store in
back for discounted Mallo Cups and Geoffrey B. chocolates (plus free samples)
between 9:00 A.M. and 5:00 P.M. Tuesday through Saturday. Then head south
on U.S. Business 220 (Pleasant Valley Boulevard, which becomes Plank Road).
Turn right at, and follow the signs along, Logan Boulevard to head even farther into the past: 1849, when iron, not steel, was king, and the railroad hadn't
yet reached Altoona. The **Baker Mansion** (operated by the Blair County Historical Society, 814–942–3912) on Oak Lane, just off Logan, is undergoing

You're right at rail level at one of the world's engineering marvels: the Horseshoe Curve.

restoration but is still magnificent. The Greek Revival mansion still features some of its original decor, including hand-carved oak furnishings that the original owner, Elias Baker, imported from Belgium. (Tours are available Tuesday through Sunday 1:00–3:30 P.M. between Memorial Day and Labor Day; also check for ghost storytelling.)

LUNCH: Return to Logan Boulevard and continue following the signs to Kittanning Point Road (SR 4008) and the **Horseshoe Curve National Historic Landmark** (814–946–0834). Stop first for sandwiches at the **B&C Boxcar** snack bar (814–425–8666).

Afternoon

While you're here at the Curve, find out just how important it was, and how they did it, in a brief film and exhibits. This wonder of the world was built by hand in 1854—building up low spots, cutting down high ones, blasting tunnels through the really big ones—to carry trains over a gradual ascent and descent. Then take the funicular (included in the $3.50 admission) up to the track to see how it's working today. There are still dozens of trains daily, but unfortunately the posted schedule is more optimistic than accurate. (Open 10:00 A.M.–7:00 P.M. every day between April 1 and October 31; 9:00 A.M.–4:00 P.M. Tuesday through Saturday from November 1 through December 31.)

Go farther up the line (take SR 4008 for 4 miles, then make a left onto SR 1015, Coupon-Gallitzin Road) to get up close and personal with the highest and longest tunnels of the Pennsy line at **Gallitzin Tunnels Park** (814–886–8871). Walk through a caboose (free admission) and watch the trains pass through the newly rehabbed 1854 Portage Tunnel. (Open 11:00 A.M.–5:00 P.M. daily except Monday, unless it's a Monday holiday.)

Proceed south along Tunnelhill Street past the U.S. 22 interchange to the **Allegheny Portage Railroad National Historic Site** (814–886–6150), which re-creates what must have been a bizarre idea even when it was a success. Early in the nineteenth century, Pennsylvania sought to build a cross-state canal to rival New York's Erie Canal, but came up against the Allegheny Mountains. The solution was to build (by 1834) a sort of giant incline—actually ten of them, a string of five on the sides of the mountains—to haul the canal boats, with freight and passengers, up and over. It worked, cutting days off the trip, but was obsolete in little more than twenty years. Now it's a sizable, attractive park with a re-created engine house, a historic tavern, and the traces of long-ago tracks, plus scenic walking trails, open till 5:00 P.M. (6:00 P.M. in summer) every day except Thanksgiving, Christmas, and New Year's ($2.00 admission).

DINNER: Now it's time to make tracks back to U.S. 22 to the **Cottage Restaurant & Inn** (4554 Admiral Peary Highway; 814–472–8002), a local favorite just outside Ebensburg. Start with homemade soup, and try the ribs.

Evening

LODGING: Right in Ebensburg is the **Noon–Collins Inn & Restaurant** (114 East High Street; 814–472–4311). This carefully restored 1833 mansion features modern comforts and serves as a home base for exploring the historic area of the Cambria County seat (founded 1797) and popular nineteenth-century resort area. Such illustrious visitors as Andrew Carnegie were attracted by the natural springs, clear mountain air, and scenic beauty.

DAY 2

Morning

BREAKFAST: Enjoy a breakfast of changing entrees and baked goods at the Noon-Collins.

The resortlike towns of Ebensburg and nearby Cresson inspired the Gilded Era tycoons of Pittsburgh to build a more private mountain hideaway, the **South Fork Hunting and Fishing Club.** Take U.S. 219 to the Saint Michael exit; turn right off PA 869 to the Historic District to see what remains of that monument to hubris. The two remaining "cottages" are privately owned, but you can visit the restored Clubhouse (maintained by the South Fork Fishing and Hunting Club Historical Preservation Society, 814–539–6752), where members like Andrew Mellon and Philander Knox (future secretaries of the treasury and state, respectively) dined, socialized, and relaxed.

It's a short drive off PA 869 to the **Johnstown Flood National Memorial** (814–495–4643), the site of the club's man-made lake, created by a dam originally built for the Portage Railroad in 1839–52 and long neglected until the club bought it in 1879. The club owners further compromised the safety of the dam—until it burst on May 31, 1889, unleashing a 35- to 70-foot-high wall of water and debris. You can get an idea what this looked like from the giant sculpture filling the ceiling of the visitors center. A film and exhibits retell the story, and you can walk along what remains of that dam. (Open daily 9:00 A.M.–5:00 P.M., till 6:00 P.M. in the summer. Admission is $2.00.)

Return to U.S. 219 and take the Johnstown Expressway (PA 56) into the city, but head first to the **Inclined Plane** (814–536–1816) near the War Memorial Arena at the downtown end. The steepest incline in the world (71.9 percent grade) is big enough for you to drive your car on board ($5.00 one-way), but you'll just want the $3.00 pedestrian round trip.

LUNCH: At the top, enjoy the view along with sandwiches, salads, and chili at the **Inclined Station Restaurant and Pub** (814–536–7550). For dessert, try the local ice cream, Galliker's, at the restaurant or the ice cream stand near the incline's gift shop.

Afternoon

On the observation deck, an explanatory photo of the view in front of you helps you visualize what happened that Memorial Day in 1889, when the wall of water—mighty enough to sweep away whole houses, locomotives, and boxcars—crashed down the Conemaugh River onto the Stone Bridge, which held, and still stands today. The leviathan wave then crashed back onto the town, and the debris (perhaps ignited by a damaged oil car) caught fire. The final death toll, by drowning or by flame: Of 35,000 inhabitants, 2,209 men, women, and children died.

Return downtown via the Incline, and it's a short stroll to 304 Washington Street. The **Johnstown Flood Museum** (814–539–1889) features regular showings of *The Johnstown Flood,* which won the 1989 Academy Award for best documentary short subject. Besides the exhibits explaining the dam's construction and the course of the floodwaters, you'll hear the story of how Johnstown rebounded. From around the nation came volunteers, including the new American Red Cross, for which the flood was its first major relief effort. More than $3.7 million in pre-inflation funds was contributed by eighteen nations as well as by citizens across the United States—including a relief committee of South Fork Club members, who were never held liable for any of the disaster. One member, though, Andrew Carnegie, did donate a new library building, which now houses the museum. (Open daily 10:00 A.M.–5:00 P.M., till 7:00 P.M. Friday and Saturday in summer. Admission is $4.00.)

A few downtown buildings actually survived the flood, most notably the **First Methodist Episcopal Church** (now the Franklin Street United Methodist Church), credited with breeching the wave and thus protecting several buildings behind it, along with the dozens of people who fled to them for safety. You can take an easy walking tour of downtown Johnstown, including the restored Central Park and notable flood sites, on your own (download the map at www.visitjohnstownpa.com/walkingjohnstown.html) or with a Flood Museum docent (814–539–1889; at least twenty-four-hour notice required). Also of note is the postmodern **Crown American Corporation headquarters** designed by the world-renowned Michael Graves.

DINNER: Follow PA 271 up the hill out of downtown, veering left onto Barnett Street as PA 271 curves away from the river, then turning left onto Southmont Boulevard at the bottom of the hill. The **Boulevard Grill & Warehouse** (165 Southmont Boulevard; 814–539–5805) serves updated American cuisine in a hodgepodge building. The structure started with two relocated floors of the Merchant's Hotel of flood fame, and added elements of buildings from as far away as Newark, New Jersey. There's live music on weekends, too.

The easiest way to return to Pittsburgh is to take U.S. 219 south to the Pennsylvania Turnpike and home, about two hours away.

THERE'S MORE

Grandview Cemetery. The Plot of the Unknown honors the 777 never-identified victims of the Johnstown Flood. In Johnstown (814–535–2652).

Chestnut Ridge Golf Club. *Golf Digest* awarded 4 stars to both public courses, Chestnut Ridge and Tom's Run. In Blairsville (724–459–7188 or 800–770–0000).

Southern Alleghenies Museum of Art. Changing exhibits of regional artists rotate from the museum at Saint Francis University in nearby Loretto to its satellites in downtown Altoona and the Johnstown branch of the University of Pittsburgh (814–472–3920).

Lakemont Park. Ride the world's oldest roller coaster or opt for the water park, $7.95 all day. In Altoona (814–949–PARK or 800–434–8006; www.lakemontparkfun.com).

Baseball. Catch old-fashioned minor-league action in intimate ballparks. Altoona Curve, a Pirate farm club, plays in the Blair County Ballpark, next to Lakemont (814–943–5400; www.altoonacurve.com). And the Johnstown Johnnies rule the Frontier League from Point Stadium (814–536–TEAM; www.johnniesbaseball.com).

Fort Roberdeau. The reconstructed fort near Altoona re-creates the frontier days of the French and Indian War and the Revolution. ($3.00 admission; 814–946–0048).

Rail-trails. Scenic former railroad rights-of-way welcome bikers, walkers, and equestrians. The 16-mile Ghost Town Trail (cross-country skiing also permitted; 724–463–8636) links Cambria and Indiana Counties. The 11-mile Lower (rhymes with *flower*) Trail (814–832–2400) links Blair and Huntingdon Counties.

Windber Coal Heritage Center. Relive the life of a mining town of a century ago in this interactive museum (814–467–6680).

PREVIEWS OF COMING ATTRACTIONS

Heritage centers. In the works are several more historic museums. Johnstown's opened in March 2001 in the former Germania Brewery Building in the Cambria City National Historic District (888–222–1889). Coming in 2001 are heritage centers for Portage and for Hollidaysburg (featuring its most famous export, the Slinky).

SPECIAL EVENTS

Memorial Day. Flood-related historical groups host a variety of commemorative tours and special events at the Saint Michael and Johnstown sites (814–539–1889).

June. Friendly City PolkaFest brings four days of music to various Johnstown locations (814–536–7993 or 800–237–8590).

Early August. The six-day Tour de 'Toona, one of the Western Hemisphere's largest cycling races, runs from Johnstown to Altoona and back again via Hollidaysburg and Martinsburg (814–237–8590).

Labor Day weekend. The Cambria City Historic District hosts music and food from around the world at the Johnstown FolkFest. Free admission (814–539–1889).

October. Altoona Railfest takes worldwide rail fans to "backstage" tours of the Pennsy (814–946–0834; www.railroadcity.com).

OTHER RECOMMENDED RESTAURANTS AND LODGING

Allegro Ristorante. This popular Italian dinner spot is on the way to the Curve at 3926 Broad Avenue, Altoona; open for lunch Friday only (814–946–5216; www.allegrorestaurant.baweb.com).

U.S. Hotel Restaurant & Tavern. The recently restored 1835 hotel in Hollidaysburg is a favorite local spot, especially for Sunday brunch, served 10:00 A.M.–2:00 P.M. (814–695–9924; www.theushotel.com).

Dillweed Bed & Breakfast & Trailside Shop. Take your bike and hop on the Ghost Town Trail at the Dilltown Trailhead (814–446–6465; www.dillweedinc.com).

Station Inn B&B. The truly dedicated railhead enjoys being close to the tracks in Cresson and hearing the trains at all hours. Watch the Main Line from the front porch (814–886–4757 or 888–886–4757).

FOR MORE INFORMATION

Allegheny Mountains Convention and Visitors Bureau, Logan Valley Mall, Route 220 and Goods Lane, Altoona, PA 16602; 814–943–4183 or 800–84–ALTOONA; www.alleghenymountains.com.

Greater Johnstown Cambria County Convention and Visitors Bureau, 1 Market Place, 111 Market Street, Johnstown, PA 15901-1608; 814–536–7993 or 800–237–8590; www.visitjohnstownpa.com.

INTO THE HEARTLAND

Happy Valley

IN THE CENTRE OF IT ALL

---

1 NIGHT

Art • Victoriana • History • Ice Cream

Maybe the bumper sticker has it right: God must be a Penn State fan, not only for making heaven in the school's colors—blue and white—but also for creating such spectacular scenery around idyllic small towns. State College, the hub of Happy Valley, is the quintessential "small town with big-city amenities." The largest borough in the commonwealth is home not only to the main campus of Penn State University, but also to arts and cultural resources (as well as that famous football team) that many cities would envy. Its status as a major research institution has given it a wealth (in quantity, quality, and variety) of accommodations and a sophistication in dining options that you don't normally associate with a college town.

Penn State is but a newcomer to the attractions of the Centre County area, tracing its history only to 1855, when an initial donation of 200 acres created a modest agricultural school. The nearby towns of Bellefonte and Boalsburg were then already thriving, etching their names in American history long before Penn State had its first cow. The former, home to seven governors of three states (Kansas and California besides Pennsylvania), is a Victorian jewel in the mountains alongside its *belle fontaine*—or so a French visitor called the "beautiful fountain" of Spring Creek. Boalsburg dates even farther back in history, not merely to the eighteenth-century founding of the town but to the discovery of America itself.

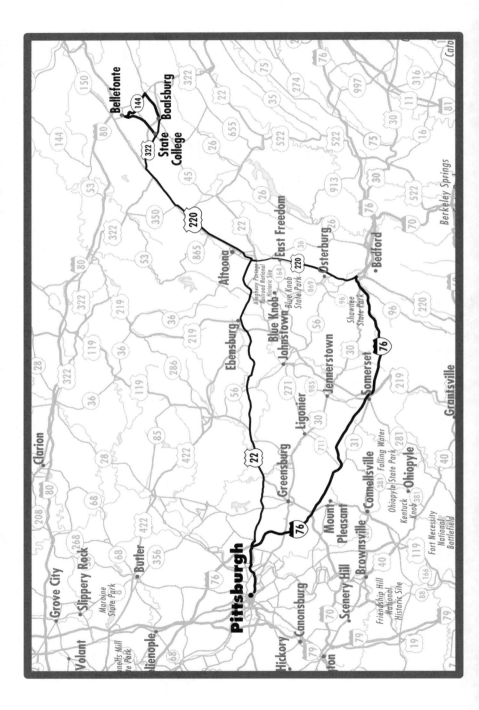

DAY 1

Morning

The time-honored route to Penn State is the Parkway East (I–376, U.S. 22/30). Go past the turnpike entrance in Monroeville, into Murrysville and **Dick's Diner** (4200 William Penn Highway; 724–327–4566).

BREAKFAST: This popular diner has expanded quite a bit over the years, but it still serves huge, inexpensive breakfasts all day, though some breakfast specials like eggs Benedict or cornmeal mush are available 6:30–10:30 or 11:00 A.M. only. (Open 6:30 A.M.–10:00 P.M. every day except major holidays.)

Soon the strip malls evaporate and much of U.S. 22 is divided highway to I–99/U.S. 220, which whisks you through Blair County and deposits you at Bald Eagle (I–99 is scheduled to connect with I–80 in 2003; check updates at www.penndot2.com/route26/), about two hours from Pittsburgh. Continue on U.S. 220 for about 12 miles to U.S. 322 east. (Or go the "back way": Turn right at Port Matilda onto SR 3017, then left onto PA 550 at the top of the ridge. This will take you past the farm stands of Half Moon Valley.) In about 5 miles, U.S. 322 turns into the limited-access Mount Nittany Expressway. Exit at Park Avenue and turn right, but rather than heading to Beaver Stadium, turn left onto Porter Road to the new **Centre County Visitors Center** (Porter and Park Avenues; 814–231–1400 or 800–358–5466; www.visitpennstate. org). Opened in summer 2000, this vast center is made of limestone, with a meeting room lined in wood rescued from a local barn. You can not only pick up a variety of the usual tourist brochures but also plan your visit with the help of the floor's giant map and various interactive computer screens, and then check out historical exhibits and vintage photographs. In one corner, by the window that overlooks Mount Nittany itself, is the story of Nit-A-Nee, the Delaware princess who protected her people even in death: After she was buried, her grave grew into the mighty mountain that bears her name. (Open Monday through Friday 8:00 A.M.–6:00 P.M., Saturday and Sunday 9:00 A.M.–6:00 P.M.)

Continue on Porter Road for a few blocks, then turn right onto College Avenue, at the **Centre Furnace Mansion** (1001 East College Avenue; 814–234–4779). The residence (1842–91) of iron master Moses Thompson is now a house museum and home of the Centre County Historical Society. (Free admission. Regularly open Sunday, Monday, Wednesday, and Friday, 1:00–4:00 P.M. and by appointment.)

College Avenue (PA 26) is the main street of **State College,** with a bustling downtown of shops and restaurants to your left, the University Park campus to your right. Free walking maps for the dozens of shops and for historic sites are available from the Downtown State College Partnership (814–238–7004; www.downtownstatecollege.com). Browse through thirty clothing shops (generally sportswear and Penn State garb), seven bookstores, and interesting gift shops. (Most are open Monday through Friday 10:00 A.M.–5:30 P.M., till 8:00 P.M. Thursday; also Saturday 10:00 A.M.–5:00 P.M. and Sunday 11:00 A.M.–5:30 P.M.)

Whether you head for the shops or follow the still-being-developed historic path, you'll come to the oldest building in State College. Built in 1857 as a private house, it was soon known as Jack's Road House, then the Nittany Inn, but since 1922 it's been the State College Hotel (814-237–4350), home of the **Corner Room** (11 West College Avenue; 814–237–3051) restaurant since 1926.

LUNCH: The Corner Room serves basic but memorable "comfort food," and has been popular with generations of Nittany Lion fans. (Open Sunday through Thursday 7:00 A.M.–10:00 P.M., Friday and Saturday 7:00 A.M.–midnight.)

Afternoon

For the full **Penn State** experience, skip dessert and walk into campus through the Allen Street Gate and one of the nation's largest remaining stands of American elm trees, past **Old Main,** right onto Pollock Road, and stop by the HUB (Hetzel Union Building) to pick up a campus map; it's a huge place with more than 17,000 undergrads. Turn left onto Shortlidge Road and left onto Curtin Road, then follow the crowd to the **Creamery** (814–865–7535), the oldest (1892) academic ice cream research institute in the world. You can "research" a cone or a dish ($1.55 each) of exceptionally rich, fresh (average four days from cow to cone) ice cream. Don't be daunted by the long line; it moves very quickly, as you place your order and pay first, then choose a single flavor to be hand scooped for you. The single-flavor rule was bent only once: Not knowing the rule, 1996 commencement speaker President Clinton ordered two flavors, Peachy Paterno and Cherryquist. (Open late enough that you can stop back before you leave to pick up university-made cheeses or ice cream, which can be packed in dry ice for up to twelve hours of traveling:

Monday through Thursday 7:00 A.M.–10:00 P.M., Friday 7:00 A.M.–11:00 P.M., Saturday 8:00 A.M.–11:00 P.M., Sunday 9:00 A.M.–10:00 P.M.)

Finish your ice cream before you continue down Curtin. You'll first see columns with narrow bands of bright colors at the top; around the corner are the distinctive giant lion paws (and popular photo op) that mark the entrance of the **Palmer Museum of Art** (814–865–7672), home to 3,500 years of art with some 4,000 works. The most ancient pieces include painted miniature earthenware from eighth- to fifth-century B.C. Greece, coins from fourth-century B.C. Israel, and early Roman bronzes. Of more recent interest is the notable collection of modern ceramics, exquisite twentieth-century works that redefine folk traditions while breaking the mold (so to speak) of mass-production aesthetics. You'll find more remarkable ceramics (third century B.C. to nineteenth century A.D.) in the Asian collection. Don't forget to stop in the outdoor sculpture garden, and check what's in the **Zoller Gallery** and the student exhibition spaces in the School of Visual Art in the Patterson Building next to the Palmer. (Free admission. Open Tuesday through Saturday 10:00 A.M.–4:30 P.M., Sunday noon–4:00 P.M.)

Cross Curtin Road for a glimpse of the university's **Ag Hill** complex, four buildings from the early twentieth century that comprise the smaller and older of two national historic districts on campus. There's no shortage of historic plaques to let you know some of the history of these Renaissance-style structures, including one of the world's two respiration calorimeters. The larger historic district, the **Farmers' High School/Penn State Old Campus** complex, is comprised of some forty early- and mid-twentieth-century buildings a short stroll west. From Curtin, turn left onto Frager Road to the beaux-arts-style Carnegie Building—yup, formerly the school's library, given by Andy in 1903. Across the quadrangle is the Burrowes Building, which features a notable mural inside and (to literary types) a more notable plaque outside about such writers as Joseph Heller and John Barth teaching here. Nearby is the Richardsonian Romanesque Old Botany, the oldest building on campus (1887). There's plenty more to explore, but eventually you'll want to head north on Burrowes Road, and soon you'll see the **Nittany Lion Shrine,** built on the spot in 1942 from a thirteen-ton block of Indiana limestone and one of the most famous landmarks on campus. Continue north on the path to a Dutch Colonial–style hotel and through the side door of the **Nittany Lion Inn** (200 West Park Avenue; 814–865–8500 or 800–233–7505; www. nli.psu.edu/html/nittany.html).

DINNER: Service is as exquisite as the food in the inn's **Dining Room** (814–865–8590), which features local produce, including fresh trout, plus venison, its famed crabcakes, and a good selection of wines by the glass. Desserts include an exclusive Creamery ice cream, Inn Berry Swirl. (Open every day: breakfast is served 6:45–10:00 A.M., lunch 11:30 A.M.–2:00 P.M., dinner 5:30–10:00 P.M.; Sunday brunch buffet is served 9:30 A.M.–2:00 P.M.)

LODGING: The Nittany Lion Inn provides 237 comfortable rooms in colonial style.

Evening

Stretch out in the inn's Alumni Fireside Lounge, or check what's playing at the campus's two entertainment venues, the **Bryce Jordan Center** (814–863–5500; www.bjc.psu.edu) and the **Center for the Performing Arts** (814–863–0255; www.cpa.psu.edu).

DAY 2

Morning

BREAKFAST: No matter when you arise, **Ye Olde College Diner** (126 West College Avenue; 814–238–5590) is ready for you with breakfast—and a 1950s aesthetic—twenty-four hours a day. Whether you opt for the traditional omelettes, the trendy breakfast wraps or the homemade quiche, you'll want to leave room for the World-Famous Grilled Sticky—I'd call them sticky buns or pecan rolls. They also show up as dessert with ice cream and as a popular take-out item at every hour of the day and night. (No credit cards.)

Head east on PA 26 then PA 150 north to **Bellefonte,** the county seat founded in 1785 at the site of the Big Spring, which gushes 13.5 million gallons a day. Enriched by its iron industry in the 1800s, Bellefonte was the biggest and most influential town between Pittsburgh and Harrisburg, and that legacy still shows in one of the nation's best-preserved Victorian districts with more than forty structures. The hardy of leg can get the best view on a walking tour of this rather steeply situated town. A popular starting point is Talleyrand Park, next to the railroad station (built 1869), now a mini museum and starting point for various excursion rides offered by the **Bellefonte Historical Railroad Society** (814–355–0311). Most rides take only about forty-five minutes (weekends, Memorial Day through Labor Day, plus special excursions). Up the hill is the **The Benner-Linn house,** now home to the

Bellefonte Museum (133 North Allegheny Street; 814–355–4280; www.
bellefonte.org/museum), a growing history museum with changing exhibits.
(Open Friday through Sunday 1:30–4:30 P.M.)

Enjoy more mountain scenery by heading south on PA 144 and joining
up with the **Brush Valley** scenic route. There are four such routes outlined
for fall foliage enjoyment in the visitors guide. As you head down the mountain, watch for the turnoff on your right to the **Mount Nittany Inn**
(814–364–9363).

LUNCH: Also a B&B, the Mount Nittany Inn features home cooking and a
spectacular view. (Open Sunday through Thursday 11:30 A.M.–9:00 P.M., Friday and Saturday 11:30 A.M.–10:00 P.M.)

Afternoon

The bottom of the mountain takes you into tiny **Centre Hall.** A left turn
onto PA 192 would take you into the Old Order Amish communities of
Madisonburg and Rebersburg, but for this tour, continue on PA 144. In just
a couple of miles, turn right onto PA 45 to head west into **Boalsburg.**
Though not officially recognized as such, Boalsburg considers itself the birthplace of Memorial Day, because folks here were the first to celebrate a Civil
War remembrance day.

Once in town, follow the signs to the **Columbus Chapel and Boal
Mansion Museum** (814–466–6210; www.vicon.net/~boalmus). This house
museum is unique in that the family still lives in it—the ninth and now tenth
generations—so only parts of the first floor are included on the tour, which
takes in family portraits as well as historical artifacts dating back to 1789. The
family has been international in outlook (and marriage); in 1908 Mathilde De
Lagarde Boal inherited the Columbus family chapel and had it shipped and
reconstructed here. The Columbus Chapel includes Christopher Columbus's
admiral's desk, religious art dating to the fifteenth century, and two pieces of
the True Cross. Also on the grounds are exhibits of antique weapons, military
artifacts, and clothing. (Admission is $10. Open May 1 through October 31,
Tuesday through Sunday 1:30–5:00 P.M.; between Memorial Day and Labor
Day weekends, Tuesday through Saturday 10:00 A.M.–5:00 P.M., Sunday
noon–5:00 P.M.)

Historic Boalsburg Village makes for a lovely stroll, with specialty shops
like **A Basket Full** (814–466–7788) on "the Diamond" along Main Street.
Most are open Monday through Saturday 10:00 A.M.–5:00 P.M., Sunday

Discover Christopher Columbus's family chapel in Boalsburg.

noon–4:00 or 5:00 P.M., although the **Ken Hull Studio & Gallery** is generally open just Saturday 11:00 A.M.–4:00 P.M. and by appointment (814–466–3139).

DINNER: Built 1819, **Duffy's Tavern** (113 East Main Street; 814–466–6241; www.duffystavern.com) features loads of history, 22-inch-thick walls, microbrews, and both casual and fine dining. (The tavern is open Monday through Saturday 11:30–1:00 A.M., Sunday 11:30 A.M.–9:30 P.M. Fine dining, Monday through Saturday 11:30 A.M.–2:00 P.M. and 5:00–10:00 P.M. On Sunday the lunch menu is served 11:30 A.M.–9:30 P.M., dinner 4:00–9:30 P.M.)

Whether you hit the Creamery again or not, the best way home in the dark is to return to I–99 and follow it all the way south to Bedford, then take the Pennsylvania Turnpike.

THERE'S MORE

Penn State museums. Other than the Palmer, weekend hours vary, but visits can often be arranged in advance, especially during the school year. The **Earth and Mineral Science Museum** (814–863–6427) is home to not just a wonderful mineral and gem collection but also paintings of Pennsylvania's mineral-related industries. The **Pasto Museum** (814–863–1383) showcases early tools of agriculture. The **Frost Entomological Museum** (814–863–2865) houses thousands of insects, with a notable butterfly and moth collection. The **Matson Museum of Anthropology** (814–863–3853) includes collections of prehistoric Pennsylvania, Meso-America, and world ethnology.

State recreation areas include **Bald Eagle** (814–625–2775), **Black Moshannon** (814–342–5960), **Poe Valley** (814–349–2460), and, a particular favorite, **Whipple Dam** (814–667–1800) State Parks; **Bald Eagle, Sproul, Moshannon,** and **Rothrock** State Forests; and several state game lands. Explore hiking and snowmobile trails, fishing, hunting, boating, and more (www.dcnr.state.pa.us).

Toftrees Resort and Conference Center. A 4-star golf course (schedule your tee time online at www.toftrees.com) plus a popular hotel and restaurants 3 miles from campus (in Pennsylvania 800–252–3551; out of state 800–458–3602).

Penn's Cave. The nation's only underwater cave, plus a wildlife sanctuary, just outside Centre Hall. Closed January (814–364–1664; www.pennscave.com).

Lincoln Caverns. Another cave, closer to the Spring Creek fishing area, along PA 45 in Huntingdon (814–643–1358; www.lincolncaverns.com).

Pennsylvania Military Museum/28th Division Shrine. Outside are somewhat formidable tanks and memorials to veterans; inside are exhibits about the state's military history. Open year-round, but weekends only from December through February (814–466–6263; www.psu.edu/dept/aerospace/museum).

SPECIAL EVENTS

January. Winter festival in Black Moshannon State Park (814–342–5960).

May. Big Spring Festival celebrates the water source in Bellefonte's Talleyrand Park with music, water events, food, et cetera (814–355–2917).

Boalsburg's A Day in Towne celebrates Memorial Day weekend with a Civil War encampment, entertainment, crafts, and a parade (814–466–6311 or 814–466–6865).

July. Central Pennsylvania Festival of the Arts offers five days of visual and performing artists all over State College (814–237–3682; http://arts-festival.com).

The Peoples Choice Festival is crafts oriented, on the grounds of the Pennsylvania Military Museum, Boalsburg (814–466–6263).

August. Centre County Grange Fair: five days of serious agricultural competitions and exhibitions in Centre Hall (814–364–9212; www.pafairs.org/centrecountyfair).

December. Five-day Festival of Trees features more than one hundred decorated holiday trees, entertainment, crafts, and such at Penn State (814–231–1400 or 800–350–5084).

Bellefonte Victorian Christmas includes crafts, train rides, music, decorated houses, more (814–353–0656).

OTHER RECOMMENDED RESTAURANTS AND LODGING

The Tavern. In downtown State College, popular for Italian, steaks, chops, and Toll House pie since 1948; local wine. Dinner only (814–238–6116; www.thetavern.com).

The Deli. Right off campus with popular sandwiches and salads (814–237–5710; www.dantesinc.com/thedeli).

Spats Cafe and Speakeasy. Cajun and Creole in downtown State College (814–238–7010).

Schnitzel's Tavern. German rathskellar food and brew seven days a week downstairs in the historic Bush Hotel, across from Talleyrand Park, Bellefonte (814–355–4230).

Penn Stater Conference Center Hotel. The newer hotel on campus, in Penn State's Research Park, includes the Gardens restaurant (814–863–5000 or 800–233–7505; www.nli.psu.edu/html/pennstater.html).

Pa-Reservations.com. A network of inns, B&Bs, and rooms in private homes (814–466–2001 or 888–466–9955; www.pa-reservations.com).

The Atherton Hotel. It's where Bob Dylan, Garth Brooks, Phish, Nelson Mandela, Gloria Estefan, and the London Symphony stayed when at Penn State. Tarragon Restaurant is notable as well (814–231–2100 or 800–832–0132; http://atherton.statecollege.com/).

Carnegie House. A popular country inn at Andrew Carnegie's former Pond Bank Farm near Toftrees. The dining room features bison and other creative dishes (814–234–2424 or 800–229–5053; www.carnegiehouse.com).

Spruce Creek and J. S. Isett Bed & Breakfasts. A quick cast into some of the best fly-fishing waters a few miles southwest of State College (814–632–3777; www.sprucecreekbnb.com).

FOR MORE INFORMATION

Centre County Convention and Visitors Bureau, Centre County/Penn State Visitor Center, 800 East Park Avenue, State College, PA 16803; 814–231–1400 or 800–358–5466; www.visitpennstate.org.

INTO THE HEARTLAND

Elk County

GETTING OUT OF A RUT

---

1 NIGHT

Elk • Beer • Wine • Woods

For about six weeks in September and October, the largest free-roaming elk herd east of the Mississippi is in rutting season. Bulls weighing up to 800 pounds compete for females by charging at each other, butting heads and antlers. The thousands of humans who come to watch often display similar behavior, jostling for space in prime viewing areas and in area accommodations.

Combined with spectacular fall foliage in the Allegheny National Forest area, rutting season is certainly the most dramatic time to see the 700 or so elk, but it's not the only and certainly not the easiest, for either you or the animals. In November the now-calmer elk move around in larger herds, and in areas easier for people to see: You're pretty much guaranteed good elk sightings. Golden eagles also return to the area, and white-tailed deer start their own breeding season. The elk are pretty easy to see throughout winter and spring—when the area offers plenty of snow sports—though the bulls start losing their antlers in March. The only time it's really tough is in hot weather, when the elk keep cool in the woods and wander into the open only at dawn and dusk. Remember not to get too close, and be extra careful driving. Even the "babies" are likely to be bigger than you.

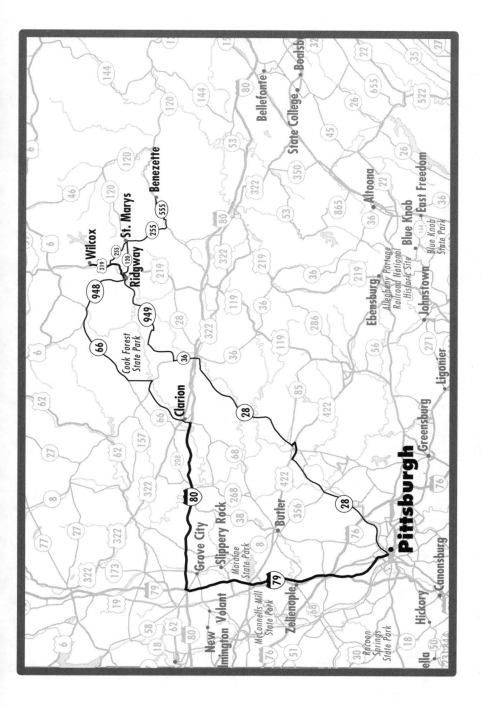

INTO THE HEARTLAND

DAY 1

Morning

Follow PA 28 northeast past Kittanning, where it becomes a two-lane country road. At Brookville, continue straight north (thus switching to PA 36). Turn right onto PA 949 past Clear Creek State Park to drive to **Ridgway,** a pretty little town bisected by the Clarion River, one of America's most scenic waterways. Canoeing is big—and biking is too now—along the new 18-mile Clarion–Little Toby Creek rail-trail to Brockway. On U.S. 219, just after you cross the railroad tracks, turn left to park, then recross the bridge to the Pennsy Restaurant. You've been on the road for about two hours.

BREAKFAST: A classic diner in cuisine if not decor, the **Pennsy** (157 North Broad Street; 814–772–9935) makes its own bread as well as soups and pies. Try to get there before the cinnamon bread runs out. Order the homemade sausage, and do get a side of homefries without a speck of grease. (Opens at 5:45 A.M. Monday through Saturday, 7:00 A.M. Sunday; closes at 11:00 A.M. Monday, 1:00 P.M. Saturday, and 1:30 P.M. all other days.)

Given the shortage of Sunday hours for most places in the county, you'll have to weigh attractive but not spectacular antiques shops in Ridgway against one of the best beers in the country. My choice is to hightail it on PA 120 to **Saint Marys** for the **Eternal Tap** before it closes at 1:00 P.M. **Straub Brewery** (303 Sorg Street; 814–834–2875), a family-owned brewery for five generations, prides itself on "honest beer" with no sugars, no salts, no preservatives. It's best fresh, and you can't get any fresher than to head for the source, walk up the few steps to the office, and draw yourself a cold one from the Eternal Tap. The trendiest (and pricey) beer in New York is yours for free—just remember to wash your glass. (Free tours are offered Monday through Friday 9:00 A.M.–noon. The Eternal Tap and brewery gift shop are open 9:00 A.M.–5:00 P.M., until 1:00 P.M. on Saturday. The drive-up beer store is open Monday through Thursday 9:00 A.M.–8:00 P.M., till 9:00 P.M. Friday and Saturday.)

Walk it off in "downtown" Saint Marys, a fairly small town yet the biggest in the county, which boasts that it has more trees than people. Antiquing here is more of the "collectible" variety, but you may find unique old jewelry or dolls at the two houses comprising **Victoria's Vintages** (133 West Mill Street; 814–834–4599) or enjoy the scents of candles and wreaths at **Village Peddler** (14 Erie Avenue; 814–834–1095).

You can see some magnificent houses in a walking tour of Ridgway.

LUNCH: Just how far do you have to get from Pittsburgh before the steak salad comes without fries? Farther than Saint Marys, obviously. The **Station Inn** (322 Depot Street; 814–834–1010) puts homefries on its steak, chicken, and Black Diamond Steak Salads, and makes its own soups and chili. (Open Monday through Saturday 11:30 A.M.–midnight.)

Afternoon

Now it's time to head south on PA 255. Before you go elk hunting, about 3 miles from the restaurant, watch on your right for **Becker's Chapel,** built in 1856 and a contender for title of smallest church in the United States. It's real, and a National Historic Landmark open most of the time for visitors.

After your photo op, continue south on PA 255, then turn left onto PA 555 to Benezette, the small village closest to the elk herd. Turn left at the Benezette Hotel and head 3.5 miles up Winslow Hill (there are signs) to the

elk viewing area. There's plenty of parking and even portable rest rooms, because folks tend to stay for a while to take in the great vista and some easy walking trails. The more adventurous can try exploring trails in the 200,000-acre Elk State Forest (814–486–3353) and neighboring state game lands.

When you're ready for dinner, retrace your steps to Saint Marys. Near the center of town, turn right onto Saint Marys Street for the Bavarian Inn.

DINNER: In case you haven't guessed, this area was largely settled by Germans—the town name was originally Saint Marien Stad—and the **Bavarian Inn** (33 Saint Marys Street; 814–834–2161) maintains the tradition. You'll find imported German beers as well as the favorite homebrew, Straub's, to wash down the wursts, sauerkraut, and spaetzle. Also includes a motel. (Open Monday through Friday 7:00 A.M.–10:00 P.M., Saturday 4:30–10:00 P.M.)

Evening

Return to Ridgway via PA 120, turn right onto Main Street, and drive through downtown. West Main Street becomes PA 948 and turns right, up the hill, at the first light after the bridge. Or just follow the signs to Faircroft.

LODGING: On the outskirts of town, practically next door to the Allegheny National Forest, **Faircroft B&B** (814–776–2539) offers quiet and its own seventy-five acres of grounds for walking and, in winter, cross-country skiing. Winter getaway packages are available.

DAY 2

Morning

BREAKFAST: Country eggs and baked goods will wake you up whenever you want them. Get stoked up for a stroll.

The county seat, Ridgway is home to a respectably grand courthouse, built in 1879 and spruced up in 2000. Just about everything except the churches (and there are quite a few of them, many architecturally significant) shuts down on Sunday. But arm yourself with a free **Historic Ridgway** map for a walking tour of some of the gorgeous private homes, businesses, and churches, all noted on the map. Make sure you take a look at the massive granite house at 344 Main Street, and get a glimpse of the Tiffany windows on the house at 21 East Avenue.

Head back toward Saint Marys. Just outside of town is **The Gothic Gallery** (814–772–5675), for all your gargoyle needs. You'll find plenty of medieval reproductions (cherubs, columns, urns) for garden decoration or to spice up the library. (Open Monday through Saturday 10:00 A.M.–7:00 P.M., Sunday 1:00–7:00 P.M.)

LUNCH: Back in Saint Marys, grab a quick meal at **South Street Bagel Co.** (240 Depot Street; 814–834–6872). You'll find sandwiches on freshly made bagels, with a rotating selection of such unusual bagel flavors as orange-pineapple, salsa, and raspberry-chocolate. (Open Monday through Friday 6:30 A.M.–2:00 P.M., Saturday and Sunday 7:30 A.M.–2:00 P.M.)

Afternoon

As you head out of town on PA 255, note the **Saint Joseph Monastery** on your right. This Benedictine community, dating to 1852, is one of the oldest in the country.

From PA 255, turn right (north) onto U.S. 219; pass through Johnsonburg on the way to Wilcox. **The Winery at Wilcox** (814–929–5598) serves as a visitors center as well as a winery and shop. Most customers like the sweeter fruit wines, especially Peach Mist, but there are some respectable varietals. I like the Chambourcin. Tours are available, but not regular. (Open 10:00 A.M.–6:00 P.M. daily.)

Take the scenic route now—officially scenic, that is—through the **Allegheny National Forest** (814–362–4613; www.fs.fed.us/r9/allegheny/). More than 513,000 acres, the only national forest in Pennsylvania is home to more than eighty species of trees (mostly northern hardwoods such as cherry, oak, and beech, seventy to a hundred years old) and critters from beavers to wild turkeys to bears, plus plenty of deer, of course. Return to Ridgway (south) on U.S. 219, then head north on PA 948, which merges with PA 66 (west). Stay on PA 66 through the depths of the forest. Turn left at Vowinckel onto SR 1015 (the turnoff is marked with a COOK FOREST sign), which joins PA 36. You've reached the Cook Forest State Park (814–744–8407; www.cookforest.com), which has administratively merged with Clear Creek State Park.

The Cook Forest, Pennsylvania's first protected wilderness and the second largest stand of old-growth pine east of the Mississippi, includes more than 6,600 acres along the Clarion. The place hasn't really changed a great deal since today's boomers were first brought here as kids, and the outskirts retain the 1950s homeyness/tackiness of souvenir shops and mini theme parks. But to attain a real sense of the woods (and a little Zen), park near the log-cabin visitors center and follow the Longfellow Trail to the **Forest Cathedral,** a National Natural Landmark. It's a little steep in places, but worth the climb. If you're into hugging trees, you'll need help. It took three of us to encircle some of these 250- to 300-year-old pines and hemlocks, which can be 5 feet in diameter and about 200 feet tall.

As you leave the visitors center, turn right onto PA 36, then take the first left onto SR 1005 and follow the signs south to Clarion. When you reach Main Street in this university town, turn left and park along Sixth Street for the Captain Loomis Inn.

DINNER: Captain Loomis (540 Main Street; 814–226–8400), in a historic former hotel, is more for faculty and visiting parents than a hangout for students. The service is undergraduate, but the prices are good for straightforward chicken, fish, and steak. (Open Monday through Thursday 11:00 A.M.–9:30 P.M., till 10:00 P.M. Friday and Saturday; Sunday 7:00 A.M.–7:00 P.M.)

It's getting dark, so the interstates, though more roundabout than the country roads, are a better bet home. Follow the signs south to I–80, head west to I–79, then south to Pittsburgh.

THERE'S MORE

Clear Creek State Park. Along the Clarion between the Allegheny National Forest and Clear Creek State Forest, its 1,676 acres get less use than nearby Cook Forest, but it's just as pretty (814–752–2368).

The Queen of the Herd. View the world's largest fiberglass cow (15 feet high, 20 feet long, 5 feet wide, 1,200 pounds) at the Ayrshire Dairy Farm on Old Kersey Road, near Saint Marys.

Elk Country Adventures. Guided hiking, biking, auto, helicopter, and horseback tours of elk habitat (814–371–3530; wildside@penn.com).

Pennsylvania Shoppe. Antiques, Amish quilts, and furniture in Ridgway (814–772–6823).

Elk County Council on the Arts. Changing exhibits of local artwork in Ridgway (814–772–7051).

Hollywood Exchange. Seven rooms of antiques in the former Hollywood Tavern, south of Saint Marys (814–637–5953).

Flying W. Ranch. Sponsors rodeos, powwows and stagecoach holdups, cowboy and horseback riding packages. There's also a western-style restaurant and accommodations. In Tionesta, near the national forest (814–463–7663).

The Cook Forest Sawmill Center for the Arts. Arts and crafts classes for children and adults, along with theater and crafts shows (814–744–9670; www.sawmill.org).

SPECIAL EVENTS

July. Winery Anniversary Weekend, Wilcox (814–929–5598).

September. Saint Marys Hometown Festival (814–834–3723).

October. Fall Festival, Elk County Historical Society, Ridgway (814–834–3723).

OTHER RECOMMENDED RESTAURANTS AND LODGING

Royal Inn. A restaurant (closed Sunday) and guest rooms along U.S. 219 just outside Ridgway (814–773–3153).

The Towers Victorian Inn. Period antiques set off this Italianate mansion just outside downtown Ridgway (814–772–7657).

Benezette Store arranges stays in private homes in Benezette (814–787–7456).

The Towne House Inns. This National Historic Landmark Georgian mansion offers accommodations and a full restaurant (closed Sunday) in Saint Marys (800–851–9180).

FOR MORE INFORMATION

Elk County Visitors Bureau, P.O. Box 838, Saint Marys, PA 15857; 814–834–3723; www.elk-county.com.

Magic Forests Visitors Bureau, 175 Main Street, Brookville, PA 15825; 800–348–9393; www.magicforests.org.

INDEX

ABOUT THE AUTHOR

MICHELLE PILECKI has covered Pittsburgh-area arts, entertainment, sports, science, government, business, and other facets of local life for a variety of publications. Currently, she is executive editor of *Pittsburgh,* a multi-award-winning regional magazine. The editor of two cookbooks, *The Best of QED Cooks, Vols. I* and *II,* Michelle brings to *Quick Escapes Pittsburgh* her knowledge of wine, beer, and food, as well as her interests in handmade glass, distinctive nature preserves, and quirky historical sites. Researching the book helped her to add to her famous collection of hats.